PEOPLE, PERFORMANCE, AND PAY

THE FREE PRESS

New York   London   Toronto   Sydney   Tokyo   Singapore

PEOPLE, PERFORMANCE, AND PAY

Dynamic Compensation for Changing Organizations

THE HAY GROUP

Thomas P. Flannery

David A. Hofrichter

Paul E. Platten

The Free Press
A Division of Simon & Schuster Inc.
1230 Avenue of the Americas
New York, N.Y. 10020

Printed in the United States of America

printing number

      8 9 10

Text design by Carla Bolte

Library of Congress Cataloging-in-Publication Data

Flannery, Thomas P. (Thomas Patrick)
   People, performance, and pay: dynamic compensation for changing
organizations/ The Hay Group: Thomas P. Flannery, David A.
Hofrichter, Paul E. Platten.
     p. cm.
   Includes bibliographical references and index.
   ISBN 0-02-874059-9
   1. Compensation management.   I. Hofrichter, David A.
II. Platten, Paul E.   III. Hay Group IV. Title.
HF5549.5.C67F57   1996
658.3'22—dc20   95-24746
                                        CIP

For our wives and children,
who more than compensate us daily with their love and patience:

Debbie, Jessica, and Jonathan

Carol, Kristin, and Matthew

Pamela, Rachel, and Melanie

Jeanne, Mary Lu, Wil, and Joel

Contents

Foreword

Pay is one of the most effective tools available today for motivating an organization during a time of change. I know, because an innovative, dynamic pay strategy was a critical step in transforming the Santa Fe Railway from an underperforming, traditional railroad into a fast, flexible, customer-focused transportation company that has dramatically improved its profitability.

The year was 1990. We at Santa Fe were in the throes of a major restructuring, selling off our natural resource assets and returning to our core business: running a railroad. It was not an easy transformation. The organization was, to put it bluntly, in disarray. Our margins were too low, our costs too high. To make matters worse, we were losing business to the highways and other railroads because of our poor service.

If we were to survive and prosper during the era of deregulation—our goal was a billion dollars of new revenue annually —we had to eliminate the old "utility mentality" of tolerating rising costs and merrily passing them on to customers. If we were to achieve our new vision of being a leader in the transportation industry, dedicated to growth by consistently meeting our customers' expectations, then we had to change and change quickly. Downsizing alone was not the answer. We had to become a low-cost, high-quality producer. We had to improve the performance of every Santa Fe employee.

Much as we would have liked, we couldn't achieve these goals by merely rethinking our strategy and reengineering our structure. We also had to change our culture. We had to pull together as a true team. We had to take more risks and create processes for improving quality and meeting the changing demands of our customers. We had to become faster and more flexible. Ultimately, we had to change how people worked and behaved—which meant replacing our old ways of thinking about compensation. A system that gave everyone a healthy base salary and an annual raise whether or not it was deserved and that offered incentives to only a few people at the top did not support our new values.

We began by slicing the wages of our 2,400 salaried employees. The cuts ranged from 4 percent for those at the bottom of the organization to 25 percent at the very top. At the same time, however, we established a potentially lucrative incentive program for all of these employees and granted them stock options. Although initially our performance continued to suffer and no one received incentive pay that first year, by 1994 we were paying our salaried employees $35 million in incentives. During that same period, our income from operations rose from $158 million to $429 million, and the price of our stock grew over 50 percent compounded annually. After we added measures of on-time performance and safety to our incentive program, we increased our on-time record for customer shipments from 65 to over 90 percent, and we became an industry leader in safety.

The Hay Group was instrumental in helping us design our new compensation program, and many of the suggestions that the Hay consultants passed on to us are now shared in the book you are about to read. I believe *People, Performance, and Pay* is an important book because it views compensation not as a narrowly defined human resources "subspecialty," but in the context of the entire organization. The authors show how work cultures have evolved and how those cultures must support an organization's changing strategy. They describe a number of highly effective approaches to pay. Most importantly, they make an airtight case for the critical need to align compensation and culture if an organization is to effectively weather change and improve performance.

Their innovative, total approach to compensation, which addresses not just pay, but the entire range of people issues, makes a lot of sense. Having gone through the process with Santa Fe, I can tell you the concepts they put forth and strategies they suggest are right on target. And if our results at Santa Fe are any indication, other organizations going through change would do well to heed their advice.

In many ways we are still a traditionally structured organization. But in two years, we were able to transform a 125-year-old organization into an innovative, flexible, customer-driven company. Our shareholders, who are finally getting the results they want, are extremely satisfied, and our salaried employees are performing better and making more money than they ever did under the old compensation plan.

If your organization is still searching for a higher level of performance and improved results—and what company isn't—then I strongly recommend that you read on. The way you pay people says a lot about what you expect in an organization.

Robert D. Krebs
Chairman, President and
Chief Executive Officer
Santa Fe Pacific Corporation

Preface

We've heard it on trains and planes. We've heard it in executive offices and in boardrooms around the world. Whenever our firm is mentioned, the question is invariably asked: "You're those comp guys? Right?"

It's a natural assumption. After all, for the past fifty years, Hay Management Consultants has been helping organizations develop compensation strategies to support their business values, their work cultures, and their strategic goals. Our point-based pay system, known as the Hay Guide Chart®-Profile Methodology, has set the standard for compensation programs around the world, and continues to be the workhorse of pay for many organizations.

Yet much has changed since Ned Hay developed his methodology in the early 1950s. New forces in the marketplace, new organizational values, new work cultures, and new business goals have reshaped the structures, strategies, and human resource processes of most organizations. Nothing has escaped unscathed from these forces of change. That includes compensation.

All too frequently, however, pay strategies have lagged far behind other organizational changes. Most organizations frankly don't think of compensation as a dynamic, evolving process. After all, they've been using the same, one-size-fits-all pay strategy for the past thirty years. It has always worked fine. So why bother changing it now? We've witnessed this problem first-hand: While a number of our clients have adopted highly effective people- and performance-centered pay programs, others have steadfastly clung to compensation strategies that were designed twenty or thirty years ago.

The growing chasm between organizational change and compensation also can be seen in the results of a recent Hay survey. Of more than five hundred large and medium-sized U.S. organizations reporting, 91 percent had significantly shifted their organizational culture. While a number of organizations, including many of our clients, were among the 54 percent that had begun to realign their pay programs to reflect those changes, close to half the organizations surveyed had not yet addressed compensation. Not that they weren't aware that a problem exists: 73 percent said their salary programs needed to be revamped, 84 percent and 74 percent, respectively, said they needed to change their short- and long-term incentive plans, and 56 percent said they needed to change their benefits programs.

As the frustrated compensation manager of a Fortune 100 company told us: "We seem to be somewhere in the middle of an evolution. Every major area is undergoing change." Every area, that is, but pay. While his company—and most others—are moving heaven and earth to change processes, structures, strategies, even the players, they still haven't come to grips with the issue of pay.

This troublesome gap between traditional pay strategies and contemporary organizations has led to some misguided generalizations about the role compensation should play, and criticism about the continued dependence on traditional approaches—approaches one popular business magazine termed "clunky." Author Peter Block, in his book *Stewardship*, terms it "pay for empire," and sums up his concerns this way:

"For what it was asked to accomplish, this system has done an elegant and durable job. But we must question exactly what it was we asked the Hay system to do—to pay people based on the size of their territory, number of subordinates, budget size, level of authority. . . . Soften it if you like, but these are measures of empire, not contribution to the organization."[1]

Certainly there is truth in Block's statement. Indeed, as the title of our book suggests, people and their performance—their contribution both as individuals and as members of the organizational team—are the linchpins of any effective compensation strategy.

But that title and statement do not, despite what our critics might say, signal a sudden shift in our philosophy about pay. The fact is, we've always believed that people and how they performed constitute the foundation of any successful business strategy. We've always believed that compensation is an important element of a successful human resources equation that puts people first. And as for that "clunky" Hay system, when it is properly used in the right circumstances, it can still be very effective in creating people- and performance-oriented pay programs. (It is perhaps no coincidence that the Hay system was created in Philadelphia by a devout Quaker.)

Unfortunately, the point many organizations miss in the criticism of traditional pay strategies is that the solution lies not in simply scrapping an old program for a new one, but rather in integrating pay with the other organizational changes and aligning it with the organization's other people processes. For some organizations, that means modifying their current Hay-type program, tailoring it to fit their changing cultures. For others, it means creating entire new strategies that focus on competencies, teams, and performance-based rewards. Whatever the situation, the challenge with pay systems is keeping them viable and continually refocusing on the premise on which they were founded.

We have, during the past decade or so, worked with organizations that range over the entire spectrum: those that refused to change, those that modified their programs to their specific needs, and those that created entire new strategies. In working with these organizations, and in our ongoing research into compensation strategies, two issues became clear—two issues that convinced us of the need to write this book:

- *Issue One*: You cannot talk about organizational change without talking about people and people processes.
- *Issue Two*: You cannot talk about people processes without considering compensation.

Make no mistake, pay is an important part of the change process, but only if it is viewed in terms of its impact on people. Which brings us back to our "comp guys" label. Like many of the generalities about pay today, it is, while based on truth, nonetheless a misleading label. The fact is, we're really "people people"—experts in helping organizations achieve competitive advantages through people. And yes, it so happens that one of those key people processes—and one of our key areas of expertise—is pay.

One of the recurring themes you'll find in the following pages is that of the changing dynamics of the organization—the move away from individual performance and responsibility to the efforts of groups such as teams and networks. The creation of this book is an excellent example of that sort of dynamic at work. We simply could not have told the story you are about to read without the help of a number of individuals, both within and outside Hay, who came together to share their experiences and expertise.

Most important were the clients that you will read about. They are the real heroes of our book. Not only have they continually challenged and stimulated our thinking, "raising the bar" of our performance ever higher, but also their insight and innovation, their bold actions, often in the face of adversity, their emphasis on the importance of people, have—again and again—given them a competitive edge in their markets and industries.

We also want to thank our colleagues, whose personal and professional support has been indispensable in the creation of this book. Dan Glasner, a nationally recognized thought leader on compensation strategies, was one of the first to articulate many of the concepts and principles on which this book is built. His insights and contributions were invaluable.

Others within Hay who provided much-needed insights, data, and examples include Marie Dufresne, who heads our benefits practice; Steven Gross, who has pioneered team-based compensation strategies; Kathryn Cofsky, who has shared her expertise in competencies and competency-based compensation with a number of clients, including LEGO Systems, Inc. and Holiday Inn; Robert Ochsner, who has written extensively about executive compensation strategies and the need to emphasize ownership and performance; Bruce Pfau, who played the leading role in the creation of our highly successful Culture-Sort Methodology; Michael Thompson, who heads our compensation practice; Katherine Vestal, who led Hay's early work transformation and reengineering efforts, and who now heads our health care practice; and a number of consultants, including Phillip Blount, Diane Gerard, Craig Rowley, Robert Sachs, and Leslie Smith.

Because compensation is an issue that impacts organizations around the globe, we also want to thank our international colleagues, including Mark Jankelson in Australia, Damien Knight in the United Kingdom, Steven Morris in Singapore, Lawrence Watson in Belgium, and Vicky Wright, who oversees our consulting efforts in the United Kingdom.

Also, our thanks to Beth Anderson, our editor at the Free Press, whose attention to detail and expertise in matters of language and publishing were critical. And finally a special thanks to Scott Spreier, who not only helped us research and prepare the manuscript, but whose dedication, perseverance, and insight have helped us to eloquently translate our thoughts and concepts into reality.

1

The Compensation Lag

I t had survived two world wars, a national depression, and one earth-
quake, but in 1994, the World Series, the highlight of America's national
pastime, was finally brought to its knees—broken by a players' strike
over the issue of pay.

The controversy that canceled the World Series and angered fans from
coast to coast involved a handful of superstar athletes and an even smaller
group of wealthy team owners arguing over already astronomically high
salaries. Yet it nonetheless pointed to a basic dilemma facing every organization—large and small—around the world today: How, in the face of
dramatic change, can we continue to motivate our employees, satisfy our
customers, improve the quality of our products and services, increase our
productivity and profit margin, and all the while stay on top of the competition? And what role, if any, should pay—a powerful but often
misunderstood force—play in the process?

The solution thus far has been elusive, despite a growing army of experts and ideas. You only have to pick up a business magazine, watch
television, or go to a bookstore to see what a booming business the business of rebuilding business has become. Not that there is anything wrong
with reading such books, many of which are excellent, or listening to the
growing number of experts, many of whom offer outstanding advice.

The problem is that most offer only a single answer, a small piece of the puzzle, one organizational strategy, perhaps. So, instead of trying to integrate new business strategies with new company goals, new organizational designs, and the changing values and attitudes of people, many organizations have simply kept adding the latest bells and whistles, the latest solution *du jour*.

As a result, they have created organizational monsters more dysfunctional than Dr. Frankenstein's, structures and strategies more complex and less efficient than a Rube Goldberg schematic. And, after more than a decade of pursuing the latest "business trends," many companies have, like the car-chasing mongrel that just discovered a superhighway, either been flattened by progress or collapsed in a tail-dragging, tongue-tied heap by the side of the road, exhausted, bewildered, and mad as hell.

FLOPPING FADS, FIZZLING PHILOSOPHIES

The Wall Street Journal put the issue into perspective with a page 1 story headlined "Many Companies Try Management Fads, Only to See Them Flop." The article was a well-documented indictment of some of the most highly touted business and management trends—including those in compensation—of the 1990s.

"Process re-engineering, benchmarking, total quality management, broadbanding, worker empowerment, skill-based pay," it began. "The labels abound when it comes to the trendy remedies executives are using to try to breathe new life and competitive fire into their companies.

"But while these approaches may promise more motivated work forces and greater productivity, the results often fall far short. When this happens, companies find they must sharply modify, abandon, or find antidotes to programs that bring sweeping changes to organizational and human-resource management."[1]

That is not to say that all business initiatives are mere fads, corporate alchemy that combines business school philosophy and consulting concepts to produce little more than fool's gold. Most successful companies, for example, are not giving up on quality simply because their early initiatives failed. Rather, they are looking for new and more effective ways of achieving their goals. And, they are looking beyond the normal demands of business in an effort to improve efficiency, productivity, and profits.

COMPENSATION: OVERLOOKED IN THE EQUATION

In the rush to change, many organizations have overlooked or mishandled what could well be one of the most effective tools at hand—compensation. Never mind that pay is a major cost of doing business—over $17 per employee hour worked. Never mind that compensation can be a critical force in supporting change. The fact remains, in most organizations compensation has largely been ignored.

This oversight, to a large extent, can be blamed on a lack of understanding of the changing role of pay and its impact on people. When we talk about compensation and its importance in motivating people and enhancing performance, our critics often turn to that business guru of gurus, W. Edwards Deming. "But Dr. Deming," they begin, "said that you can't motivate people with extrinsic rewards."

Although a brilliant management strategist, Deming unfortunately didn't fully understand the role compensation can play in today's organization. And most of the critics who quote him don't fully understand the point he was trying to make—a point he made very well in a newspaper interview a few years ago. "We are all born with intrinsic motivation, self-esteem, dignity, an eagerness to learn," he said. "Our present system of management crushes that all out . . . by replacing it with extrinsic motivation, by constantly judging people."[2]

Deming is right in touting the merits of intrinsic motivation. Indeed, many organizations have stifled that aspect of performance—and they have often done it through lousy pay and performance management strategies, as well as bad supervision and bureaucratic administrative practices. But to say that all extrinsic rewards are therefore bad is to miss the point. The fact is, a well-designed compensation program that is fully and properly aligned with an organization's values and culture does wonders for self-esteem and an eagerness to learn, not to mention performance.

There is no doubt that money directs behavior. If you think otherwise, just pick up today's newspaper. People switch jobs, trade stock, go on strike, even break the law, to get money. As the infamous Willie Sutton is reported to have replied when asked why he robbed banks, "Because that's where the money is."

In Western society, in particular, money has taken on a complex and significant role in defining and communicating the essence of both individuals and groups. With the possible exception of religion, there is no stronger force in determining identity, status, and personal value. In essence, pay is a proxy of self-worth. What else—right or wrong—has the power to communicate everything from where you stand in an organization to what you've done, to what you are able to provide your family, to how you are able to live, to your place in society? For most people, that power flows from their job or role—from the work they do and from the compensation they receive for doing it.

That is not to say that compensation should in any way diminish the intrinsic rewards. They too, of course, remain a critical motivational tool. (Just ask the felonious Mr. Sutton, who in his autobiography admitted that money wasn't everything. "I loved it," he said of bank heists. "I was more alive when I was inside a bank, robbing it than at any other time in my life.")[3]

PAY'S ROLE IN THE ZEITGEIST OF CHANGE

Not only is compensation often misunderstood, frequently it also is misapplied. And, more often than not, it is completely out of synch with the rest of the organization's values and processes. The reason is clear: Although organizations have undergone dramatic changes, the strategies for assigning, administering, and implementing compensation have until very recently been frozen in time. As a result, compensation is no longer aligned with the organization's evolving organizational structure, work cultures, values, and business strategies.

It is a critical failing. Only now are people beginning to realize that pay in the current Zeitgeist of organizational change should play a much more significant role than in the past. Pay can no longer be seen as a mere expense and cost of doing business, but instead must be viewed as an investment that is closely linked to the long-term success of the organization.

Organizations are beginning to understand that pay should no longer be considered only in terms of specific jobs and current financial results. Compensation must inextricably be tied to people, their performance, and the organizational vision and values that their performance supports. Two of the most important factors influencing performance and results are an organization's climate—its values and culture—and its management practices, which include compensation. But, based on our own research, management practices hold more than twice the power of climate in influencing performance, and indeed, can heavily affect changes in the climate itself.

A force as powerful as pay cannot be trivialized. Think about the time and energy an organization puts into an executive compensation program and then multiply that by the number of employees in the organization. That's the sort of effort that must go into today's compensation program. An effectively designed, carefully aligned compensation strategy certainly won't make all of an organization's employees happy or satisfied. Nor will it eliminate all of an organization's behavioral problems. Such a strategy, however, will go a long way in improving performance and results.

Given such influence, compensation must be considered a long-term investment, which pays "returns" far beyond the current fiscal year, rather than a short-term cost of doing business. Take, for example, the company with the $10 million payroll. From a cost-of-doing-business perspective, a 4 percent increase is viewed as a one-time, $400,000 expense. If viewed from an investment perspective, however, it must be considered as a continuous $400,000 expense, which will only be compounded when another 4 percent increase is added next year. In this light, the need for continued individual and group growth, the need to continually "raise the bar," so to speak, and ask people to share the risks as well as the rewards becomes much more significant.

In many organizations, unfortunately, not everyone shares this enlightened "investment" vision of pay. Line managers, who are constantly driving home the message of continually improving speed, efficiency, and quality, are among the first to grasp it. But senior leadership, which often remains focused on cutting costs and increasing profits, usually has a tougher time seeing pay as anything more than a margin-reducing expense. And the human resources and compensation professionals often see pay purely in terms of attracting and retaining talent.

It is among this last group—those most closely involved in pay—that resistance to compensation change is the greatest. While they enforce and administer pay, they have not yet grasped this new concept of its importance in supporting changing values and improving the performance of people.

In a recent Hay survey of more than 1,500 human relations professionals, for example, improving quality and productivity were ranked as the top priorities for the coming year by 41 and 42 percent of the respondents, respectively. Yet only 25 percent thought linking pay to individual performance was a top priority; only 22 percent said linking pay to team performance was critical; just 14 percent thought tying pay to quality improvement was a major goal; and a mere 9 percent thought it was critical to survey employees about the company and their work.[4]

So much for pay and performance and the importance of people in the equation. No wonder the human resources department is often viewed as a minor player in the organization—out of touch with goals and values. No wonder more than one human resources or compensation vice president has had his or her head "taken off" by the board of directors for merely suggesting a pay increase based on traditional survey comparisons within the market—a practice that worked fine in the past. Why, the VP is asked rather bluntly, is their organization hobbled in lockstep with market pricing when it had a worse—or perhaps better—year than the competition?

Good question. It isn't that the traditional pay strategies—programs that worked so well for so long—suddenly turned on us. What shifted were organizational values, work cultures, and business strategies. Although they largely have been overlooked, dramatic changes in the organizational rules have frequently rendered traditional compensation strategies ineffective.

Employees today are expected to work in teams rather than solely on their own. They are expected to keep learning new skills and to assume broader roles. They are expected to take more risks and responsibility for results. As a consequence, we are slowly coming to the realization that we may be paying for the wrong things, sending inconsistent messages about the company to its employees, or creating artificial expectations of continued advancement and raises, no matter how well the company performs.

This need to change compensation is in no way limited to U.S. organizations. In early 1994, for example, Hay held a number of conferences around the world to introduce the concepts of dynamic pay strategies. At that time, we found that many organizations in many countries were far behind what we were doing in the United States and some parts of Europe. On a similar tour less than nine months later, however, the mood had shifted dramatically. Everywhere we went—Europe, Latin America, Asia, the Pacific Rim—we found organizations clamoring for new compensation strategies. The waves of change that we had earlier experienced in the United States and parts of Western Europe had very quickly, we found, reached their shores. Today, we are helping many of those organizations design new compensation strategies that are aligned with their changing cultures and business strategies. Among them are a large Australian petroleum firm that is transforming its culture so that it can aggressively develop new markets and increase customer service, an electronics firm in Singapore that is developing new leadership competencies so that it can improve managerial effectiveness, and a Venezuelan utility that is beginning to use skill-based pay in order to boost performance, broaden the roles of employees, and eliminate a culture of entitlement.

A GROWING NEED FOR CHANGE

It's not just compensation that must change, of course. In most organizations today, there is an increased awareness of the need for a total rethinking of the traditional ways of doing things, a revolution of the workplace. The cutbacks, downsizing, and layoffs that are such prominent features of the corporate landscape can no longer be viewed as solutions to short-term economic problems. Rather, they call for a fundamental change in the way we think about work and pay.

Among those traditional concepts that are beginning to be jettisoned is the view of work from a "scientific" management perspective that broke it down into its respective parts, and then broke those parts down into specialties and subspecialties. Take, for example, the traditional human resources department that continues to be used in many organizations. Within that department there is usually a benefits department. And within the benefits department there are "subspecialists"—individuals who deal with health care benefits, retirement benefits, and compensation.

Increasingly, organizations today are giving up this multitude of specializations—and the multitude of staff they require—in favor of smaller staffs of generalists, supplemented when necessary by specialists from outside the organization who are brought in on a temporary basis. Thus the paradigm of specialization is beginning to shift. As this shift takes place, we have stopped defining jobs in a tight, vertical, functional manner, and have begun to ask people to do things more horizontally, a move that sacrifices depth but provides a team of broader, more well-rounded players.

This shift signals dramatic, and in the view of some, dire consequences for a lot of people. Many of those jobs and positions that daily we read are being eliminated are just that: gone forever. And no economic boom, however rosy, is going to bring them back. The successful organizational employee—the one who will not only survive but move ahead in this brave new workplace, will be the one who can learn and expand his or her knowledge, skills, and competencies. It will be the individual who will be able to perform a variety of functions and frequently work as a member of a larger team.

Those who want to remain specialists will become "contract" players, the consultants, freelancers, and part-timers who will be used by the organization on a temporary basis. These individuals will leave the role or relationship after they have accomplished their mission or special project, whether it lasts two days, two weeks, or two years. As noted organizational expert Charles Handy wrote, "Less than half of the work force in the industrial world will be in 'proper' full-time jobs in organizations by the beginning of the 21st century. Those full-timers or insiders will be the new minority. . . ."[5]

One early example of this move toward utilizing a combination of "core" and "contract" employees was seen in the health care industry. A decade ago, during an industry-wide shortage of nurses, hospitals created their own registries in order to attract and keep the best available nurses. These hospital registries allowed nurses to sign up for a certain number of hours or days a week, rather than work a standard forty-hour-a-week schedule.

Today, of course, the acceleration of change is forcing most health care organizations to reengineer their core processes and redefine the roles of their core employees. In many hospitals today, the raft of "specialists" ranging from the housekeeper to the head nurse has been replaced by a small cadre of multiskilled people who—as a team—provide the full range of patient care.

Although still foreign to many traditional organizations, new approaches such as team-based processes and core/contract networks are slowly gaining acceptance in modern organizations that recognize the need to change.

SIX CHANGES AFFECTING EVERY ORGANIZATION

While every organization and industry finds itself undergoing a unique set of changes, there are at least six major changes that are common to almost every organization. They are:

- rapidly expanding technologies
- growing global competition
- increased demand for individual and organizational competencies and capabilities
- higher customer expectations

- ever-decreasing cycle times
- changing personnel requirements

Each of these has been examined in great detail by other authors, but a brief review here is warranted in the context of changing organizational values and compensation strategies.

Technologies: Faster, More Accessible

Although the explosion of technology is widely acknowledged and accepted, many of the specific technological changes that have occurred have been either misread or not fully appreciated. The computerization of offices, for example, was initially viewed primarily as a way to enhance productivity. And productivity was defined as individuals being able to do more or higher quality work in a given span of time.

What occurred, however, was a much greater revolution. That piece of cable now linking employees had absolutely no respect for organizational charts or rules, and information began flowing freely across what had previously been impenetrable boundaries. New and ever-expanding networks were created linking employees not only with employees in other rooms, offices, even countries, but also with suppliers and customers. So, what began as an improvement of the traditional, specialized individual paradigm (it is, after all, called a *personal* computer) soon was itself creating new paradigms—"nodes" of influence that emphasized networks and groups rather than the lone employee punching a keyboard. Ultimately, what started as a tool to improve individual productivity has become a tool to facilitate group communications. And, with such developments as local area networks (LANs) and the Internet, the dynamics of those group communications are continually expanding.

In a few short years, the computer has fundamentally changed jobs. The electronic spreadsheet alone eliminated huge numbers of jobs. What before the advent of computers had been done by roomfuls of mid-level analysts in finance, marketing, sales, and human resources can now be handled by one clerical person with a machine and software that can be purchased for a few thousand dollars from any discount electronics store.

And personal computers aren't the only technology to impact organizations today. Mobile telephones, fax machines, satellite links, and commercial air travel are playing a big role in reshaping the organization, reducing the significance of specific times and places for work (or almost any other activity), provided output is delivered on time. Flexible schedules, job sharing, telecommuting, and the growth of the virtual office all reflect this change.

Global Economics: Expanding Its Impact While Limiting Labor Costs

These technologies have given rise to a new breed of businessperson, a globe-trotting transnational who, although affiliated with one region or country, is really playing in a world marketplace. Indeed, the borders and barriers that traditionally have restricted the global market are coming down at a dazzling pace. In five short years, we have seen the Berlin Wall crumble, the former Soviet Union fall, a large part of Eastern Europe plunged into economic and political turmoil, the rapid growth of the European Economic Community, the signing of the North American Free Trade Agreement, the General Agreement on Tariffs and Trade, and the explosion of the Asian/Pacific market. Whether or not we support these changes, the fact remains: They are reshaping the global marketplace.

Increasingly, organizations—even those that don't feel the impact of global pricing—are being reshaped by forces outside of what they perceive as their market. Take, for example, the small business with a sales effort that is limited to one region of one country. It may not view itself as a global player. Yet, if the product it sells is produced in the United States, and the business's customers can get that product for less money or faster through another source in, say, Taiwan or Vietnam, then this small company may soon face the impact of global economics even though it considers itself a local player.

Over time, these global economics are narrowing the cost of labor as a percentage of a product's cost. As a result, a finite range of labor costs is evolving, beyond which an organization cannot stray and expect to remain competitive. In light of such change, many organizations are restructuring around teams and processes rather than individual jobs to increase cost effectiveness, as well as improve flexibility, speed, and service. These more efficient organizations require fewer employees, but employees with multiple skills and competencies. As Charles Handy wrote, the new organizational equation for success today is:

$$1/2 \times 2 \times 3 = P$$

Translated, it says that in today's marketplace, profit and productivity are best created by half the workforce, paid twice as well, producing three times as much.[6]

Competencies and Capabilities: More Important Than Products

With increased competition, companies are rapidly finding that a good product or service alone does not ensure success. Instead, they must distinguish themselves by focusing on fundamental competencies and capabilities that will set them apart from the pack. To achieve this, organizations must maximize individual, unit, and organizational competencies—those underlying attributes or characteristics that can predict superior performance. These competencies range from tangible attributes, such as skills and knowledge—technical know-how, for example, or the ability to operate a sophisticated computer—to intangible attitudes and values, self-image, traits, motives, and behaviors—attributes such as teamwork and flexibility. These competencies will become a part of the organization's foundation and will be the focus of everything from hiring and training to marketing.

Take, for example, large service organizations such as insurance companies or health care providers. What will set them apart from the competition is no longer simply the quality of the insurance policies they write or the level of health care they provide, but also how fast they are in processing claims or providing treatment, and how sincere and friendly they are in addressing the needs of policyholders or patients. Organizations are increasingly differentiating themselves in terms of focus and strategic competencies rather than specific products, services, or markets. One electronics company, for example, may not think in terms of the particular pieces of equipment it makes, but in terms of its competency in miniaturization. Another may think in terms of dominating competition through time-based superiority—emphasizing speed to market, simplicity, and self-confidence.

Customers: Driving Organizational Designs and Strategies

Next to technology, customers may be the most powerful force changing organizations. Being first to market with a product or service is no longer enough. Today's customers are demanding better service, faster response, higher quality, and a heightened sensitivity to their needs. They require products and services to be customized or individualized—without erosion of accessibility, functionality, or reliability.

Consumers have quickly gone from accepting "any color as long as it's black" to "having it their way." Take ice cream: It is no longer enough to have vanilla, chocolate, and strawberry. It is not enough to have thirty-one flavors, or even the flavor of the month. Now you can go to the ice cream store and order chocolate-chip-cookie-peanut-butter-cherry-pie ice cream. It doesn't make any difference whether you are a commercial or retail customer. You can require and receive products tailored to your tastes and requirements.

When it comes to service and accountability, customers today also are less willing to recognize the geographic and ownership limits of an organization. "If you sell a product to me," they reason, "then you are responsible for making sure it works. Don't bother me with your problems or principles, I don't really care. My bottom line: Either stand behind your product or service, or I'll find someone else."

Sound a little strong? Perhaps. But you would be surprised how many people are committed to this philosophy. Just ask anyone who has consistently maintained a successful automotive dealership over the past ten years. The ways in which imported attitudes forced U.S. dealers to shift their emphasis from sales and style alone to continuous high-quality customer service could themselves take up an entire book. A few have even turned to pay. One luxury car dealer in Texas, a client of ours, is creating a team-based reward program in which pay is in large part determined by customer satisfaction. Unquestionably, this is a very different paradigm from the car sales of old.

This increased emphasis on customers extends beyond what is traditionally thought of as the customer—the retail or wholesale buyer of goods and services. Today, it also extends to the "internal customer," the supplier perhaps, or the coworkers in other departments or divisions. And it works in a variety of settings—even in the middle of the ocean. Although it was named Black Magic, the yacht that New Zealand sailed in its lopsided America's Cup victory was successful because of its approach to business and not because of any curses or wand-waving. While other designers labored over their plans in isolation, the Kiwis involved most of the fifty-five-person crew—who in effect were the designers' customers. The crew, for example, came up with the boat's deck plan.[7]

As the challengers who were left in Black Magic's wake quickly discovered, organizations that reinforce bureaucracy and preengineered responses are rapidly being overtaken by those that provide customers with the best tailored solutions in the shortest time. To meet this shift in focus and attitude, new organizational designs are evolving that are aligned with customer needs and emphasize customer/company partnerships. As a result, new leadership skills must be developed, along with new measurement systems that not only integrate customer satisfaction and financial performance, but also facilitate strategic planning with key customers.

Boeing Co. took such an approach when it built its state-of-the-art 777. Not only did it involve a team of experts in design, manufacturing, and tooling, but it also brought airline customers into the planning sessions. So well did the approach work that the first plane built went together almost perfectly. Said the general manager of the 777 division: "It was just like Fisher-Price toys going together on Christmas Eve."[8]

Speed and Simplicity: Keys to Competitive Advantage

Why have customers become so demanding? Part of the "problem," if you want to call it that, goes back to technology. Not only are today's customers more knowledgeable and aware, but they also have been spoiled rotten, brainwashed if you will, by the Religion of Real Time. They have come to expect everything from their hamburgers to their health care right now! If they can have a war brought into their living rooms, live from Baghdad, then, by gosh, they do not expect to wait around for a burger and fries, a new water pump for the family van, or a liver transplant for Uncle Fred.

You cannot blame them. We are living more in a real-time environment than ever before. The lag-time of yesterday ("We'll have a decision for you in a couple of weeks, Mr. Dithers. As soon as the information is mailed to us from the home office, we'll mail it to you.") has been eliminated by technology as simple as Federal Express and telephones. ("We'll have a decision for you in a couple of hours, Ms. Jetson. As soon as the information is faxed to us we'll modem it to you.")

While most of us are still struggling with the ever-increasing speed at which change buffets our organizations, we have come to accept that speed when it comes to reduced turnaround times and shorter product cycles.

To survive and compete in such an environment, organizations must move through their product/service life cycles at a faster pace. This ever-quickening rush to market can be found in a number of industries, especially those that dance on the cutting edge of technology. Locked into a battle-to-the-death with Nintendo Co. and Sony Corp. for control of the video game world, and hoping to "get the drop" on both, Sega Enterprises, Ltd., advanced by four months the scheduled release of its latest game player in the United States. Its marketing slogan for its new product said it all: "It's out there."

But speed to market alone doesn't insure success. At the same time, organizations must find simpler, more customer-friendly ways to deliver services and products. Control-oriented organizations filled with barrier-laden bureaucracies, time-consuming committees, and cumbersome approval processes are being scrapped. Instead, work is being redesigned and reengineered to increase flexibility and efficiency and empower employees.

People: Greater Diversity, More Value, Less Loyalty

Whatever their structure, whatever their business strategy, organizations are quickly coming to the realization that it is the performance of their "human assets," their people, that can make the difference between success and failure. Yet, as the organization and nature of work has changed, so too have the workers.

With the increased emphasis on technology, quality, and service, we are quickly moving away from a purely "mechanized" workforce to an "intellectualized" one. Consistency is no longer king. We no longer want people to act like robots, but rather to make their own informed, intelligent decisions, use good judgment, and assume more responsibility for the organization's performance. Such a dramatic change requires that people accept new values, behave differently, learn new skills and competencies, and often take more risks.

Empowering those people is a critical element of effective organizational change. As Gary Hamel and C. K. Prahalad argue in their book *Competing for the Future*, "Delegation and empowerment are not just buzzwords, they are desperately needed antidotes to the elitism that robs so many companies of so much brain power."[9] Unfortunately, next to reengineering, empowerment *has* become the most overused and misunderstood business buzzword of the 1990s. In too many offices in too many corporations, it has become a hollow battle cry, a phrase paid only lip service by many managers and openly laughed at by employees still waiting to be somehow "blessed" with this new mantle of responsibility.

A major reason for these problems is organizational change itself. Few organizations in America today have avoided the throes of downsizing or reorganization. And even the most loyal employees may find it difficult to believe that they are an empowered, valuable asset when all around them other "valued assets"—most likely their friends and coworkers—are being cut from the ranks.

The problem is not just with those people who have lost their jobs or who fear losing them. As the workforce continues to shrink and more is required of everyone—from the hourly worker to the CEO—each person must add measurable value to the organization. That means acquiring new knowledge, new skills, new competencies, and new behaviors. Employment is no longer viewed as a lifelong commitment, but rather as a performance contract that is continually renewed. Employees are being asked to do more, do it differently, and share in the organization's risks and rewards. For most of us, that is a bitter pill to swallow. After all, we had come to expect a continually improving quality of life, along with continually increasing paychecks and continued job security.

Just how much damage these changes have done to the employee psyche can be seen in the results of several recent studies. A 1993 study by a group of Fordham University social scientists found that Americans' sense of well-being had dropped to a twenty-year low. This Index of Social Health, which looked at sixteen categories including unemployment, came in at a weak 36 out of a possible 100 points—less than half the 1972 high of 79. A companion Index of Social Confidence, which examines how Americans evaluate national performance in areas that shape the quality of life, including education, occupation, and living standards, came in at 34.[10]

The results of a recent Hay study of employee attitudes were little more encouraging. Top management, for example, got favorable ratings from less than half of the four employee groups surveyed: middle management, professional/technical, clerical, and hourly workers. Less than 40 percent of each group felt that their company provided them with the training to advance. And 50 percent or less of each group said they were satisfied with their pay.[11]

For companies that had gone through a downsizing in the past two years, the view was even worse. Employees in those companies thought they were treated with less respect and had less job security than employees in organizations that had not faced such cutbacks. The survey showed that 60 to 80 percent of the employees (depending on the group they were in) at downsized organizations still liked their jobs and the kind of work they did. Yet only 30 to 40 percent thought that the job made good use of their skills and abilities; 40 to 50 percent thought they had good job security, and less than 25 percent thought they were treated with respect.

Those are scary numbers, considering that many organizations are pinning many of their hopes for the future on the belief that employees will take a greater role in the decision making and a greater responsibility for the success—or failure—of the organization. We're not talking about just the few leaders and "star" performers, but the "average ideal" employees who, if truly empowered, become superior performers and drive the organization.

This sort of true empowerment, however, requires much more than new titles or even shifts in jobs, roles, and organizational structures. It requires a commitment not only to help employees obtain the new skills and competencies they need, but also to reward them when they use those skills and competencies to help the organization achieve its goals. One company that stands out in this regard is LEGO Systems, Inc., the manufacturer of those little plastic bricks that many of us—or our children—played with while growing up.

A recent employee attitude survey at the company's Connecticut plant, which garnered a 98 percent favorable response rate, is just one indication that the organization is doing something right. That something, according to managers and employees alike, is a transformed company culture, structure, and pay program that emphasizes teamwork and responsibility. In the packing department, for example, the traditional assembly line operation has been replaced with self-directed work teams, eliminating the need for several layers of supervision and creating a heightened sense of pride and responsibility on the part of the employees.

"There is a very positive atmosphere about this company," says compensation manager Raymond Patton. "You can sense it when you walk in here. You can sense it on the floor. People just love this company to death." Yet as glowingly as Patton describes the company, he is the first to admit that achieving a high level of employee empowerment is not something that happened overnight. It was—and remains—a slow, continuously evolving process that has not been without its share of problems. It is not a process, however, that most companies to this point have been willing to sustain.

Greater workforce diversity is another "people" issue that organizations are struggling with. Perhaps the best "snapshot" of the changing face of the American worker was taken by the Hudson Institute in its landmark *Workforce 2000 Study*. Among the study's findings, many of which already are proving accurate, between now and the turn of the century:

- The population and the workforce will grow more slowly than at any time since the 1930s.

- The average age of the population and workforce will rise, and the pool of young workers entering the labor market will shrink.
- More women will enter the workforce.
- Minorities will make up a larger share of new entrants into the labor force.
- Immigrants will represent the largest share of the increase in the population and workforce since World War I.[12]

The impact of this increased diversity can already be seen in workplace attitudes. According to the latest Hay employee data, for example, minorities express more favorable attitudes than their counterparts in their commitment to their company and their chances of achieving career goals. But they are less positive than their nonminority coworkers when it comes to issues such as job stress, discrimination, and the fairness of pay. Although the survey noted few differences between men and women employees, issues such as flextime, job sharing, child care, and maternity leave have become critical as more women have entered the workforce. And, despite this supposed age of enlightenment in which we're living, the issue of equal pay for women remains a hurdle for many organizations.

Workforce diversity, like many of the changes assaulting organizations, is a two-edged sword. There is no doubt it has created a number of new management issues that range from the variety of food served in the cafeteria, to the need for flextime, to the facilitation of teamwork. Employee relationships, for example, more critical than ever in this time of teams, can be considerably more complex in a highly diverse workforce.

Despite these new management issues, diversity has quickly proven itself critical to organizational success, adding an important and much-needed dimension to our workforce. For starters, it has given employers a larger, more diverse pool of talent from which to choose—especially important in a global economy. Depending on the type of organization, they may select independent creative self-starters, or more controllable, detail-oriented people. These choices can more easily help change the way work is designed. Perhaps more important, diversity also has introduced a broad variety of values and perspectives that were solely lacking in the white, male-only organization of the past—values and perspectives that are not only required in today's more diverse marketplace, but also are critical in facilitating change.

RESPONDING TO CHANGE: FOUR AREAS OF EMPHASIS

How organizations react to these major changes varies, of course, depending on their business goals and strategies and which of the changes are exerting the most "pull" within their environment. Yet if we examine their structures, cultures, and values closely, we see that in general there are four primary areas that organizations focus on in order to achieve their desired results.

These types of responses are not new. They have, to one extent or another, been around for literally hundreds of years. Yet the importance of each and the role it plays must continually change and evolve along with the rest of the organization. These four areas of focus or emphasis are:

• *Technology*. Broadly conceived as "ways of doing things," these responses range from low-tech approaches such as manual labor to state-of-the-art, high-tech computerized information systems.

• *Customer Focus*. Many organizations respond by granting the customer a key role in determining the culture and strategy of today's organization. How an organization perceives, understands, relates to, communicates with, and works toward satisfying customers is critical to its strategy and success. And the "customer base" is far bigger than the retail or wholesale buyer. It includes suppliers, contractors, even other divisions or departments in the organization.

• *Flexibility*. Speed and adaptability are of the essence in today's global marketplace. Cycle and turnaround times continue to shrink. How quickly and effectively an organization can change the things that don't work, or improve those that do, is critical to keeping it competitive and profitable.

• *Reliability*. Despite all the new demands driven by change, such as better customer service, more efficient processes, and faster response times, an organization can't forget the major area of focus that has traditionally ruled an organization. Reliability, the ability to continually meet high standards, be they for quality, service, speed, or dependability, is essential in today's market.

The degree to which organizations utilize one or more of these key responses leads to the creation of broad strategies within and between industries. If they are to be competitive, organizations must make strategic decisions on work systems and design, management processes, and human resource practices (including compensation and benefits) based on these touch points.

OUTCOMES: BROADER MEASURES, LONGER VISION

Many of the changes already discussed also are forcing organizations to rethink their outcomes—to reconsider how they measure value and success. Traditionally, organizations have measured their performance primarily through relatively short-term financial results: sales, growth, profitability, and key ratios such as earnings per share, return on investments, and return on assets. While these measures are still valid, today's faster paced, more competitive business environment is pushing organizations to find ways that better predict their long-term viability and shareholder value— in terms of both financial performance and less tangible assets such as name, brand, image, levels of quality, and customer satisfaction.

To that end, organizations must now look at the behaviors, organizational cultures, and business strategies that will generate long-term value— everything from responsiveness and customer service to acquisition and organizational integration.

To better determine their long-term shareholder value, a number of organizations are turning to economic value added (EVA) models, which look at the total cost of the organization's true capital—everything from machinery and real estate to what the organization is spending on research and development and employee training.[13] Such measures, organizations are finding, while not "magic bullets," are much better predictors of their long-term success and viability.

THE ROLE OF DYNAMIC COMPENSATION
STRATEGIES IN THE CHANGE PROCESS

As we have already noted, to this point most organizations have dealt with the forces of change through very narrow, specific strategic initiatives, such as quality, teams, and reengineering. Unfortunately, when organizations finally begin to rethink their pay strategies, they frequently continue taking a somewhat reactionary approach—overlooking the connection to the overall structure and strategy of the organization, or to any other processes.

That is not surprising considering that, traditionally, compensation, like many other human resource processes, functioned somewhat independent of other organizational strategies. And, because most businesses—although different in size, scope, and even industry—tended to be organized along similar, very functional lines, most embraced a fairly standardized approach to pay.

Take the pay-for-points methodology made famous by our firm. The Hay Guide Chart Profile Method, a system that compares the value of jobs based on know-how, problem solving, and accountability, has been used since the early 1950s by literally thousands of organizations in a wide variety of industries around the world. Yet while the Hay system continues to work well in many of these organizations, others are finding that—at least in its current form—the traditional guidelines for pay no longer support their business and organizational needs.

As a result of this continuing disconnect between pay and other processes, a plethora of pay strategies somewhat miscast as "magic bullet" solutions has been developed, creating what we call the "Pay for _____ Syndrome"—pay for skills, pay for teams, pay for competencies, pay for the latest management solution to come down the pike. And, because each of these strategies is considered in a vacuum, companies often find themselves jumping from one "pay for" program to another, searching for The Answer to all their needs.

Not surprisingly, with the scope and diversity of the changes that are taking place, there is no longer a single, ideal pay strategy for all organizations. Any number of these new approaches to pay can be very effective if they are tailored to—and aligned with—an organization's evolving needs, goals, and work cultures. In the "one organizational model, one compensation strategy" paradigm of the past, alignment was a virtual no-brainer. Today, however, it has become a major part of the equation. To jump into a brand-new pay strategy without fully understanding its fit with your particular organization is like attempting to tune a Ferrari after working for years on Model Ts.

AN ISSUE OF ALIGNMENT

There is no doubt compensation should play an important role in supporting changing organizational values, business strategies, and work cultures. An effective compensation strategy, although often overlooked, can be critical in effectively harnessing the forces of change and moving the organization forward. Nonetheless, the key is not in finding the newest, most innovative, or even the most mechanically efficient of these pay solutions. The key is in first assessing an organization's culture and then aligning it with its strategic goals: What kinds of people does it want? What does the organization want them to do? Only after those people have been selected and their expected goals and responsibilities identified can the organization design supporting and stimulating reward programs—not trends, not fads, but dynamic pay programs that can evolve and change as the organization evolves and changes.

The solution to compensation, we strongly believe, lies not in tossing out the old standardized approach in favor of a new standardized approach. To be successful, organizations must take dynamic approaches that blend the body of compensation knowledge developed during the past fifty years with the latest, leading-edge approaches. But before they can even take that step they must—as we have already noted—carefully tailor compensation programs to their evolving needs, goals, and cultures.

Does this approach work? A number of organizations certainly believe so. Consider Trident Regional Health System, part of Columbia/HCA, the huge health care management organization. Saddled with a performance management system and merit pay plan that did not reflect its true mission and quality-driven values, the Charleston, South Carolina-based health system—a beta site for TQM efforts—developed a performance management and pay strategy based, to a great extent, on behavioral competencies such as teamwork, communications, and customer-mindedness. The results were very positive. As one of the senior executives told us: "A majority of employees are responding to what they need to improve upon. They feel they are more in control of their own destiny, because they are able to talk openly and honestly with their supervisors. After the first review cycle, not one employee came to us complaining about their pay."

He went on to add: "I don't know what it is going to look like in five years. But we've got a base to work from and continuously improve, and we have a feedback system that is going to allow us to effectively do that. I believe it is going to lead us closer toward something that is going to fit the high-quality hospital of the 1990s and beyond."[14]

His organization obviously understands what many others are just be-ginning to grasp: that while compensation can help support change, to be effective it must be aligned with the organization's values, culture, and stra-tegic goals. In the next chapter we will take you through the first step in achieving that alignment: assessing and understanding your organization's culture.

2
Work Cultures

I t is a frequently repeated scenario: A client or a potential client, often the vice president of human resources or the compensation director, calls. Their organization wants to design a new compensation program. The company has gone through major changes in the past eighteen months— a large staff reduction and a significant management restructuring. But problems persist. Productivity remains low. The recently implemented quality initiative is stalled. Employees are insecure and unmotivated. Top leadership is convinced pay is a big culprit and wants a new pay program— one of the new strategies they have read so much about—implemented by the end of the third quarter.

So we set up a meeting. But instead of immediately launching into a discussion about the compensation program they've asked us to design, we begin talking about change, work cultures, and the alignment of key business and human resources processes. At first they often appear a little perplexed. Yes, they say, they understand change. Now can we please get on with the subject at hand—compensation. After all, isn't that what we are the experts in? Isn't that why we were called in the first place?

Well, yes and no.

Before any new compensation program is designed, there must be a clear understanding of the organization: its current values, its structure, its people, as well as its goals and vision for the future. Without that knowledge, it is all but impossible to successfully change from the traditional, tightly conforming, highly rigid organization of yesterday into the flexible, diverse, continually evolving organization of tomorrow.

How does an organization establish a position from which it can chart such a course? The most effective way is through a thorough assessment of how its work is organized, how its people behave, interact, and relate to the organization, and what values and forces shape the organization's vision, mission, and strategic goals. Together, these dynamics make up what we call the organization's work culture.

CULTURE AS AN ORGANIZING CONCEPT

Mention the word "culture," and most managers and mid-level executives raise an eyebrow. It may be a fine phrase for the current management literature, perhaps, but a bit too touchy-feely—too "soft"—for the bottom-line-ruled world in which they must operate. It's a natural response. After all, most of us are grounded in technical expertise. And the application of that expertise, we believe, is what will move us—and our organizations—ahead.

No doubt such "hard" technical expertise is still important. But success in today's business environment requires a much broader vision, not only of the organization itself, but of the people that make up the organization, their skills and competencies, their relationship with each other, and their relationship to the organization—in short, their work culture.

"Culture," in this context, is far more than the "warm and fuzzy" attitudinal concept popularized in the 1970s. Nor is it merely a "fashion statement" that can be used to typecast or differentiate organizations. What we are describing is an organizational concept that encompasses how work is done and how people are selected, developed, managed, and rewarded.

Our research has shown that, given specific market dynamics, an organization must adopt certain work cultures if it is to become—or remain—a high-performing market leader. Health care organizations, for example, are quickly discovering that the market dynamics of managed care and capitated costs are forcing them to make widespread changes in the way they do business. The traditional, highly departmentalized, functional approach is neither cost-effective nor customer-friendly. If they are to be successful, they have to be more customer-focused, caring for patients through a series of seamless processes that eliminate functional barriers. At the same time, they must broaden their concept of what health care entails and redefine their role through the creation of networks or alliances with everyone from insurers to physicians.

All of these changes require a major culture shift. When Metropolitan Life Insurance Co. and Traveler's Group, for example, joined forces to create MetraHealth, a managed care company, they quickly determined that the new organization could not succeed by maintaining the highly functional, segmented culture of its parents. To be a force in the marketplace, MetraHealth instead would have to be a flexible, process-driven, team-oriented organization. Kennett L. Simmons, chairman and CEO, envisioned what he called a "gazellelephant"—a big organization that could turn on a dime. To create such an organization, MetraHealth is first establishing a culture that encourages—rather than impedes—change. As Simmons noted in a letter to employees: "Our organizational structure, our use of information and communications technology, our compensation and evaluation systems—all are being developed with the express goal of facilitating change."

The need to shift culture is not limited to a specific industry or organization. Indeed, as organizations scramble to keep up with changes, many seek decisive cultural adjustments. Eastman Kodak Company, for example, which dominated the photography industry for years, attempted a major culture shift after losing ground to foreign competition. If it was to regain its competitive edge, Kodak's leadership determined, it had to replace its highly functional, multilayered bureaucratic culture with one that was flatter, more flexible, and faster to market.

It should be noted, however, that a new work culture won't make a poor strategy effective. What it can do is provide critical support to the organization's chosen strategy so that its people continually deliver the desired results—be they in terms of productivity, quality, speed to market, or profits—in the most efficient, cost-effective manner possible. The most effective work culture is one that supports the organization's strategy by aligning behaviors, processes, and methods with the desired results. And, as many organizations have found, it is not just achieving results, but the method through which they are achieved, that is critical to long-term strategic success.

THE ELEMENTS OF A WORK CULTURE

Work cultures are made up of a variety of elements. In our own culture-modeling methodology, for example, we have identified more than fifty attributes that can be used in helping organizations determine their culture. These attributes, which range from "encouraging innovation," to "maximizing customer satisfaction," to "providing secure employment," can then be prioritized so that organizations can begin to determine both their current and future cultures.

While such methodology can provide a highly detailed picture of a work culture, it is not essential—at least in the initial stages of assessing one's organization. Indeed, although the "resolution" may be less well defined, an organization can begin to create a good likeness of its cultures by answering the following questions:

- What is the overriding strategic intent of the organization?
- How is the organization structured?
- What are its values?
- How is work organized?
- How are decisions made?
- How are resources allocated?
- What behaviors are encouraged? What behaviors are prohibited?
- What kind of people work for the organization?
- What are their values?
- How do they think?
- How do they act?
- How much power do they have?
- How much risk are they allowed—and do they wish—to take?
- How are they selected and developed?
- How are they rewarded?
- How is pay viewed? Is it seen as an investment, or merely a cost of doing business?

By answering these questions, an organization can begin to understand its work cultures and how they are evolving. From that point, it can begin to determine which compensation strategies would be most effective in supporting those cultures. Yet it is this assessment that organizations frequently overlook or ignore in creating many of today's so-called "pay for" programs. Instead, most new compensation strategies are based on simplistic, snapshot assessments that often lead to static, one-dimensional pay solutions. "We have teams! So let's implement a team-based pay program," exclaims the director of human resources. "No," cries the CEO, "knowledge and skills are becoming more important, so let's create a skill-based compensation plan."

A more dynamic cultural assessment, on the other hand, offers the multidimensional "live picture" that is needed to design a carefully aligned, ever-evolving pay program. This analysis, however, cannot be limited to the organization as it currently exists. Its "future vision" and the cultures that will be needed to achieve that vision must also be examined.

THE EVOLUTION OF FOUR CULTURES

Work cultures, despite their newfound popularity, have been a part of organizational life for years. Certain functions have always lent themselves toward different ways of organizing work, and different ways of structuring and relating jobs. Engineers and industrial psychologists have long walked the floors of factories and plants, searching for ways to better organize work and thus increase productivity, reduce cycle times, and ultimately boost profits. Effective leaders have continually sought ways to better link the role of the individual to that of the organization, so that the individual would feel that he or she had a greater stake in the organization and would assume more responsibility for the organization's success.

Yet because most organizations were highly functional and similar in structure, most conformed to a single culture—one with a rigid hierarchy emphasizing specialization and equity. This single-culture paradigm effectively eliminated the need to diversify jobs, work, organizational structures, and compensation. Instead, compromise ruled. A single, unified approach was used by most organizations. Jobs were analyzed and measured, placed into a single table, and from that table a pay plan for the entire organization was developed. These were what the jobs should look like. These were the tasks, the outcomes, the kind of training needed, the range of rewards. The result: a comfortable conformity—not to mention a good deal of compromise—in how organizations rewarded people.

Eventually, however, as global competition intensified, and the demand increased for better quality, more speed to market, and more intellectual labor, most organizations began to find this "one-size-fits-all" approach no longer acceptable. Why, they asked, should we be content to look like companies A, B, and C, when we can increase productivity—even a few percentage points—by refining our measures, redesigning work, and, finally, redefining how we reward people for that work? Take sales, for example. Although it has traditionally been treated as a function—with a sales department, sales representatives, a sales strategy—in reality it tends to be a continuous process, the culmination of many activities that cut a wide swath across the entire organization.

This questioning of traditional values and compromises has led many organizations to begin—perhaps for the first time—critically examining their work cultures not only in the context of their organizational structure and business systems, but also in the context of their overall strategies, goals, and—most important—their people. As a result, a more systematic pursuit of work cultures is evolving.

Our research of work cultures has resulted in the identification of four major "cultural models" that are operating in organizations today. These include the traditional, functional culture along with the three newer, evolving cultures: process, time-based, and network.

As Figure 2–1 shows, these cultures are driven and shaped by the changes described in Chapter 1, and by the four primary areas that organizations emphasize in order to achieve their desired results in the face of those changes: reliability, customers, flexibility, and technology.

What this static, two-dimensional figure does *not* reflect is the complexity and ever-changing dynamics of work cultures. For that reason, it is critical that as we discuss these cultures in detail, we keep in mind three important caveats: First, while work culture classification is critical, the models we have identified should be used as a yardstick and not a micrometer. Second, few organizations are "culturally pure." A natural initial response to the cultural assessment is to try to identify your organization with *one* of the four models. "Aha," you'll exclaim, halfway through this chapter, "we're a process (or network, or time-based) organization!" Resist this temptation to place a single label on your organization. Why? Because organizations seldom—if ever—fall completely within the parameters of a single model. Rather, they are variations and hybrids, such as a process/time-based culture, or a time-based/network culture.

Third, these four models should not be construed as the only ones at work in organizations today. No doubt others will evolve and are evolving as this is being written. The only thing we can say with certainty is that the traditional, one-paradigm work culture of the past is no longer relevant.

Figure 2–1

Changing Work Cultures

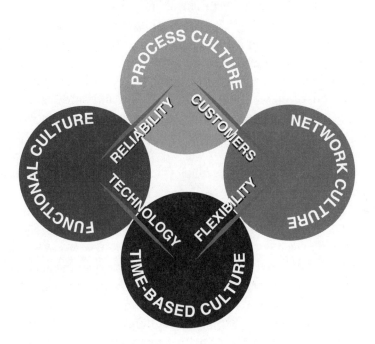

What *Fortune Magazine* predicted in a cover story on "How We Will Work in the Year 2000" has in fact already become reality: "Many of the industrial colossi, long the pillars of our economy, will have broken up or hollowed out. Taking the place of the hierarchically layered giants will be not just one type of organization but a variety of them. . . ."[1]

Despite these three exceptions to the rule, these models provide excellent vehicles for defining cultures and for demonstrating how they function within an organization. They offer a point of reference not only for determining an organization's present identity and personality, but also for creating a blueprint for building its future.

THE FUNCTIONAL CULTURE

Perhaps the easiest way to understand work cultures is to view them in anthropological terms: Just as the cultures in societies vary and continually evolve, so too do the cultures within organizations. As we've noted, for most of the past hundred years, indeed until about twenty years ago, a single culture dominated. Work, at least in the United States, was organized along functional, hierarchical lines. Stability, reliability, and consistency were the watchwords of the organization; customers were passive, cycle times lengthy, competition limited.

Although technology was slowly accelerating organizational processes, there was little need to rush things to market. Instead, this traditional work culture focused on what the organization did and on doing that consistently. It was driven by the need to accumulate resources of applied technology and limit risks by building highly reliable productivity. Long-range planning was the key. It was very reasonable to look ahead ten or even twenty years and be able to tell where an organization was headed.

The leading minds in business, people like Frederick Taylor, Henry Ford, Alfred P. Sloan, Jr., and Chester Barnard, staunchly defended and advanced this belief in the importance of stability of business patterns and markets. You were in a business; you knew what that business was. You knew your customers, and those customers tended to be passive. You also knew your competitors, who were usually limited by geography or industry. Banks, for example, didn't compete with insurance companies.

As Figure 2–2 shows, the primary attributes of the functional culture reflect these values—attributes such as minimizing the unpredictability of business results.

Work in the traditional culture was designed around the specialization of individuals. It was identified by management hierarchies in which decision making was clearly set apart from execution: bosses bossed, workers worked. Performance was measured in terms of size, return on equity, and industry reputation.

The successful employees were those with professional expertise—self-controlled people who valued discipline, security, and order. Chances are, they stayed with the same company—or, at the very least, the same industry—from the day they entered the workforce until the day they retired.

Despite the evolution of cultures, however, the functional culture remains alive and well, and continues to be an important—if not predominant—force in many organizations today. Yet in many of these organizations, the culture has evolved. Negative characteristics—such as rigid command and control structures—have been replaced with more positive approaches that emphasize people and performance.

Figure 2–2

Key Attributes of a Functional Culture

**To a Great
Extent**

- Being highly organized
- Using proven methods to serve existing markets
- Maintaining clear lines of authority and accountability
- Limiting the downside of risks
- Minimizing unpredictability of business results

- Providing secure employment
- Establishing clear, well-documented work processes
- Treating employees fairly and consistently
- Establishing clear job descriptions and requirements
- Respecting the chain of command
- Being precise
- Minimizing human error

- Supporting the decisions of one's boss
- Maximizing customer satisfaction
- Providing employees with resources to satisfy customers
- Delivering reliably on commitments to customers
- Using limited resources effectively
- Participating in training and continuing education
- Quality checking employees' work
- Supporting top management decisions
- Being loyal and committed to the company
- Achieving budgeted objectives

**To Some
Extent**

THE PROCESS CULTURE

About twenty years ago, cracks began to appear in the foundation of this one-culture paradigm that had ruled business for so long. The explosion of technology, along with the emergence of flexibility and customers as dominant marketplace forces, drove organizations spinning out of the traditional cultural orbits. As a result, new ways of organizing work, a redefinition of relationships with employees, and new sets of organizational values began to gain popularity.

For most organizations, this shift in trajectory was not a conscious move based on a sudden revelation of effective, new organizational strategies. Indeed, they knew only that their traditional strategies and values were no longer working, and they began an often aimless search for ones that were more effective. Nor did most organizations suddenly switch from a traditional, functional culture to one that they perceived to be more effective. Instead, they slowly began to evolve into some sort of a cultural hybrid, depending on their specific and very individual needs and how the major forces of change were affecting them.

Not surprisingly, with the increased emphasis on quality and customer satisfaction came the need to emphasize processes and group efforts rather than specialization and individual performance. As a result, one of the first new cultures to evolve was the process-based culture.

As the name implies, work in process-based organizations is designed around processes for meeting obligations to customers and continually improving quality. As such, a team approach to work dominates the culture. Planning, execution, and control are integrated as close to the customer as possible. Suppliers, the teams that carry out the processes, and customers, are linked through the decision-making process. Customers also play a role in measuring employee satisfaction.

Successful employees in process cultures are those who value service and who want to be affiliated with a group or team—tenacious people who work best when "influenced" rather than "directed" or "ordered." Strategic priorities obviously put customer satisfaction first, followed by reliability, technology, and finally, flexibility. The predominant attributes of the process culture, as shown in Figure 2–3, include maximizing customer satisfaction and continuously improving operations.

The process culture is growing in popularity in American business today, and may well be on its way to becoming one of the dominant work

Figure 2–3

Key Attributes of a Process Culture

To a Great Extent

- Maximizing customer satisfaction
- Demonstrating understanding of the customer's point of view
- Delivering reliably on commitments to customers
- Continuously improving operations
- Gaining the confidence of customers

- Providing employees with resources to satisfy customers
- Maintaining existing customer accounts
- Establishing clear, well-documented work processes
- Responding to customer feedback
- Participating in training and continuing education
- Acquiring cross-functional knowledge and skills
- Pushing decision making to the lowest levels

- Using proven methods to serve existing markets
- Treating employees fairly and consistently
- Tolerating well-meaning mistakes
- Limiting the downside of risks
- Encouraging teamwork
- Capitalizing on creativity and innovation
- Organizing jobs around capabilities of individuals
- Being precise
- Being loyal and committed to the company
- Achieving budgeted objectives

To Some Extent

cultures of the next ten to twenty years. Just how pervasive and effective this culture has become can be seen in its application to three very different organizations: a company that manufactures carbon black, a greeting card maker, and a large health care organization.

Cabot Corporation: From Product to Process

For many years, the Cabot Corporation has been one of the world's largest producers and suppliers of carbon black, a fine black powder that is critical to a number of industrial processes, including the manufacture of tires. As successful as it was, Cabot found its sales strategy—a single staff responsible for everything the company manufactured—did not lend itself to today's highly competitive, customer-oriented market. By focusing on traditional markets it was ignoring new sales, new markets, and, ultimately, new revenues—all the while making it easier for competitors to enter the market.

To address the problem, Cabot segmented its sales force by market to handle both existing and potential customers. Now, teams made up of individuals from sales, manufacturing, and research and development handle a single market—automotive products, perhaps, or construction. These teams not only sell products, but also are qualified and empowered to help design and manufacture them. In effect, Cabot transformed its sales function into a broad platform from which it can serve the customer's multiple needs. The result is a sales department that focuses not on projects, but on processes that emphasize speed, quality, and most important, customer satisfaction.

Hallmark Cards: From Function to Team

Even though it long ago established itself as a highly successful, innovative company, Hallmark Cards, like Cabot, continually searches for ways to better meet the needs and requirements of its customers.

Consider, for example, the creation and production of its greeting cards. Traditionally, this was a highly functional, departmentalized process. The artists were concerned solely with creating the perfect design and color. The writers focused their talents on the perfect verse. The printing and graphics departments worked to match the color. Average time to get a card to market: twenty-four months.

To improve both speed to market and at the same time continue to enhance the quality of its product, Hallmark, like Cabot, took a team approach. Now a group of artists and writers, along with representatives from the graphic and printing departments and unit control, sit down and create the card from design and color to words. Time from the first meeting until market: three to six months.

What Hallmark created, in essence, was a process-based culture. It replaced its rigid, traditional order, which was driven by the variety of specific functions needed to make a greeting card, with one in which work is designed around processes for meeting obligations to customers, and is executed through empowered team efforts.

Hallmark even carried the process a step further, converting the distribution of its Ambassador brand in large retail outlets from a traditional supplier/merchant relationship to a team/merchandiser approach. These teams work closely with the retailers, concerning themselves with issues such as profitability per square foot and number of returns. They constantly monitor what is being sold, obtain point of sale information, and feed the information back to the artists and editors. By shifting its strategy toward processes and away from functions, the company has successfully created a true partnership in which everyone—including the customer—benefits.

Harvard Pilgrim Health Care: A Process Approach to Care

Process cultures aren't limited to manufacturing. Many service industries also are adopting this approach. Harvard Pilgrim Health Care, for example, a large, Boston-based HMO, developed such an approach for caring for its patients. Rather than see a single physician who might refer them to a specialist, but who had little interaction or say in their overall treatment, patients are now served by a primary care physician who also serves as the ongoing "gatekeeper." This primary care physician channels and coordinates the full program of care as needed with an ever-changing ad hoc "team" of specialists and subspecialists who can provide the highest quality, most cost-effective care. As a result, everyone benefits—a key design criterion of the process culture. The HMO member benefits from better care and faster relief, and the customer—the employer or purchaser—from more cost-effective care management.

Harvard Pilgrim Health is not alone in its approach. Many hospitals and health care management organizations are reengineering today in an effort to cut costs, improve patient care, and stay ahead of the health care reform curve. Such approaches improve the quality and cost effectiveness of care, not to mention the work life of employees, through the redesign of work, the creation of new cross-functional roles, and the integration of the full range of services.

THE TIME-BASED CULTURE

While emphasis on quality and customers has driven many organizations away from the traditional functional organization toward one that is driven by processes, two other cultures have evolved in the past twenty years and are gaining prominence in business. They are the time-based and network cultures.

The time-based culture first gained attention in the early 1990s. As the marketplace became more global and technology more accessible, companies were no longer satisfied to rest merely on the laurels of quality and customer satisfaction. They had to search for additional ways to reduce costs and move new products and services to the market at an ever-quickening pace.

Keyed to maximizing the return on fixed assets, flexibility, and technical agility, time-based cultures limit the levels of management hierarchy while increasing the use of program and project work groups that cross functional boundaries. Individuals in time-based organizations are encouraged to develop multifunctional expertise and competencies. Rather than using traditional accounting measures such as return on assets, organizational performance is assessed through more dynamic measures such as economic value added (EVA) and by the competitive position that new products or services achieve in the marketplace.

The strategic priorities of time-based cultures are first flexibility and agility, then technology and customer needs, and finally reliability and quality. These priorities are reflected in the critical cultural attributes seen in Figure 2–4, which include maintaining a high sense of urgency and capitalizing on windows of opportunity.

The time-based approach was developed in organizations such as General Electric Co., which wanted, on a global basis, to be Number One or Two in each of its areas of business. Utilizing human and financial resources to the best advantage possible, such organizations strive to dominate markets in their high-profitability phases, and then move toward new opportunities as those markets reach a mature, lower-return stage.

In many cases, time-based cultures are far ahead of the customer in defining new applications, opportunities, and products that create new

Figure 2–4

Key Attributes of a Time-Based Culture

To a Great Extent

- Significantly decreasing cycle times
- Developing new products or services
- Maintaining a high sense of urgency
- Capitalizing on windows of opportunity
- Adapting quickly to changes in the business environment

- Being flexible and adaptive in thinking and approach
- Anticipating changes in the business environment
- Increasing decision-making speed
- Pioneering new ways of doing things
- Taking action despite uncertainty
- Promoting one's point of view strongly
- Applying innovative technology to new situations

- Maximizing customer satisfaction
- Demonstrating understanding of the customer's point of view
- Acquiring cross-functional knowledge and skills
- Capitalizing on creativity and innovation
- Organizing jobs around capabilities of individuals
- Encouraging innovation
- Rewarding superior performance
- Taking initiative
- Attracting top talent
- Establishing new ventures or new lines of business

To Some Extent

markets and generate new sources of value. Take, for example, the development of laptop computers, personal stereos, and VCRs: Until these products were created, no market for them existed. Indeed, a key to the success of time-based culture is its effectiveness in anticipating potential new market opportunities and then developing those markets.

Understanding that flexibility and agility are critical to maintaining a competitive edge, a number of organizations are adopting time-based cultures. One of the most highly publicized time-based success stories is the Chrysler Corporation. Driven by the need to reduce the time it took to get a new model to market from five or more years to a competitive three, Chrysler in the late 1980s "retooled" its traditional process for developing new cars. The sequential, functional process—from styling, to engineering, to parts procurement, to manufacturing—was replaced by four cross-functional teams, each of which had almost total responsibility for a particular segment of the market—small car, large car, minivan, and Jeep.

These teams are responsible for designing, engineering, and manufacturing in those key market segments. According to company officials, the time-based strategy not only worked, but has played a major role in the automaker's continuing success.[2]

THE NETWORK CULTURE

By the early 1990s, change was no longer viewed as a once-in-a-lifetime, once-in-a-decade, or even once-in-a-fiscal-year phenomenon. Instead, it had become a constant force. And with that consistency of change came the emergence of the "virtual corporation" and a fourth work paradigm, the network culture.

Work in the network culture is designed around alliances that bring together the necessary proficiencies and competencies to successfully complete a specific venture—the development of a new product, perhaps, or the production of a new movie. The traditional management hierarchy is replaced by "producers" who coordinate and direct the efforts of the network through the specific venture's life cycle.

Because the work in a network culture focuses on the completion of a well-defined venture or project, the roles are situational, lasting only as long as the project, and focused on achieving specific aspects of the venture. Relationships, not structures, rule the day. The emphasis is not on how specific jobs are designed, or where they fit into the organizational structure, but rather on how effectively people can work together. After all, the goal of a network culture is to assemble a group of highly effective and talented people and then give them the freedom to act, creating, in essence, situations where $2 + 2 = 5$. Power in these cultures flows to those with the critical capabilities, and is derived from the partnerships and strategic alliances of people and organizations—alliances which, unlike the teams in process cultures, are usually only temporary.

The forces that propel such organizations are innovation, mobility, and market creation and penetration. The people who are successful are innovative individuals who can quickly build relationships with others, exploit their mutual and collective talents, and who are confident of their own capabilities. These people also are highly skilled, providing top performance from Day One of the venture. In the network culture there is little need—or time—for individual training or development. The focus is on the successful orchestration of the team's collective efforts, usually under limited time constraints.

Flexibility and agility tend to head the strategic priorities of network organizations, followed by customer responsiveness, technology, and reliability. The key attributes needed to support these priorities, as seen in Figure 2–5, include building strategic alliances with other organizations and using resources outside the company to get work done.

Many network cultures are designed around the creation of new products, markets, or businesses. Once those markets or businesses are developed, however, they often are better managed by functional, process, or time-based organizations.

The network culture is not really new. It has been around for hundreds of years in various forms. Take guerrilla warfare, for example: If you wanted to start a revolution you simply went out and hired a band of mercenaries. After the revolution, the mercenaries went their way, you went yours. Today this "hired gun" approach is used in much more sophisticated and peaceful ways. One of the best examples is the development of the Macintosh computer, in which a group that included system designers, ergonomists, and marketing people was brought together for the sole purpose of creating a new computing platform.

But the network model is not limited to high-tech organizations. Two established industries have been using this approach successfully for some time. The modern entertainment industry brings together a production team that includes a variety of skills and competencies (direction, sound,

Figure 2–5

Key Attributes of a Network Culture

To a Great Extent

- Developing new products or services
- Capitalizing on windows of opportunity
- Establishing new ventures or new lines of business
- Building strategic alliances with other organizations
- Using resources outside the company to get things done

- Adapting quickly to changes in the business environment
- Being flexible and adaptive in thinking and approach
- Pioneering new ways of doing things
- Applying innovative technology to new situations
- Capitalizing on creativity and innovation
- Encouraging innovation
- Attracting top talent

- Maintaining a high sense of urgency
- Anticipating changes in the business environment
- Taking action despite uncertainty
- Promoting one's point of view strongly
- Maximizing customer satisfaction
- Organizing jobs around capabilities of individuals
- Rewarding superior performance
- Gaining the confidence of customers
- Selling successfully
- Finding novel ways to capitalize on employees' skills

To Some Extent

lighting, acting, set and wardrobe design) for a single project. The construction industry takes a similar approach; a general contractor links a number of subcontractors with diverse skills and competencies.

THE CULTURE-AS-SPORT ANALOGY

At this point, the four work cultures we've just described may still appear a bit murky in concept. Perhaps one of the easiest ways to better understand and clarify work cultures is by examining them in the context of various sports. We don't particularly like business/sports analogies— they're overused, perpetuate the myth that sports are a reflection of life and therefore should be taken just as seriously, and reinforce the sexist perception that both sports and business are best left to the menfolk. But they nonetheless are often an effective way of explaining confusing "management-speak." And in our defense, a recent survey of newspaper-reading business executives noted that a third turned to the sports pages first, compared to only 2 percent who started with the business section.[3]

As we go through this work-culture-as-sports theory of business management it is important to remember that just as in assessing business work cultures, these examples are based on roles and the execution of work—how the game is played—not on management's view of how the team is run.

Football: A Functional Game.   If there ever was a functional sport, it is football. Everyone is a specialist, responsible for a single, individual role. There are separate defensive and offensive teams, not to mention specialty squads. And within each of those teams, players are given specific tasks and assignments. The quarterback is responsible for implementing a specific play. His backs and ends are responsible for running a specific route. The offensive linemen are responsible for specific blocking assignments on each play. While everyone is concerned about the organization's success, as individuals they must concentrate on their own assignments. Football also is very hierarchical. The coaches (the executive team) call the plays. The quarterback (middle management) is responsible for making sure they are executed by the rest of the team (the employees).

Basketball: A Time-Based Contest.   At first glance, basketball appears to be process oriented, with everyone performing specific roles on a single team. But a closer examination reveals a time-based culture. True, players start out as specialists—point guards, centers, forwards, and the like—based on their size and skills. But as the game rapidly unfolds, those functions, along with the team dynamics, change. Not only does the team constantly move from offense to defense and back, but the roles of the individual team members moving up and down the court also are situational. Cross-functionality is key. You may be the point guard, by title, but if you are standing in the paint and a teammate misses a shot, you forget play-making and shooting for the moment and become a rebounder. (Talk about being multicompetencied!) And, while the coaches would like to believe that they are in charge, once the clock starts, a basketball team has to be self-directed. Like other time-based organizations, speed and flexibility are critical in basketball. The goal after all is speed to market—scoring more points than the competition within a limited window of opportunity.

Soccer: A Process Sport.   While soccer may appear to be similar to basketball, there is a subtle distinction that makes it more process oriented. The difference is this: Unlike the constantly shifting roles of hoops, the individual members of a soccer squad not only function as a single team, but also constantly maintain their position or role on that team. The goalie's role is to protect the goal. The fullbacks are primarily defensive; the forwards primarily offensive. At the same time, however, unlike football, in which each player has a very specific assignment for each play, in soccer the team as a whole continually shifts its position in response to the ever-changing demands of the customer (the ball) and the position of the competition (the market).

Baseball: The Great American Network.   While it can be argued whether baseball is a sport, a pastime, pure entertainment, or an unscrupulous business, there is no doubt that it is the quintessential network organization. Think of a game not really as a competition between one entire team and another, but rather as a series of interactions or relationships between two, or at most three, players—all members of a network. First, the pitcher throws the ball toward the catcher. The moment the batter swings, and slaps a hard grounder down the third-base line, the network shifts. Now the interaction is between the runner, the third baseman, who fields the ball, and the first baseman who takes the throw. The rest of the network is standing by, but is uninvolved in the play. (Like many business networks, there is frequently a lot of downtime for many of the members. Just ask any Little Leaguer who has spent hours daydreaming in left field, with nothing to do, just waiting, waiting, and waiting.) Indeed, baseball has a lot in common with another traditional network culture, sales. Both are highly situational, focus on statistics and odds (number of sales orders, number of hits), and are driven by strategies for improving the odds (the pitching strategy used against a certain hitter based on his previous batting performance, the sales strategy used with a certain client, based on that client's previous order). There are other similarities, too. Managers in both baseball and sales tend to be not coaches, but producer/strategists, individuals who pull the team or sales force together, plot the game plan, and then stand back and let the "experts" do their thing, only offering support when it is needed.

Track and Field: A Cultural Combo.   Most sports, of course, like most organizations, have in reality a number of cultures at work. Take a track team, for example. Most of the competition takes places in individual, functional terms: The pole vaulter vaults; the high jumper jumps; the sprinter sprints. Yet a few events require other work cultures. A relay team, for instance, could be considered a time-based culture, with everyone playing a specific role, but working together with a high degree of flexibility and speed, to win the race.

Off the playing field, this mix of cultures is even more obvious. Free agency has turned many professional football teams into network organizations of sorts. Each season, teams try to pull together the ensemble of "stars" that they think will best help them achieve their venture—a national championship. Such was the case, one could argue, when the San Francisco 49ers lured Deion Sanders to the West Coast to help them win the 1995 Super Bowl.

THE ORGANIZATIONAL MELTING POT

Like football, many business organizations are finding the need to consciously develop very specific hybrid cultures based on their mission, vision, and strategic goals. These are not merely juxtapositions of the models, but genuine hybrids.

Many functional organizations, for example, tend to move toward process as they begin to deal with issues of quality and customer service, while a number of time-based organizations are realizing that one of the best ways to increase cash flow without tying up all their assets is to create joint ventures and strategic alliances. The time/network hybrid already dominates some organizations, especially those in the highly competitive high-tech and communications/information industries, where alliances and networks have become a natural way of doing business.

There is, of course, no set, pre-established route through the cultural spectrum. Cultural movement really depends on the goals and vision of the organization. Take the case of BHP Petroleum, one of Australia's largest employers. Faced with diminishing resources and changing customer needs, BHP determined that it needed to begin shifting its culture. Rather than remain a purely functional "oil and gas company" that was driven by traditional supply-side economics, BHP is now evolving into a time-based organization that is focused more on the demands and needs of customers and the changing energy markets. It is capitalizing on new technology and emphasizing its core competency of deepwater drilling to develop new resources, while at the same time boosting customer service and repositioning itself as a global energy company.

Nor are these evolving organizations shunning their roots. The functional organization may not be the king it once was, but it still plays an important role in many organizations. Take, for example, Hallmark Cards. While the organization is developing an overriding process-based culture, elements of the three other cultures have been added or maintained in order to ensure its continued success:

• The manufacturing arm of the organization tends to be time-based. Speed is critical. Cards must be printed and packaged according to a tight schedule. And the product—the cards themselves—is continually changing. Therefore, the printing, graphics, and packing functions must be organized in a manner that makes them flexible and agile, able to shift product lines quickly and continually meet deadlines.

• Even with the use of merchandising teams, the distribution of Hallmark cards is network-oriented. The distribution department must deal with an ever-changing alliance of "customers"—those merchants (including their own retail stores) who are selling Hallmark products. They must be innovative and flexible, able to create and penetrate markets quickly, and negotiate productive partnerships and strategic alliances.

• The artists and editors, while now incorporated into teams responsible for a bigger piece of the business picture, still require very specialized, individual skills. As a result, "centers of excellence" have been established, through which both artists and writers rotate to receive further training and enhance their technical abilities. This element of the Hallmark culture, in which the goal is learning and applying very specialized skills, can be described in classic, functionally based terms.

Another example of this hybridization or diversification of work cultures within a single organization can be found in Reuters, the long-established, highly successful international news agency. At first glance, Reuters may appear to be a simple news service, which gathers and disseminates information. But in reality, its role is much broader. Not only must it gather the news and information at one end of the process and distribute it at the other, but in between it must sort the information, process it, package it, and ultimately sell it. In this broader sense, the organization encompasses a complex information system.

Like Hallmark, Reuters embodies a variety of cultures. At the "information gathering" end of the organization, the network culture dominates. A continually evolving worldwide alliance of correspondents collects the information.

This information is then processed by editors working in bureaus in major cities. Although highly specialized and functional in their individual roles, they tend to form time-based cultures that emphasize speed and flexibility, as they sort, process, and package the information.

Finally, the information must be pumped into the offices of thousands of subscribers, from print and electronic news outlets to investment houses and other organizations that rely on timely updates from around the world. Such a sales and distribution effort was once structured along very functional lines. The Reuters salesperson might have called on a potential subscriber who needed the service up and running via customized software within a few days. The salesperson would pass the order on to the installation group, which worked under different—and perhaps less immediate—priorities, and who in turn would pass it on to the software development department, which operated under yet a third set of priorities. As a result, the customer might not have received the service as quickly as he or she might have wished. Today, however, this cumbersome hierarchy has been replaced by process-based product delivery teams that handle all three functions—sales, installation, and software development. Reuters' process-based culture recognizes the importance of customer requirements for both accessibility and accuracy.

THE LINK BETWEEN CULTURE AND COMPENSATION

So what does all this talk about evolving work cultures have to do with the subject of compensation? No doubt the models are helpful. No doubt they can be used as sort of a cultural sextant to determine or "fix" an organization's position. But what do they have to do with pay?

Everything.

In today's rapidly changing world, compensation must assume the critical role not only of rewarding and motivating individuals, but also of moving the organization forward. And attempting to shift an organization's cultures, as many leaders are discovering, can be a difficult challenge. Kodak Chief Executive George Fisher, for example, found that no matter how many meetings he had or how much E-mail he personally answered, the company's plodding operating mentality was tough to overcome. "The mind-sets here have to be worked on," he noted. "But you can't change a culture just by decree."[4]

Fisher is right, which is why it is so important that today's pay strategies be aligned with the culture—or cultures—of an organization in order to successfully support and drive its employees to achieve its strategic business goals. And, since each culture and its people is different, each requires different pay strategies. One size no longer fits all.

Although the alignment of pay with culture will be discussed in much more detail in Chapters 4 and 5, it is worth noting here very briefly how some of the various aspects of pay, such as internal equity, external market comparisons, pay grades or bands, variable pay, and even benefits, vary from culture to culture:

Functional organizations, which focus on stability, routine, reliability, resources, and specialization, need compensation programs that attract and retain individuals, provide security over the long haul, and recognize differences in individual jobs and responsibilities. Such programs tend to focus on narrowly defined jobs and individual performance. They often consider both internal equity as well as outside market comparisons, which are especially important for attracting new people. Because of the emphasis on individual specialization, compensation programs in functional organizations tend to encompass numerous and very narrow pay grades. Variable pay plans, or incentives, are limited to those individuals who have a definite influence on the bottom line—people in departments such as sales or who are at the top of the organization in key leadership positions. Benefits are extremely important to the functional organization, steeped as it is in values of career-orientation and long-term security.

Process organizations, with their focus on the customer, also emphasize internal equity, but for the comparison of teams more than individuals. External comparisons with what the rest of the market is paying are important only when it comes to attracting new talent. Once people are in the organizations, their pay increases commensurate with their performance and acquisition of new skills and competencies.

What makes certain roles and teams more valuable than others is their impact on the customer. Members of a team dealing with quality control in one small aspect of an organization, for example, may receive less for their team performance than a large cross-functional team that is responsible for the organization's entire customer service operation.

Pay bands or grades tend to be wider than in traditional organizations, since there is less emphasis on individual specialization. Incentives—for both individuals and teams—are more widespread throughout the organization. There may be small, quarterly incentives to motivate individual team performance, as well as broader, annual incentive programs that link everyone in the organization with its overall performance and customer service mission.

Time-based organizations, which emphasize flexibility and speed rather than long-term relationships, place little emphasis on internal equity. Because of their need to get the right people in the right roles right now, they are much more sensitive to comparisons with the external market. As in process organizations, many employees are probably going to be eligible for incentives, but the standards for payout are going to be much tougher, since the focus here is much more on getting results and getting them now. Unlike the process organization, where the incentives are ongoing, and usually short-term (a year or less), the incentive programs in time-based cultures often are periodic, lasting only through the duration of the project, and paying out based on the results of the project.

Pay in time-based organizations tends to be divided into a few broad bands rather than a large number of grades. One band, for example, could encompass all the professionals within an organization. Individuals can frequently advance within a band, based on the acquisition of new skills, competencies, and responsibilities. They will only jump to another band, however, when they have moved to a level that adds appreciable value to the organization. For example, an engineer might remain in an organization's "professional" band throughout most of his or her career, but advance to the "senior professional" or "leadership" band upon developing the competencies needed to lead multidisciplinary teams responsible for creating new products. That individual now brings added value to the organization through not only his or her professional and technical expertise and leadership skills, but also through the ability to lead a diverse, cross-functional group of employees.

Network organizations, with their emphasis on alliances and ventures, care little about internal equity. Because each individual is paid for what he or she brings to the table for one particular project, much more attention is paid to competing market rates or individually established value. Indeed, pay in the network organization is somewhat bipolar. The "stars"—the real talent—may be paid huge salaries, may be totally on commission, or given equity in the enterprise, while the extras are paid scale. Because employee/employer relationships may last only a few weeks or months, benefits tend to be very limited in both duration and scope.

ASSESSING YOUR ORGANIZATION'S CULTURE

Seeing how these different compensation strategies support different values and work processes, one can begin to understand the need for assessing an organization's culture *before* designing and implementing any new pay program. The fact is, an effective culture assessment is perhaps the most critical step in developing an effective compensation program. Without an honest, unbiased, thorough evaluation, the entire pay initiative will more than likely be cursed by that old computer adage: "garbage in, garbage out."

How and by whom an organization is assessed should depend on the organization's size and scope. A small, very tightly focused business, with perhaps a single overriding culture, will no doubt be easier to assess than a corporate giant. In both cases, however, it is critical that those doing the assessment not only have an excellent understanding of the major cultures and the forces that shape them, but also are well-versed in the dynamics and protocols of the assessment process itself.

A self-assessment, for example, might be a good first step, especially for a small, narrowly defined organization or business unit. But beware: Internal audits are frequently skewed by barriers, biases, misconceptions, and the rogue agendas of both individuals and groups. Most often, it helps to utilize an impartial outsider who can bring an objective, unbiased view to the proceedings, and who is unafraid to ask some pointed and uncomfortable questions about the organization's strategic cultures. Our own Culture-Sort methodology, for example, utilizes both a self-assessment and outside analysis. The self-assessment is usually completed by the senior leadership team or key members of the team, although it is sometimes done in several levels of the organization. Each participant prioritizes the fifty-plus cultural attributes mentioned earlier both in terms of the organization's current culture, and what they perceive the future culture should be. We then analyze the results, identifying not only the gap between the current and desired cultures, but also perceptive and visionary gaps among the members of the leadership team, or between the leadership team and other levels of the organization.

Interestingly, when applying our Culture-Sort methodology, we find that there tends to be much more consensus around where people want to go than there is around where they are. Executive team members often agree on what their target culture should be, but disagree on to what degree and with what speed the organization must change to achieve it. In some cases there is even basic disagreement over fundamental issues, such as whether achieving budgeted objectives is a key priority of the organization.

While such sophisticated tools are extremely helpful in accurately assessing where an organization is and where it wants to go, we often find that the easiest way of initially getting clients to look beyond compensation and focus instead on their organizational work culture is simply to ask them a few questions:

1. Why do you want to implement a new pay program?
2. What has changed within the organization that requires you to change your compensation strategy?
3. What has triggered those changes?
4. What behaviors must people engage in for the organization to be successful?
5. What corporate competencies are required for the organization to be successful, and what individual competencies must be aligned with these corporate needs?
6. What are the outcomes that you want to reward?

Take Hallmark Cards, for example. When they told us they needed a new job measurement system, we asked why. What had changed within their organization that required a new system? Their response, after some careful thought: "Well, jobs have changed." And, along with the changes in job responsibilities came changes in goals and values. Hence, new goals and values needed to be established that more accurately reflected how the card company measured work and motivated and rewarded new behaviors.

In Hallmark's case, it was fairly easy to determine that, in moving to the team-based approach, a lot had changed. In other organizations, however, we find a lot of smoke and mirrors, but little real change. People may have a new job description that tells them they are now empowered, when in reality they are doing the same things they have always done. There are new labels, but no real changes in the culture. People have no more access to resources or information. They have no more decision-making authority. And, they are not rewarded for the decisions they do make or the results they achieve. Or, they are told that they are now part of a team that works together to achieve broad goals. Yet they are actually still performing a narrowly defined task, still worrying only about their own technical specialty, still focusing on individual rather than group success.

SEPARATING FUNCTION FROM FORM: ASSESSMENT CRITERIA

Separating such window dressing from reality is critical in assessing an organization's culture. So, too, is an examination of the major individual components of an organization—the governing system, the product or service development and delivery system, the operations system, and the financial system. At first blush, these systems all appear to be functional. In reality, each component may have its own culture that is different from the others. For that reason, it is important to focus not only on *what* each component does, but also on *how* and *why* it does it. This is perhaps best done by looking at each component of the organization using four criteria—strategy, structure, systems, and staffing. These criteria help define behavioral expectations that are needed for success and thus the cultures required for that success.

Strategy.   What is the organization's purpose? What are its values? What are its business goals? A strategy encompasses the goals and processes used for achieving the organization's vision. In determining a strategy, an organization must look not only at its unique characteristics, such as specialization, flexibility, or customer satisfaction, but also at its tactical focus—how it turns these goals into reality. This focus might be operating continuity, market penetration, or market domination.

If an organization is hell-bent on capturing market share, for example, it will probably want to be time-based, since moving quickly and devising new opportunities for value creation is critical to increasing its numbers. If, on the other hand, an organization wants to extend a core product as long as possible to meet changing customer needs, it probably wants to create a process culture. Or maybe an organization's primary focus is the establishment of new markets or a new global position. Then, a network culture, based on strategic alliances with designers, suppliers, manufacturers, investors, and even competitors may be necessary.

At the same time, an organization must examine its critical elements of performance, such as productivity, added value, operational effectiveness, efficiency, customer satisfaction, and market integrity. It must also look at its measures of effectiveness, be they market share or penetration, return on investment, economic value added, or cash flow. All of these are indicative of one of the four cultures. If performance is measured primarily by integrity and specific return measures, for example, it most likely is a functional organization. If true customer satisfaction is its main focus and measure of success, it probably is process oriented. Market share and expanded sources of economic value added indicate a time-based focus. If the success of a specific venture or "betting the business" is the main driver, then the organization almost certainly requires a network culture.

General cycle time for products, processes, and decision making also are indicators of an organization's culture. Lengthy cycle times to assure exacting reliability lend themselves to functional organizations, while shorter cycle times reflect process, time-based, or network cultures.

An organization must also examine its core competencies. Is functional excellence in a broad range of products or services critical? If so, the organization is most likely functional. If the critical competencies focus on partnering with customers, then it is at least in part process driven. If, however, doing key things better than any other competitor is critical, the culture is most likely time-based or network.

Structure.   The next step in identifying an organization's culture is examining its structure and basic organizational design. Does it comprise a number of highly specialized functions? If so, it is probably functional. Is it organized around the customers' needs and requirements and supported by teams? Then it is process-based. If components and programs are clearly linked through strategic business units designed to address specific business sectors or product/service lines, then it more than likely is time-based. If each essential phase of the operation requires a unique effort, then a network structure is probably being utilized to bring together the key competencies to ensure the success of the venture.

The organization must also examine the dynamics of its authority. If it is a typical corporate hierarchy, with managers, supervisors, and clear chains of command and control, it undoubtedly is functional. If, however, the authority rests with teams or truly empowered work groups, then it probably is a process or time-based organization. If most of the authority is in the hands of a producer or director who works with key alliances and joint ventures, then it is in all likelihood a network organization.

The number of levels within the organization also is critical. If there are as many levels as there are specialties, then it probably is functional. If only the absolute minimum are in place, then it is probably process-based. The mere absence of levels, however, is not an absolute diagnostic criteria. We have seen a number of organizations that have reduced levels but have not gone to the next step of truly empowering people and expanding their roles.

Work design also indicates culture. If work is divided by function and specialty, then it is probably functionally oriented. If work is organized primarily through permanent teams that are responsible for an ongoing process, such as sales, or packaging, then it is more process-based. If teams or multicompetencied project groups are created to handle a new initiative or complex assignment from beginning to end, such as Chrysler did in the design of its new cars, then it is time-based. Finally, if strategic partnerships and alliances are created for a single event or project, then a network culture is at work.

It also is important to look closely at group efforts within an organization. While we often associate teams with process organizations, group efforts exist in almost all organizations. In traditional organizations, those efforts usually are in the form of committees and task forces. In process organizations, teams tend to be stable and replace many functional hierarchies. In time-based organizations, teams tend to be operational and change quickly, with individuals moving from one project or enterprise to another. And in networks, of course, temporary affiliations, alliances, and partnerships tend to dominate the organization and be the principal forces for creating value.

Systems.   How does the work in an organization flow? What sort of communications are in place? How are decisions made? How is performance measured? These are the systems of an organization. Take the decision-making process, for example. In functional organizations, decisions are often left to the top leadership or internal experts, while in process cultures, the customers' or clients' needs are the primary consideration. In time-based organizations, the rapid creation of value is critical and guides the decision process. In networks, the venture or product drives the decision making.

Communications tend to be formal, regularly scheduled, and mostly one way—top-down—in functional organizations. In process and time-based organizations, where more people need to know more things in order to be effective, communications tend to be less formal, more constant, and decidedly multidirectional. There is, for example, usually frequent communications among teams and work groups in such organizations. In networks, communications tend to be largely informal, sporadic, and "on demand." Information is available when it is needed by someone in the network, not when someone in leadership decides it should be communicated. Thus, communications are built around "nodes of influence" which integrate a wide variety of data and information.

Performance in functional organizations tends to be measured by tracking results against a number of more traditional comparative industry standards. In process organizations, the emphasis is on continued progress and improvement, and on reaching new levels of customer satisfaction and partnering. Very specific market share/penetration goals are critical to measuring performance in time-based organizations, while milestone events—the completion of a project or product design, for example—are the key measures of networks.

Other criteria important in considering systems include the focus on cycle times (product, process, and business), quality, and the organization's attitude toward risk.

Staff.   Much can be said about an organization's culture by looking at the people within it. Do they value the discipline, focus, established parameters, and long-term security of a functional environment? Are they more comfortable in the team roles and interaction of process cultures? Are they driven by the recognition of the enterprise achievements of time-based cultures, or do they like the autonomy and innovation of networks, even though the length of the specific job or project may vary?

How people are empowered also says a lot about an organization. In a functional organization, power is channeled through individual assignments and increased technical skills, while in process cultures, it rests with the collective action of teams. In time-based organizations, people are empowered based on their broad competencies and multiple roles, while in network cultures, power is derived from the talent and expertise individuals bring to the venture, as well as the ability to complete the venture—whatever it may be—in the shortest period possible, with the best possible results.

Selection and development of people also varies from culture to culture. In functional cultures, people are hired based on their know-how and ability to learn, and then are encouraged to refine and upgrade those specific skills over time. In process cultures, skills and knowledge are supplemented by competencies that foster teamwork and flexibility. People are encouraged to continually improve and expand those capabilities in the context of the key processes of the business. In time-based organizations, expertise and the drive to achieve are critical. Individuals are encouraged to develop those competencies that will increase their ability to contribute directly to the organization's goals in the most timely way possible. Finally, networks seek individuals with already developed strengths that can be immediately applied to the venture. Growth tends to be self-supported and self-directed.

UNDERSTANDING YOUR CULTURE IS ONLY THE FIRST STEP

You may already have begun to apply the culture criteria we have outlined to your organization. Remember as you are doing it, however, that the goal is not just understanding what cultures are at work in your organization. The objectives are first, to make sure you have a culture that is aligned with your business goals, your values, your strategy, and your vision for the future; second, that you have business processes—including compensation, human resources, performance management, and communications—

that are aligned with and support that culture. It is this alignment that creates the right culture necessary for success, optimizes the value of individual competencies, and encourages the behaviors required to achieve the expected results.

Just because you understand your current work cultures, and just because they are aligned with other key business processes, don't assume that they happened naturally, or that even though they have been effective in the past, they will work next month or next year. What we have found, in client after client, is that many are unaware of the cultures that are at work within their organizations. Others have discovered that while they have steadfastly clung to ideas and philosophies of the past, their organizations have changed, evolving into more contemporary cultures that are, unfortunately, not supported with contemporary pay programs. Still others have discovered that even though they have newer cultures, those cultures will not support or drive the future goals and long-term vision of their organizations.

Before moving on to the issue of aligning compensation, these organizations must take a crucial mid-step: They must set their course for the future; they must determine not only where they want to be, but also how to get there.

Of course, leaders, managers, and planners with different backgrounds often have strong ideas about which aspect of the organization—its strategy, systems, staff, or structure—should be considered first in the change process, or which should take precedence in decision making. Intuitively or rationally, one is argued as being more important than the others.

The truth is, they all are important, they all influence each other, and eventually they all must come together. Ultimately, the issue that must be addressed is this: How does the organization get its people to do the right things in the right ways at the right times, improving not only their productivity, but their satisfaction with their work as well. The solution is to create a fully aligned organization—one in which *all* the signals are consistent as to how people work, gain knowledge, skill, and competencies, and contribute.

The emphasis on changing the organization is no doubt the biggest global trend sweeping through business today. *Reengineering the Corporation* is not only the title of a best-selling book, but continues to be the battle cry for literally thousands of American businesses—both large and small. And, while *this* book is about paying people—not reorganizing them—it would be lacking a critical step if it did not address the issue of work reengineering.

For that reason, before moving on to the issue of aligning pay with culture, we have included a chapter on the cultural implications of work reengineering. Just as strategic success depends on having the right work culture, highly effective strategic execution demands that organizations take a serious and focused approach to changing their work cultures. There is really no choice if an organization wants to survive and thrive in the coming decade.

3

The Role of Pay in
Organizational Change

If you had any doubts about the degree to which organizational change has consumed our lives, those doubts were surely dispelled if you happened to watch the annual onslaught of New Year's Day college football games on American television. During at least one of the nationally broadcast bowl games recently, advertisements from a large, well-known consulting firm touting the importance of work reengineering ran side-by-side with commercials for burgers, beer, and high-tech basketball shoes.

Why a consulting firm would spend hundreds of thousands of dollars wooing an audience of football fanatics and hung-over holiday revelers is a question best left to the marketing and advertising geniuses. The fact remains, a dramatic need has been created for such services as more and more organizations attempt to solve the riddle of change. So big is this trend that James Champy, coauthor of the best-selling *Reengineering the Corporation: A Manifesto for Business Revolution*, predicted that "within the next five to ten years, every organization must fundamentally rethink its infrastructure and the way the employees do their work, or else it will be non-competitive. It's possible that reengineering will be called something else a few years from now, but it will never be a fad. It's just too important."[1]

Important? Of course. But also very difficult. Many organizations are discovering that creating effective, lasting change is one of the toughest challenges they face today. According to one estimate, between 50 percent and 70 percent of reengineering efforts do not achieve their goals.[2]

One of the most critical reasons for this high rate of failure, we believe, comes back to the issue of compensation—the fact that pay, as we've already discussed, is a frequently misunderstood or ignored step in the change process. Just how ignored was shown in our compensation survey of more than five hundred organizations: Of the 60 percent that had started or completed work reengineering, only 24 percent believed pay played a primary role; 43 percent said it played a secondary role, and 33 percent said it played no role at all.[3]

Yet, as many of that unfortunate third that ignored pay are discovering, compensation and major organizational change are interdependent. Most organizations are finding that they can't do one effectively without considering the other. Like the cultural assessment process considered in Chapter 2, neither compensation nor change initiatives such as organizational reengineering—or work transformation, as we prefer to call it—can be considered in a vacuum. Both must be viewed as important parts of a complex equation in which not only the structure of the organization is transformed, but also the strategies, systems, and—most important—the people. As author Champy said upon the release of his sequel, *Reengineering Management*: "We need their hearts and minds because we're asking them to be more accountable—we're giving them more authority."[4]

PAY: A CRITICAL SUPPORT, BUT NOT A DRIVER

As a powerful motivator, pay can be very effective gaining the hearts and minds of employees during times of massive change. If used effectively, it can hasten the acceptance of and commitment to change. It is an important tool for communicating and reinforcing new values and behaviors, supporting accountability for results, and rewarding the achievement of new performance goals. In short, it is the critical step that moves change beyond processes to people. And, as Jack Welch, chairman and CEO of General Electric Company, has noted, "No matter how many ideas we try, it all comes back to people—their ideas, their motivation, their passion to win."[5]

Yet pay itself cannot drive or lead the change process. It cannot define what the change should be. It cannot establish values. It cannot replace effective leadership. As Figure 3–1 shows, in the high-performing organization of today, pay is just one of several issues that must be addressed during any major change initiative. As the organization shifts its business strategies in response to changes in the marketplace, it frequently must also shift its culture. Not only must it embrace new core competencies, develop new competencies for its people, and reexamine its critical success factors, but it also must respond with changes in its human resources processes, including defining and articulating the organization's mission and values (its purpose or "shape"), designing work and roles to support that mission (reengineering/work transformation), selecting people, developing their performance, and, ultimately, rewarding them.

UNDERSTANDING THE BROADER
TRANSFORMATION PROCESS

Because compensation should be considered in the broad context of change initiatives and used to support those initiatives, it is critical that those involved in the development of pay strategies also understand how work and cultures are reengineered or transformed, and how compensation can effectively be linked to these change processes.

Effective work transformation is far more complicated than simply reengineering or redesigning business structures and processes. It involves far more than drawing a new flow chart, firing a few hundred employees, and then simply damning the torpedoes and moving ahead at full speed in the same direction the organization has been traveling for the past fifty years. As management guru Peter F. Drucker says: "Research, engineering, customer service, accounting, marketing, clerical work—all need to be reengineered to be freed from diversions and busy-work, to be focused on their key tasks, to be organized around the flow of the work and the flow of the information. Yet, however badly needed, neither layoffs nor reengineering are likely to restore an ailing company to health. . . . The only thing that can effect the needed turnaround is rethinking and reformulating the company's business theory and repositioning the business on a new set of assumptions."[6]

Figure 3–1

High-Performing Organizations: The Process of Alignment

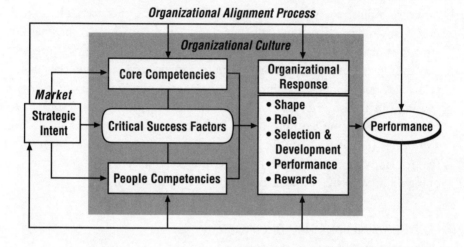

What Drucker is describing goes beyond the simplistic approach that has led far too many CEOs to think of the change process purely in terms of downsizing and cost cutting—a dangerous assumption. What Drucker describes, and what we define as work transformation, encompasses:

• redefining jobs and work processes
• reenforcing quality initiatives, such as TQM and CQI
• designing new management systems
• creating more effective work cultures
• developing performance-enhancing reward and recognition programs

Work and culture transformation is not a discrete event. To be truly effective, it is a continually evolving process that is closely aligned with the organization's strategic goals and vision. It should take an approach that is balanced by the forces of quality and customer service, cost management and employee satisfaction. Finally, it requires commitment on the part of not only top executives, but managers and employees alike.

As with compensation, work transformation requires a keen appreciation and understanding of:

- *People*—what motivates them, how they react to and buy into changes, and what competencies will be required of them for outstanding job performance in the future
- *Work*—the design of jobs, work flow, organizational relationships, teams, management systems and processes, information systems, technology, and measures of outcomes
- *Performance*—management processes, training and development, coaching, performance management, and monetary and nonmonetary rewards and recognition programs

There is an important reason why we list people first: They are the heart and soul of redesigning jobs, work, and organizational cultures. By giving them a clear vision, involving them in the design and development process, and motivating them through dynamic rewards and performance management programs, any organization can successfully transform itself into a more efficient, more effective, more competitive business.

Without their involvement, support, and attention to their needs, those same change initiatives will more than likely be doomed to failure. It is, after all, a dramatic, disruptive, frightening process, both personally and professionally. Just think about it for a moment: If your organization goes through a major transformation process, not only will your job probably change, but also the way you work and how you are paid. As one of our top change management consultants puts it: "It's like hitting people with an eighteen-wheeler."

FIVE STEPS TO A SUCCESSFUL FUTURE

Controlling that eighteen-wheeler—knowing when to brake, when to accelerate, and when to turn—is not something for the faint of heart. To ease that journey, we advise organizations to incorporate a unique, five-step approach in negotiating major organizational change. This continuous process, which covers the spectrum of change from reshaping work cultures to the creation of new compensation strategies, involves the following basic steps:

1. *Assess the organization.* This includes examining its work culture, vision of the future, and its ability to achieve those future goals, be they improving customer service, reducing costs, advancing quality initiatives, or improving the quality of job satisfaction. This assessment typically is

accomplished through executive, manager, and employee input, which is obtained in meetings, focus groups, and surveys. A series of "visioning sessions" follow, at which time executives develop an image of their future organization. During this step decisions are made about the amount of change that is warranted and the speed at which it should be implemented. Key results also are established, in order to measure the effectiveness of the transformation.

2. *Design improvements to work processes and environments.* This includes the creation of new job models, the development of cross-functional roles, if needed, and the creation of teams. In fact, the design process itself is often best accomplished through the use of multidisciplinary design teams made up of employees and managers. This unique team approach not only creates immediate employee involvement and buy-in, but it also establishes the importance of the team process.

3. *Develop details of new work and roles and an implementation plan.* This step includes all the "detailing"—everything from creating new policies and necessary training programs to designing new reward and performance management strategies. The development phase typically involves both staff and management in determining the needed resources to prepare everyone in the organization, as well as customers, for the coming transition.

4. *Implement the new processes.* During this step an organization-wide implementation plan and schedule are developed that include education and training, communication, a manpower planning protocol, a new evaluation model, a process improvement agenda, and finally new compensation strategies. Depending on the size of the change initiative, implementation may be organization-wide, or begin with two or three demonstration models and then be expanded to all areas of the organization.

5. *Evaluate and improve the processes.* During this final, but ongoing phase, the specific changes in culture and work processes are linked with established quality improvement processes, and human resources processes, including compensation strategies, are refined.

Initially, these five steps may appear to have little to do with compensation. They are, after all, about organizational change, not pay. Yet, if an organization is to be successful in implementing major change using this process, it must thoroughly understand the integral supporting role that compensation plays. Indeed, the issue of pay must be addressed at every step of the process.

ASSESSMENT: REACHING BEYOND THE LOW-HANGING FRUIT

We have already discussed the importance of understanding change and assessing an organization's culture. But understanding how and to what extent that culture must be changed is another matter—one that even many CEOs fail to grasp. An organization must look deeply into its corporate soul. It must ask itself what its business goals really are, and then determine whether its structure, its organization of work, its people—and ultimately how those people are paid—are the most effective ways of achieving those goals. In performing this self-examination, it must look not only at its history, but more importantly at its future, envisioning where it wants to be two, five, even ten years from now.

Many organizations initially aim fairly low. Most just want their people to be a little more flexible, their organizations a little less rigid and hierarchical. So they go after the "low-hanging" fruit. They start redesigning some processes, creating some teams, cutting some staff, and implementing some trendy new initiatives, including, perhaps, a new compensation program. They incorporate the latest business vocabulary and speak knowingly of sharing risks and rewards, of empowerment, of pushing decisions further down the organization. Yet they have little real comprehension of the meaning—or magnitude—of such actions.

This trickle-down approach to work culture change, while offering some temporary relief, is seldom sufficient to support lasting changes. That is why, early on, we undertake a process that we call "visioning." In one-on-one meetings, or more frequently in small groups, we start talking and working with the organization's executives. We ask them to articulate a set of compelling reasons to explain why they want to change the organization, what new results they expect to see, the reasons for operating their business as they do, and how they will select and compensate people under the new vision.

Again, it is not as if these executives haven't been thinking about such issues. They usually have. But this visioning process helps them to clarify the organization's goals and to unify the executive team—an important, consensus-building step that is key to successful change.

The first task the executive team must face is creating a clear set of descriptive visions about how the organization will be operated in the future—a road map for change, if you will. We tend to do this around cultural issues, by getting the executives to describe the future roles and behavior of individuals, of teams, and of leadership and management. We also get them to envision their future business in terms of quality imperatives, customer demands, and cost effectiveness.

Depending on the politics and power at the top of an organization, this process can range from an enlightening religious experience to something more akin to a running of the bulls through the executive boardroom. We have seen cases where, when the CEO nodded "yes," the executives nodded in unison, and when the CEO shook his head, "no," his corporate chorus collectively shook theirs. We have seen cases where the CEO demanded a secret ballot, and then proceeded to throw a tantrum when the ballots came back with a single opposing vote.

Perhaps the reddest of the flags is flown when an executive team comes together to do the visioning and the CEO doesn't show, delegates responsibility, or is there in body only, not really participating, but bouncing up and down, checking his beeper, answering phone calls, or rushing in and out. If this happens in an organizational culture in which the CEO is the primary decision maker and must sanction any effort to move forward, the odds are great that the initiative will fail. Granted, empowerment is an important part of most change initiatives, and everyone knows how busy top executives are. But this is not the time for the CEO to demonstrate his or her first act of empowerment. This is, after all, not just another initiative, but a permanent shifting of direction of the entire organization.

Everyone else on the executive team also must be involved and committed to the visioning process. If the executives cannot produce a descriptive vision of what the future culture is going to look like—because of a lack of knowledge or a failure to change or agree—then another red flag should go up, and the corporate eighteen-wheeler should remain at the loading dock. Indeed, many changes have failed because there was never consensus on what the outcomes were going to be. And, in the absence of clear results that are understood by everybody, such organizations spend years managing disappointment.

FACING THE IMPACT OF WORK CULTURE CHANGE

To be effective, the vision process must focus on sea-level issues, and not just be allowed to float somewhere in the stratosphere, eighty thousand feet above the corporate offices. If not carefully facilitated, these sessions too often rise to ethereal heights, as executives debate such issues as risk, empowerment, and cultural shifts. Granted, such discussions must at times climb to philosophical levels. But to move forward, they must eventually deal with practical decisions.

The entire executive team must have a thorough understanding of the impact of work transformation and cultural change on the current organization. Most organizations underestimate the amount of change that must take place and the amount of work and resources—financial and human—necessary to effect that change. Take, for example, the traditional organization that is moving from a highly specialized, intensely bureaucratic culture to one that is process-oriented. Just transforming decision making from a top-down process to self-directed work teams will take an enormous amount of change in everything from jobs to training to reward strategies.

Because most executives tend to be "big-picture" oriented, most tend to take a macro view of the change process and its impact on the organization. Yet almost all of the changes that determine the success or failure of the process will come at the micro level in terms of how work is processed, how people do their jobs, how they are selected, and how they are rewarded. Let's take, for example, empowerment: An organization cannot be empowered by the mere stroke of a pen. Rather, it requires a change in values, a recognition of the importance of risk and failure, new decision-making processes, new competencies on the part of both individuals and teams, and new pay strategies to reward those new competencies, behaviors, and values.

This attention to detail and acceptance of the complexity of the process is necessary if organizations are to weather the resistance, setbacks, and outright failures that beset most major change efforts. If people do not have a clear understanding of how tough it is going to be, either they bail out of the process because it is harder than they thought and not worth the effort, or the organization itself kills the process because it cannot cope with the changes.

Make no mistake, major organizational change initiatives are worth all the time, hard work, and trauma that is involved in such projects. But they must be carefully, expertly, and objectively managed if they are going to be effective over the long term.

CRISIS, COMPLACENCY, OR COMPETITION: WHY CHANGE?

Another issue on which consensus must be built early in the change process is why the organization is undertaking the initiative in the first place. As obvious as this issue may appear, it is one that is frequently overlooked, especially in the initial phases of the process. And it often comes back to haunt organizations, especially when they begin designing new work processes, creating new roles, and developing new compensation strategies.

The executive team may unconsciously understand the issue that ultimately led up to the decision to change, be it a drop in financial performance, a decline in productivity, or increased foreign competition. But sooner or later, especially if there is no obvious crisis to trigger the change, the Big Question will rise from the managerial and employee ranks like a sudden summer squall: "Why in the hell," it will rattle through the organization like a clap of thunder, "are we spending millions of dollars and hundreds of hours turning the entire operation on its ear, eliminating jobs, changing our pay, and totally disrupting our sense of security and direction?"

This is a fairly easy question to answer *if* the organization happens to be in the middle of a crisis. Take many of the health care organizations in the United States. Facing managed care, increased competition, and local and national reform, they have little choice but to redesign jobs, reengineer processes, and realign compensation strategies. If they don't, chances are, they won't be around for long. Not surprising, according to a recent Hay survey of hospitals, 62 percent said they had either begun redesigning roles and processes or had completed such initiatives.[7] As Michael Green, chief executive officer at Concord Hospital in Concord, New Hampshire, said after successfully leading his organization through a major change initiative: "At one time the luxury of large resources allowed us to develop dozens of small, specialized departments to handle patient needs. While we have the same needs and commitment to patients, those resources have dwindled."

For other organizations, however, the need to change may be less obvious. LEGO Systems, Inc. for example, faced no obvious crisis when it
began to reorganize its packing operation several years ago, taking a team-
based, process approach. It did, however, realize that the business was
changing, that because of changing customer demands the company had
to become more flexible and cost effective. High turnover, slow turnaround
times, and a need to increase capacity were all beginning to take a toll.
Still, the company was doing well financially.

So, too, was UtiliCorp United, Inc., a Kansas City-based utility, when it
decided it needed to transform itself from a traditional utility firm to a
more agile, leading-edge "energy company." But that success did not stop
CEO Rick Green and his executive team from shifting UtiliCorp's very traditional corporate headquarters culture into a more process-driven one
that utilized a team approach. As Green put it, "Given the industry deregulation of the past six or seven years, we need to change our culture to
become more competitive."

While the cultures of LEGO and UtiliCorp allowed them to make such
transitions with relative ease, it is in such "healthy" organizations where
the need for change is less obvious that the resistance to change—be it
roles or compensation—can be the greatest. In order for work transformation to be successful in such cases, it is important that the argument or
reasons for its implementation are "translated" in such a way that people
throughout the organization can understand the need to get behind the
initiative. That includes not only those employees at lower levels who may
not see the obvious connection because their "horizon of understanding"
is limited to day-to-day operations, but also boards of directors, who may
be quite happy with market share, profitability, and productivity, and who
see such change as a frivolous executive exercise. Here too, compensation
can play an important role as both a communicator and a motivator. A new
pay strategy in which people are rewarded based on new behaviors and expected outcomes can do more to move change forward than all the memos
from the president, all the "town hall" meetings, and all the over-hyped
kickoff rallies combined.

A CRITICAL MEASURE OF TIME AND RESOURCES

The assessment and visioning phase of a change initiative is also a good
point from which to examine the time and resources that will be needed,

and to determine whether or not the organization can truly commit to and follow through with the scope of the effort it is planning. All too frequently organizations overlook or underestimate the time and commitment that will be needed for education and training, the time it will take to bring people into the fold, or to develop better selection, evaluation, reward, and communication processes. LEGO and UtiliCorp, for example, both developed extensive training programs. At UtiliCorp, the entire corporate headquarters staff was required to participate in a series of training programs that covered everything from teamwork to writing and speaking skills.

In the absence of funding and the support to make such training happen, an organization can easily end up with a puzzle with only half the pieces. At LEGO, new hiring and training programs were created to help the company not only select employees with the right competencies needed for the team approach, but also teach them the necessary new skills. "Training is critical and has to be a big commitment," said Robert Truncellito, the company's director of packing production. "Once you have set up the expectation that there will be training, it is never-ending. Before our transformation we could train all the basic skills we needed in ten hours. Now it takes a hundred hours or more for the total present training."

LEGO's training schedule may sound extreme. But it is not: Remember, when an organization undertakes a massive change initiative and transforms the way it approaches work, it in effect must commit mammoth amounts of time and human resources to think, plan, and implement change, yet all the while continue running the business at full speed. People must simultaneously pursue two sets of priorities, and are expected to give 100 percent to both. Unfortunately, it is easy for people under such pressure to become distracted, disgruntled, or—very naturally—gravitate to the crisis or the most immediate need of the day rather than focus their energy on the long-term view of the organization. That is why it is necessary not only to carefully manage change, but also to focus continually on the ultimate goals and results.

A MISSION FOR WORK

Frequently organizations develop a mission or vision statement—or series of statements—that, in so many words, tries to capture their new direction, culture, and goals. There is nothing wrong with such a practice. Indeed, having the executive team draft some statements is an excellent way of helping the members reach a consensus on difficult issues, and then articulate that consensus, so that it is clear that they aren't merely agreeing with the boss, but truly understand the implications. They can then either disagree or agree with the direction the organization is taking and subsequently commit their own energy to making it happen.

Such statements also can be used as a tool for articulating the vision throughout the organization and helping employees focus on the future. According to one study, over a sixty-five-year period, eighteen "visionary" companies outperformed a control group by more than six to one. Part of the reason, says one of the study's coauthors, is that such companies set ambitious goals which are communicated to all of their employees.[8]

But beware, such statements can backfire, particularly if an organization tries to overemphasize their importance by turning them into corporate battle cries or continually quoting from them as if they were Mao's Little Red Book or God's Ten Commandments.

While they should help focus the organization, they should not be viewed as a set of inflexible, unbreakable rules, nor as a gimmicky internal "sales pitch." In fact, there is a fine line that must be negotiated when crafting vision statements: Oversimplify them and they'll have a mindless, hollow ring that will destroy credibility rather than build it; overcomplicate them, and they'll create confusion, misunderstanding, and more than a little cynicism.

Nor should they be considered the Final Word for All Time. If the world continues to change at its current pace, the vision, like the rest of the organization, will need to be revised on an ongoing basis. (At one company, we saw two different mission statements proudly displayed in different offices. No doubt such "double vision" created more than a little confusion.) Despite these potential problems, however, mission and vision statements, if used properly and if backed by other processes such as effective compensation programs, can be very effective in building consensus and communicating vision.

IGNORING MISSION IS INVITING DISASTER

Why, you may be wondering, are we spending so much time on the visioning process? Because without it, what follows in terms of change initiatives or new compensation strategies will be fraught with problems, no matter how carefully they are designed or how well they are implemented.

Just how important this process is can be seen in the example of one large manufacturing firm that attempted to implement a major work transformation initiative and a new compensation program *before* it had even completed its visioning process. The organization's CEO was impatient with an entrenched, very traditional "command-and-control" executive team that had spent six months disagreeing on how to empower its staff and create a more process-based culture. Rather than take more time—and leadership—in building consensus about the changes, he ordered the implementation of teams. So instead of a smooth transition, the middle management and staff, who were trying to implement this "foreign" culture, collided head-on with the executive team, which couldn't agree on what the culture was. The result was months of anger, distrust, and confusion—and little forward progress. The executives grew ever more impatient with the managers and staff, who—fighting their way into a new culture while still carrying out their traditional roles—saw it as another failed initiative.

Interestingly, the organization had carefully planned the training that was needed to educate its managers and employees, and had spent a lot of time and money on the process. As a result, much of the resentment and frustration came not from learning new skills and competencies, but rather from spending the time and effort to learn them and then not being provided the new forum in which to practice them.

If the CEO and executive team had taken time to clarify the vision, set the stage, make clear the expectations, link them to the strategies of the organization, and empower people to move forward, the journey would have been much different. A whole new "world order" would have been created, implemented, and accepted. Instead, barriers were erected that to this day are slowing and at times stopping the change. And the executives who sent conflicting messages and threw up those barriers have lost precious credibility.

LEADERSHIP VS. INVOLVEMENT:
A BALANCE OF EMPOWERMENT

While the need to plan and build consensus is critical, there is a second lesson to be learned from the Case of the Impatient CEO and the Executive Team That Wasn't. It is this: Know when to lead, when to delegate, and how to balance both. That may sound like a subject for Business 101, but in this age of empowerment, the line between the two is becoming more blurred.

To go back to our eighteen-wheel analogy of work transformation for a moment: Empowerment involves a lot more than merely waving a corporate wand, pronouncing the organization "empowered," and then getting out of the driver's seat. You don't have to be an organizational expert, or a trucker for that matter, to know that the odds are quite high that the vehicle will careen wildly down the road, ultimately crashing and burning. Nor does it mean continuing to hang onto the wheel in a death grip, while the rest of the organization tries desperately to wrest control.

Yet you would be surprised how frequently, when it comes to the issue of empowerment, the leaders of organizations follow one of those two courses. Take the CEO and executive team described above. While the CEO was eager to push risk and responsibility down the organization through new organizational and compensation strategies, he and his executive team not only had a hard time relinquishing control, but also failed to agree on how that control should be passed on. As a result, those staff members upon whom the mantle of power was supposedly being placed received mixed signals that translated into confusion, cynicism, and ultimately a loss of credibility in the organization's executive team. Instead of eliminating barriers, more were raised.

Other organizations have had the opposite problem. Consider the CEO who gave his executive team carte blanche control over the process. He in effect told them: "Zap, you're empowered, now get the heck out of my office and reengineer the company." He then virtually vanished from the scene, appearing only to criticize, demand results, or pass final judgment on critical issues. Needless to say, what was supposed to be an atmosphere of freedom and liberty was quickly transformed into one of fear and loathing.

Such reactions—on the part of both leaders and those being led—is not unusual. Indeed, it is quite predictable if you think about who wields power in the organization. Traditionally, power has rested almost entirely with management. The higher the management, the stronger the power. Now, all of a sudden, that power is being defused throughout the organization. To add to the confusion, decisions are not being delegated to specific individuals, but to entire teams. So the issue becomes one not only of control, but also of risk and the potential for failure. In essence, major concerns of the organization—concerns about productivity and financial performance that were once the sole turf of the top executives—are now the shared responsibility of managers and employees alike.

In this climate, the issue of trust—on the part of both leaders and employees—becomes even more critical than in the past. People must not only be rewarded based on their performance and that of the organization (a subject covered in detail in Chapters 4 and 5), but they also must be allowed to take risks—and even occasionally fail—without feeling threatened. That's not an easy task at a time when, thanks to downsizing and reorganization, the lifetime employee has joined the ranks of endangered species.

Peaks and valleys must be considered normal in the new organizational landscape. Finger pointing and a "slash-and-burn" response to failure must be replaced with a philosophy that accepts setbacks as part of a search for solutions. If, in fact, an organization can give its employees that sense of comfort and security, then it will go a long way toward empowering them.

Sharing the risk, however, is often more difficult for both employees and executives than sharing the rewards. While it is nice to get paid a few additional bucks for helping the organization achieve its goals, such rewards mean little without the security of knowing that you can occasionally fail and not be summarily fired. In organizations where the culture has been very quick to declare failures or to punish them, any kind of change is considered risky. Employees aren't going to believe that the CEO is suddenly going to accept failure after a twenty-five-year history of tearing people apart when they made mistakes.

Indeed, the idea of accepting setbacks and the occasional failure is foreign to most people. Take, for example, the company that was creating an employee question-and-answer sheet on its pending change initiative. The team in charge of writing the Q&A had no problem using the terms "layoffs" or "staff cuts." When it came to acknowledging "setbacks and failure," however, team members were at a loss for words.

Other organizations are boldly moving to change such perceptions. Some, for example, are implementing performance management systems in which no incentive can be paid unless employees and employee groups can show that they tried at least one initiative during the year that failed.

Tough decisions about such empowerment strategies, including risk and reward, must begin at the top of the organization during the initial assessment/vision process. The executive team must not only envision a new strategic plan, but also determine how the organization is going to make that plan happen. How will people do their work? How will people relate to one another? What kind of decision-making authority are they going to have? What organizational values and behaviors are going to be stressed and rewarded?

Throughout the change process the executive team must take the lead in removing barriers in the existing culture so that the new culture can thrive. An organization cannot simply push a new culture into an old one. New cultures frequently die because no one is there to either remove the old barriers or to champion new values. Organizations design new work models, merge departments, create cross-trained roles. Yet old traditions, fiefdoms, departments, and policies—including compensation—often linger, smothering everything new that comes along.

If the executives in such organizations think their only job is to run around and tell everyone how they ought to love the *new* initiatives, then the changes will probably fail. If, however, the executives reduce friction by removing the barriers of the old culture and rewarding acceptance of the new one, then the new one will probably thrive.

To that end, communication must not only be direct, open, timely, and honest, but it also must be continuous. People have to understand not only why the organization is initiating a cultural change and the process itself, but also new competencies and skills that will be needed to be successful. Not only does such communications help alleviate fear and create support and buy-in, but it helps advance the new work processes as they are designed, implemented and modified. Says LEGO's Truncellito: "Communication is probably more important than training. Even though we think we communicate well, we want to throw more out there and let them be selective as far as what's important and meaningful."

DESIGN: BUILDING THE CULTURAL INFRASTRUCTURE

Once the executives have developed a new vision and it has been communicated throughout the organization, the second step of the change process can begin: designing the framework and infrastructure that will carry the new vision and culture forward. It is here that the organization can begin thinking through the new strategies and processes that will be necessary to achieve its vision.

Not the least of these issues, of course, is compensation. At the same time organizations are beginning to create new work processes and roles, they should begin thinking how they will reward people in those processes and roles—how they will align pay with the new values, goals, and vision created in the initial assessment phase. The same careful introspection and rethinking that shaped the broader change initiative must now be applied to pay.

All aspects of a compensation plan—including merit pay, incentives, and noncash components—should be reviewed in the context of their relative contributions to desired behaviors and performance goals. This review should encompass all levels of employees—from hourly and nonexempt to executive—and be long-term in nature, asking such vital questions as:

- Which work roles will emerge as the most critical for the organization as it pursues its new objectives?
- What new behaviors will be required for peak performance by the people in those critical roles?
- How will the various work roles in the organization interact in new ways?
- Which reward mechanisms will foster the desired behaviors, on both a team and individual basis, that will lead to optimal organizational performance?

A CHANGING ROLE FOR MANAGERS

Responsibility for the design phase of the change process—be it compensation or work processes—often falls to the newly empowered mid-level managers. Yet it is here that risk and change frequently collide to create one of the biggest barriers to work and cultural transformation: middle management misgivings. Why do managers fear such change? Because they have the most at risk, including their power, their responsibilities, and ultimately their jobs. They have grown up with the philosophy that "the manager that dies with the most FTEs, wins." Now, they are being told that the old axiom is no longer valid, that their lot in life is no longer a "vertical" power trip, in which their worth is measured by the size of the department they control and their ability to protect that department from outside forces. Rather, it has become a "horizontal" journey that requires a whole new set of values and competencies, not the least of which are the abilities to coach and cooperate.

The pretransformation middle manager may not have the competencies to succeed in this broader role of posttransformation "super manager," with its additional requirements. In the past managers were expected to manage a single specialty. Now they are being asked to step out of that box and manage several. Most middle managers, unfortunately, have limited exposure to many of these new initiatives. Not that they can be blamed for this lack of vision; their success, after all, has traditionally depended on their ability to maintain a narrow, specialized vision, not on their understanding of the big picture.

Here again, executive leadership and vision are critical. With the changing roles and opportunities, additional education and training must be provided not only to give managers new skills and competencies, but also to remove barriers created by old standards and beliefs. Managers must now be taught both new values and the importance of such values in advancing their own careers. They must move beyond the fear of losing their jobs and of being limited in their ability to move "up" in the organization, and learn the importance of acquiring new skills to make them more employable both in and outside of their current organization. In short, middle and senior managers must rethink not only their current roles, but their future careers. There is simply no way around it: Downsizing and remolding the management ranks are often inevitable when new work processes and cultures are created.

For senior leadership, this transformation of management becomes a mentoring issue. Since middle managers must lead the work transformation process on a day-to-day basis, the executive team must work closely with them to insure they not only understand the process, but also embrace the decisions that are made around it. Perhaps the best way to ensure this buy-in is to consolidate and reposition managers *before* the transformation of work processes and cultures begins, rather than reducing management staff along the way. By making careful projections and selecting the new management team early in the process, an organization can eliminate the lingering fear that frequently renders old management teams ineffective. Rather than continually looking over their shoulders, those that are selected for the new roles will look ahead with confidence, and in doing so, help move the organization forward with less resistance.

DEVELOPING THE DETAILS OF CHANGE

Once the organization has established the basic design and direction of its change initiatives, the focus shifts rapidly from macro to micro, and the detail work begins. During this third phase of change, all the processes that have been created, changed, or managed must be examined in detail, so that implementation will be smooth and effective.

This "detailing" must cover every aspect of the change initiative—everything from people issues to the development of new technology, such as information systems. It is at this point that all the interrelated human resources processes must be thoroughly developed. New selection processes should be finalized, along with new developmental programs and performance management processes. And, although the implementation of any new compensation strategies to support those changes may still be several months away, it is not too early to begin detailing how pay should be aligned with the other human resource processes.

To help eliminate fear and increase buy-in of the pending changes, we strongly recommend that organizations create developmental teams of managers and employees, which are then responsible for finding solutions to the myriad problems that must be addressed when finalizing processes and policies. Ultimately their work should result in a plan for the implementation of the change initiative.

Who should be involved in the process depends, of course, on the organization and its cultures. Certainly major stakeholders in the process should have a voice. But that doesn't mean that membership on the development teams should be limited to the traditional decision makers. In redesigning processes in health care, for example, we frequently work with teams that include physicians, nurses, and even administrative support personnel. And when we recently helped a public utility develop a compensation strategy to support its shift to a process culture, we worked with a design team that included two work crew foremen. Not only did they offer a unique and important perspective, but their participation generated rapid buy-in for the project.

In addition to often overlooking good but perhaps not obvious candidates for the developmental teams, organizations also often underestimate the time, energy, and commitment needed in the developmental phase of change. Frequently it takes far longer than the earlier phases. Yet if the development and detailing of new processes and strategies is rushed or neglected, the probability of the change initiative succeeding decreases significantly.

IMPLEMENTATION: TIMING IS EVERYTHING

Implementation of the change initiative can take from a few weeks to several months, to several years. A limited reengineering effort in a small, single-culture organization might "go live" immediately after the new process was developed. More extensive, large-scale changes in huge organizations with multiple business units often take years, and are implemented in phases.

The timing of introducing new processes and strategies is critical. This is especially true of compensation. Introduce a compensation change too early, and it will be viewed as coercive. Rather than focusing people on the broader issues of behavioral or strategic shifts, it will fixate them only on doing what they are paid to do. A premature compensation change thus becomes viewed either as an entitlement or a "takeaway," depending on an individual's particular perspective. Introducing compensation change too late in the process simply robs the new pay program of any credibility, impact, or connection to the bigger change initiatives.

As Figure 3–2 shows, the optimal time to introduce the new compensation element tends to be twelve to eighteen months into the implementation of the change initiative. The organization's enthusiasm for the new initiative typically lags at this point, and the pay element helps revive the pace of change and reinforce its importance to the organization. Long before reaching this point, of course, the organization should have completed a cultural diagnosis and established its future course. Work should have been reexamined, systems reengineered, roles redefined. New leaders should have been put into key roles. The supporting human resources programs—selection, training and development, performance assessment, and administration—should also have been designed and put in place, and operating satisfactorily.

This is not to say, of course, that development of a new approach to compensation should be kept on hold for a full year into the change cycle. Pilot reward programs should be implemented in targeted units or departments in the early stages of the process to get a quick measure of how compensation can best mesh with the larger organizational and work design issues at hand.

Figure 3–2

The Optimal Time for Changing Reward Systems

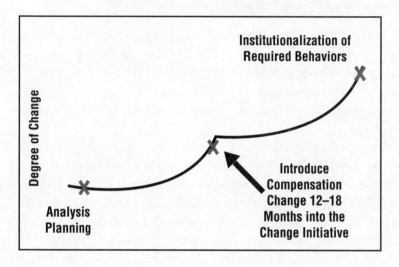

To further insure good timing, we also strongly recommend that an organization go through one full cycle of its new performance management program before implementing its pay program. This provides an opportunity not only to give the performance management program a thorough dry run, but also to create an atmosphere conducive to accepting the new pay program. The organization's top performers—usually about one third of the employees—will, by this time, begin to ask why the organization isn't paying for these new values and measures. "If these competencies, new cultures, or team approaches are so important," they'll ask, "why aren't we being rewarded for them?"

It is at that point that the new pay program can be implemented. By appearing responsive to the top third of the employees—those who already are eager to accept a new pay program, the organization will create a solid base of initial support. It can then turn its attention to the harder task of convincing the other two thirds, half of whom will be on the sidelines waiting to see if the program really will work, and half of whom will be critical, no matter how effective the program.

EVALUATING AND REFINING: A NEVER-ENDING PROCESS

As we have already noted, change has become a constant. If organizations want to remain competitive in today's rapidly shifting environment, they must never stop evaluating—and if necessary refining—everything from their broad mission and vision to their specific cultures and work processes.

Nor can they ignore the supporting human resources processes—including compensation. As much as we would like to believe otherwise, those new pay strategies that our organizations implemented three or four years ago may already be losing some of their effectiveness. That doesn't necessarily mean that they were inferior strategies, or failures. What it probably means is that our organizations, our markets, perhaps our people, have changed.

This is why it is essential that organizations develop a thorough understanding of the wide range of dynamic compensation strategies that can, in the right situation, help them successfully negotiate change. In the next chapter, we explore a variety of those pay strategies.

4

Dynamic Compensation Strategies and Tactics

t's called "FYI: Compensation." Sent out periodically from our corporate research library, it lists the latest literature on compensation. A typical issue offers a synopsis of thirty or more articles from both general publications and professional journals on a variety of pay strategies and tactics. An extremely useful tool for compensation experts, it nevertheless points to the dilemma that those in leadership and management positions face today in sorting out compensation issues: How do you select the right strategies and tactics for your organization, when there are so many to choose from—most of which appear far more complex than the traditional but ineffective pay programs now in place?

Certainly they can turn to their own compensation professionals for some of those answers. Yet in many organizations these experts have been confined—by policy, politics, processes, and training—to maintaining and administering the standard programs. They have not been encouraged to expand their knowledge and explore new options. Compensation in this traditional context frequently is cloaked in a technical mystique of sorts—a mystique that is the sole bailiwick of these "wizards of pay" with their charts, surveys, and odd terminology. Adding to that mysticism is the suspicion that they practice their magic in an organizational vacuum—with little knowledge of the people and processes or other business strategies that drive the organization.

Little wonder then that while many organizations have begun reengineering work and transforming work cultures, they have shied away from what has been called the human resources challenge of the 1990s—reshaping their pay strategies.[1]

But of course, with the right preparation, organizations can meet this challenge. This is why an understanding of not only the evolution of work cultures that we've described, but also the pay strategies that support them, is so critical. Neither can be considered in a vacuum. Both must be considered in the context of changing organizational values, structures, and goals. Just as certain cultures are more appropriate in driving and supporting certain types of organizations, certain compensation strategies are more effective in supporting certain cultures. Ultimately, of course, the alignment of both pay and culture is critical if an organization is to achieve its desired business results.

The evolution of pay and work cultures must also be considered in terms of the people's values, needs, expectations, and their behaviors—both current ones and those expected in the future. In many of our organizations, individuals have not changed as rapidly as the cultures in which they are expected to work. Many employees cling to the belief that they are entitled to ever-increasing salaries, punctual and substantial raises, and luxurious benefits packages. They are less than thrilled with this new employee/employer covenant that they are expected to sign. Taking more responsibility? Perhaps. Putting more pay at risk? Highly unlikely! Old habits, after all, die hard.

But old habits can be broken, old behaviors changed, old expectations replaced with more attractive new ones. And compensation, if properly understood, can play a major role in making these necessary changes much more palatable and much less painful.

The knowledge of new cultures and compensation strategies must not, however, be the sole property of the compensation professional. It must be shared. The generalists, including line managers, who are frequently given more ownership of and responsibility for the compensation process, must also have a clear understanding of pay strategies. And to be truly effective, the pay process must also be made clear to both supervisors and employees.

What follows is an explanation of a number of popular pay strategies, tactics, tools, and processes in use in organizations today. How these newer, more dynamic pay strategies can effectively be aligned with the evolving work cultures to achieve an organization's goals will be explained in Chapter 5.

TRADITIONAL COMPENSATION

Perhaps the best way to begin learning about specific pay strategies and tactics that are gaining popularity in the workplace is to look at how compensation has begun to evolve with work cultures—albeit at a much slower pace.

In the traditional functional organization of ten or even twenty years ago, people were paid primarily through base salaries. These salaries were usually determined by three factors: the specific job, the need to maintain a certain level of pay equity among employees in the organization, and the need to pay salaries that were competitive with those paid by other employers in the marketplace, industry, or region.

Just how much a specific job was worth became the critical factor in determining pay. As a result, point-based job measurement systems, such as the Hay Guide Chart-Profile Methodology, which ranks jobs based on three primary criteria: know-how, problem solving, and accountability, gained widespread popularity and continue to be used by many organizations. Pay was based on the specific, individual skills a person brought to a specific, individual job. Employees were not encouraged to develop other skills, nor were they rewarded for those often intrinsic attributes that we now know are so important—attributes such as flexibility, practical judgment, and the ability to work with others. The message was simple: Do your job, do it well, and we'll take care of you.

Once initial pay levels were established, pay increases for most traditional salaried employees resulted from promotions, merit, or cost of living raises. While ideally these latter two venues pay for very different values—merit for performance, cost of living for inflation—the line between the two has increasingly become blurred. Today, because of the low levels (three to four percent) of salary budget funding, most merit raises are perceived as little more than cost of living increases. Employees have come to expect them to arrive like clockwork each year, assuming they're entitled to this "merit" increase whether or not their own—or their organization's—performance really merited it.

If employees happened to be members of the organization's top management team, or if they were part of the sales department, they might also be eligible for an occasional bonus or participation in an annual incentive program. But for the vast majority, the parameters of pay were—and continue to be—a base rate, plus a merit or cost of living increase.

Often overlooked in the mix are what are frequently referred to as the "noncash" elements of the compensation picture: employee benefits and perquisites. Largely a post-World War II phenomenon, benefits started small and grew slowly. Today, however, with the explosion of benefits such as flexible spending accounts for child and health care, tuition reimbursement, and investment programs that are partially funded by employers, they comprise a significant cost to the employer as well as a significant value to the employee, and must be considered as part of the total compensation strategy.

While benefits generally have changed for the better (at least as far as employees are concerned; employers who are desperately trying to contain their continually rising costs think otherwise), other elements of the compensation equation have either stagnated or declined in the value they add to both employer and employee. A prime example of such a decline is the traditional base-pay-plus-merit-increase strategy that continues to survive in many organizations. While such programs work well in functional organizations that emphasize reliability and consistency, they do little to advance many of the values of the newer work cultures. A base pay level that is tied closely to one's specific, individual job, for example, may have little relevance in a process or time-based organization that emphasizes cross-functional teams, in which team members share the roles.

Nor does base pay, with emphasis on security and continual promotions, motivate employers in a flatter, leaner organization, where the opportunity for upward mobility is limited and security is minimal. In these more horizontal organizations, individual and organizational success hinge on performance and the "lateral growth" of the workforce—the acquisition of new skills and competencies. And, although performance, speed, and quality are the names of the game in today's process or time-based organizations, even true merit increases do little to motivate employees to work better, faster, and more cost effectively if the budgets for salary increases continue to be mired in the 3 to 4 percent range of the past few years.

AN EXPLOSION OF INNOVATIVE PAY STRATEGIES

In the past decade, organizations have slowly been coming to the realization that these traditional compensation programs have been eclipsed by their new organizational structures, strategies, and work processes. Rather than supporting the organization, they have in many cases become a barrier to growth and success. As a result, many employers have begun seeking new compensation solutions that they hope will help drive and support their new emphasis on values such as quality, customer service, teamwork, and productivity. The shift, generally, has been towards performance-based variable pay strategies. Such strategies, which include a variety of incentive programs, reward both individual and group performance. In essence, an individual's pay rises or falls depending on how well he or she performs, how well their team or business unit performs, and how well the organization as a whole performs. Measures may be tied to such issues as productivity, growth of market share, customer satisfaction, quality, economic value added (EVA), the development of new competencies, the creation of new products, or global market penetration.

Just how strong the interest in new pay strategies is can be seen in the results of a Hay survey of the compensation practices of more than five hundred companies taken at our most recent compensation conference. Fifty-one percent of the participants said they had introduced or were considering team-based pay; 48 percent said they had started or were considering pay for competencies, and 45 percent were considering group incentives.[2] While these forays into the new frontiers of pay have begun with much fanfare on the part of employers and faith on the part of their employees, the results too frequently have been disappointing and frustrating.

Take the case of an early pioneer in compensation innovation: Motorola. Concerned about the low comprehension level of some members of its work teams, the company began a skill-based compensation program that rewarded them for improving their math and reading skills. Resentment soon built among team members who had to pick up the slack when their fellow members went off for six months of training at full pay. Why, workers asked, were people being rewarded for developing individual skills, when the focus was on teamwork? Eventually, the program was replaced with an individual merit system.[3]

As with the implementation of many new compensation strategies, Motorola's problem was not the pay strategy itself or what it was intended to accomplish. There was, however, a "disconnect" between the values and behaviors it was meant to support and the behaviors and values it was perceived to reinforce. Unfortunately, it is the lack of alignment—not the pay strategy—that is frequently the culprit in such misfires. The truth is, most of today's innovative pay strategies, including those detailed in this chapter, can, in the right setting, add value to the organization. There are, however, several keys to their successful application: First, you must understand how they work—the mechanics of the strategy; second, you must know what values and behaviors they can effectively support; third, you must know how to administer and communicate the new strategies to achieve the intended results while avoiding the unintended consequences such as those experienced by Motorola, and fourth, you must know their limitations.

PAY FOR KNOWLEDGE AND SKILLS

The rapid demise of the low- and unskilled worker with limited education in highly developed nations has been well chronicled. More than a decade ago, in its now famous *Workforce 2000* study, the Hudson Institute accurately predicted that, except for those in the service occupations, the fastest-growing job categories would require more than the median level of education for all jobs. And, when ranked according to math, reading, and reasoning skills, only 27 percent of all new jobs would fall in the lowest two of six skill categories.[4]

As accurate as those figures may be, it doesn't take a team of researchers and experts to see how dramatic and rapid the shift from brawn to brain has been. Just ask someone who grew up in the early part of the twentieth century. In less than a lifetime we have moved from an ages-old emphasis on physical skills, *through* a focus on mechanical skills, and on to a time when technical and intellectual ability is of paramount importance. Take manufacturing, for example. Until the advent of steam and electrical power, most products were made by skilled craftsmen working by hand. Then came power and the assembly line and the mechanization of much of the physical labor. Today, of course, those machines are highly automated, controlled through computers that require mainly technical and intellectual skills to operate.

As author Charles Handy puts it: "The end of labor-intensive manufacturing leaves us with organizations which receive their added value from the knowledge and creativity they put in, rather than the muscle power. Fewer people, thinking better, helped by clever machines and computers, add more value than gangs or lines of unthinking 'human resources.'"[5] Just how much value these "better thinking" people add to an organization depends, of course, on their skills and knowledge. And, as organizations are quickly discovering, with fewer people doing more work and frequently sharing more roles, the rapid development and utilization of skills and knowledge is critical.

To that end, compensation programs that reward the development of skills and knowledge have grown in popularity during the past decade. Skill-based pay first gained popularity in factories and other blue-collar settings, where it was used primarily as a way to break down narrow jobs and rigid work rules such as the classic: "Only electricians can change light bulbs." Eventually, however, it came to be seen for its true value: rewarding and motivating employees in other process organizations, where speed, flexibility, and productivity were critical.

Skill-based pay strategies reward people for the skills they are required to perform rather than for a specified job. As employees acquire more skills, they become more flexible resources. Not only are they able to perform multiple roles, but they also develop a broader understanding of the work processes and thus gain a better understanding of the importance of their contribution to the organization. This flexibility and understanding is critical in organizations that are implementing job sharing and self-directed work teams.

Skill-based pay can also help employees and organizations adapt to rapid technical changes in the marketplace. An examination of any process environment today clearly shows how dramatic these technical changes are. In health care, for example, depending on what department they work in, employees must continually learn new protocols, new procedures, new drugs, and new courses of treatment. By rewarding the development of the new skills and knowledge needed in such an environment, an organization sends a strong behavioral message to its employees: "The world is changing quickly and you are expected to change at the same pace. But not to worry, we'll reward you for the necessary growth that change requires."

Skill-based pay is often presented as a radical departure from the traditional strategy of paying for the job. In reality, the radical departure—if there is one—involves the jobs themselves. The new strategy for pay, in essence, is a reslicing of the pie to better support the values and behaviors required by these new jobs. Traditional jobs were narrowly defined tasks, requiring an equally narrowly defined set of skills. Today's jobs, especially those in process and time-based organizations, tend to be wider in scope, and require a broader set of skills. See Figures 4–1 and 4–2.

Go back to the health care example for a moment. In the traditional, compartmentalized, specialized hospital the registered nurse is responsible for a very specific set of tasks—nothing more, nothing less. So, too, is the nurse's aide, the housekeeper, and the food server. But when that structure is replaced by a horizontal, integrated one, aligned with the way patients naturally move through the hospital, these jobs—and roles—change. The registered nurse now may assume the role of the "care manager," who must oversee all aspects of day-to-day care. The aide may assume the role of the "care partner," who performs routine technical work such as drawing blood and administering EKGs—tasks that previously were handled only by an RN. The housekeeper may help serve the meals. Thus, as a result in the shift of jobs and roles, everyone—the nurse, the nurse's aide, the housekeeper, and the food server—will have to develop new skills. Even the role of the physicians will change. They will do more of the managing of patient care, leaving much of the more traditional day-to-day care to nurses and physician assistants.

Or consider the home office of a large, national insurance firm, whose functional work culture with layer upon layer of managers and desk upon desk of specialized claims processors and underwriters had been rendered cumbersome and ineffective in today's computerized, service-oriented marketplace. In a move that was both cost effective and customer-friendly, the insurer eliminated several layers of management and created teams of employees that handled a wide range of tasks. Rather than be only a health claims processor or a standard life underwriter, an employee's role now may involve standard life underwriting as well as disability underwriting and medical claims processing. Like the nurse, the underwriter will have to learn new sets of skills to be able to handle the expanded role. To support these new values and the behaviors needed to achieve them, the insurance company created a pay program that rewarded employees for the acquisition and utilization of the new skills they needed.

Figure 4–1

Traditional Job-Based Design

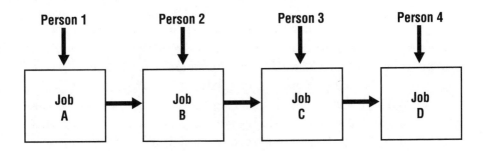

Figure 4–2

Skill-Based Pay

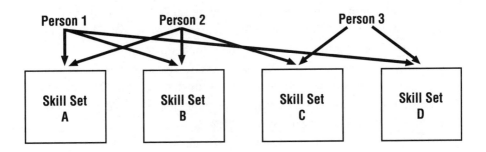

For those employees who can't or choose not to learn new skills, the options are, of course, limited. The insurance company was somewhat unusual in that it had a no-layoff policy and tried to find new roles within the organization for displaced employees. Other organizations do not have that luxury. Many health care organizations we work with, for example, create extensive retraining and education programs, while at the same time initiating out-placement efforts for those employees who will not be retained.

While skill-based pay may not appear to be a radical departure from a more traditional pay program, such programs must be carefully developed and implemented if they are to be effective. As we have already noted, a system must be created for training employees and helping them develop the required new skills. A certification process must be established to ensure that they indeed have acquired those skills. Just as important, a periodic recertification process is critical to ensure that employees maintain a certain level of skill, while a decertification process is often necessary for employees who no longer have certain skills.

Another critical issue organizations must address in implementing skill-based pay is what skills they will pay for. The goal of such a strategy, after all, is not just rewarding employees for the acquisition of more and more skills, but only for those skills that are needed for a particular role or job. To make a pay-for-skills program work, there must be a close relationship between the total value of the skills and the market level of pay. If a job requires six skills, for example, an employee shouldn't be paid at market level until he or she achieves all six skills. Nor should the employee be paid *above* market level for merely adequately demonstrating all six.

The organization also must determine the scope of skill development that will be rewarded. Should employees be encouraged to become generalists—developing more rather than higher skills—or should they only acquire higher valued skills so that jobs actually become worth more to the company? Teaching highly trained professionals word processing, for example, may broaden their skills and allow the elimination of some secretarial work, but it certainly isn't a skill that merits a pay increase. Training a secretary to handle some of the professional's tasks, on the other hand, should probably result in increased pay.

The organization also must decide whether people will get to choose what skills they learn next, or whether that will be determined by the employer, the flow of work processes, or customer demands. Still another issue that must be addressed is whether employees learn at their own pace or at a pace set by the organization, based on what is needed.

Finally, the organization also must decide whether it is going to design a program that works strictly within a single family of jobs, or whether it is going to design a plan that encourages true cross-training. In the first case, employees are rewarded for following one specific career path with a number of individual steps (more appropriate in a functional culture); in the second, they are encouraged to break off from the traditional career paths and forge new ones (more appropriate in a time-based culture). The answers to all of these questions depend, of course, on the ultimate purpose of the pay program, whether it is being used merely to add more flexibility to the organization, or whether it is needed to facilitate and support major changes in job design and work by rewarding employees for learning new skills.

While skill-based pay can effectively rank and reward today's multi-roled, skill-driven jobs and ultimately help change behavior and advance performance, it is not a radical departure from current approaches to compensation. Employees will see little actual change in their pay—at least initially—and it will be delivered in much the same manner as it has traditionally been delivered. Nor does a skill-based pay program necessarily require the creation of a new administrative process. Indeed, many of the elements may already be in place. It can, for example, still incorporate work measurement to assess skills, to price steps in the ladder, or to determine salary ranges.

Skill-based pay can be extremely effective in organizations that have re-engineered work or that want to facilitate the transformation to new ways of organizing work. By paying employees for the acquisition of the skills needed in the "new" organization, the organization can, in effect, reduce or even eliminate their natural resistance to change. Eventually, as the new values and behaviors are accepted, the acquisition of skills becomes a continuous process. Expectations are continually raised, and the skill sets needed to meet those expectations continually evolve.

Ultimately, skill-based pay can be an effective strategy for transforming a company into a more flexible, performance-oriented, team-driven organization, all the while enriching both the work lives and pay of its employees.

PAY FOR COMPETENCIES

Like the other pay strategies discussed here, pay for skills should not be considered an all-or-nothing approach. An organization may still want to maintain its merit pay program. It may want to add an incentive program based on individual and/or team performance. Or, as many are discovering, it may want to reward more than just the skills necessary for the new role.

When the toy manufacturer LEGO Systems, Inc. decided to take a team approach in its packaging department, it put together four of its best-performing, highly skilled workers, gave them some additional training, and put them to work. The results, in the words of one senior manager, were disastrous. "They had all the skills to do the job, but they couldn't interact with one another," the manager said.

When Bass PLC acquired Holiday Inn's North American operation in 1990, it found that the hotel group lacked an aggressive service-oriented culture. It needed employees who not only were skilled, but who also were energetic, service-conscious, problem solvers. Although the goals of the toy maker and innkeeper were very different, both found the solution lay in the development of not just the traditional, technical skills employees needed to successfully complete their jobs, but also in a number of less obvious *competencies*—such things as the ability to work in teams, to accomplish specific goals, to solve problems rapidly, and to understand the customers' perspectives and meet their needs in a way that really added value.

Simply defined, competencies are the sets of skills, knowledge, abilities, behavioral characteristics, and other attributes that, in the right combination and for the right set of circumstances, predict superior performance. Perhaps the best way to describe competencies is in the context of an iceberg. See Figure 4–3. Like the iceberg, a relatively small proportion of competencies are easily discernible at or above the surface. These easily visible or *essential* competencies include learned skills, such as technical capabilities and knowledge. But merely having such skills and knowledge, as every manager knows, does not necessarily guarantee the success of an individual in a particular job or role. Less visible—below the surface—are three additional levels of behavior that are crucial to superior or exceptional performance. These deeper or differentiating competencies include the *self-concepts* or vision a person has of him or herself, *traits*, or the general disposition to behave in a certain way—tenacity or flexibility, for example—and the *motives* or recurrent thoughts that drive behavior, such as a drive to achieve and perform. Although competencies are frequently used in determining an individual's ability to perform, they also can be used to predict the performance of a group, management level, specific job, or an entire organization, and can therefore be incorporated into the selection process.

Competencies have been used as an effective business tool since the early 1970s, when Harvard psychologist David McClelland first introduced

Figure 4–3

Competencies

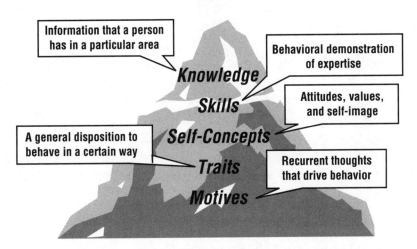

the concept. But they only recently came into their own as a popular and crucial element of successful business strategy. (It should be noted that while a lot of people these days talk in general terms about "competencies" and the word has been incorporated into popular business jargon, true competencies are those that add value and help predict success.) This rediscovery of their value was no doubt prompted by changes in organizational values and goals. In today's competitive environment, success no longer rides on the shoulders of a better product or service. What distinguishes "the best" organization from "the rest" is its superior performance in terms of quality, customer service, speed, or any other corporate attribute that establishes and helps it maintain its competitive stance.

That is equally true of employees. Organizations today are finding that they need to reconsider old notions of what kinds of workers they need, how these employees should go about their work, and how they should be motivated and rewarded for top performance in such a radically different environment. As LEGO Systems, Inc. and many other organizations have discovered, there is a pressing need for people who are not only highly skilled, but who can work together on teams, make decisions on their own, and generally assume more responsibility. It is here that the use of competencies and competency-based pay can be effective.

The use of competencies and competency-based pay need not be limited to a particular group or level of employee. Campbell's Soup Company Ltd. developed a competency-based pay program for the production workers in one of its Canadian plants. Kaiser Permanente, the huge health care management organization, is using competency-based pay in parts of its organization, and has developed competency models for its regional leaders, although it is not linking them to pay. General Electric used competencies in determining its career bands and what sort of skills and competencies were needed in each of those bands. Quaker Oats is utilizing them to sharpen the focus of its marketing operations. And Chemical Bank used them to help select and develop high-performing traders and salespeople.

The first step in developing a competency-based compensation program is to identify the competencies that create value for the organization, and thus should be rewarded. This may initially appear to be an easy task— simply creating a "wish list" of attributes that organizations would like their successful employees to have. Who doesn't want their employees to be self-motivated, achievement-oriented, customer-focused? In reality, however, it is a far more complex task than simply noting so-called "star behavior." It involves identifying the specific competencies that are needed to support an organization's strategy and that create genuine economic value added. Figure 4–4 shows how one organization aligned its vision, mission, and values with the necessary competencies it had determined generated the highest economic return for its customer service team.

Next, the organization must ascertain what qualities, attributes, and behaviors set its superior performers apart from the rest of the pack. To that end, several questions must be answered. First, for each job, role, or family of jobs, "superior performance" must be defined. Second, what the best performers do—more often and in more situations—to achieve those results must be analyzed. Finally, the behavior characteristics that predict this outstanding performance must be identified. Figure 4–5, for example, shows the competencies one organization determined were needed for the teamwork and cooperation that would create value.

Determining these behaviors—most of which are not readily visible— requires careful, thoughtful, disciplined analysis. It is one thing to test an individual to determine his or her knowledge about a particular subject or

Figure 4–4

Linking Competencies to Strategy

VISION	
Most trusted	Customer service orientation, listening and responding, organizational commitment
Responsive and helpful	Listening and responding, flexibility, interpersonal understanding
Error free	Concern for order/quality
No broken promise or unkept promise	Customer service orientation
No late delivery or incomplete shipment	Customer service orientation, concern for order/quality
No processing errors or billing mistakes	Listening and responding, concern for order/quality
No missed response time or incomplete answer	Achievement motivation, information seeking, analytical thinking
MISSION	
Personalized service	Customer service orientation, listening and responding, flexibility
Customer service as a way of life	Customer service orientation, organizational commitment, achievement motivation
Gain personally and grow professionally	Developing others, teamwork, and cooperation
Ownership of vision	Organizational commitment, teamwork and cooperation
SHARED VALUES	
Integrity though our actions	Customer service orientation, organizational commitment, self-control
Mutual respect	Teamwork and cooperation, self-control, interpersonal understanding
Cooperation	Teamwork and cooperation, flexibility, organizational commitment
Professionalism	Listening and responding, self-control, organizational commitment
Innovation	Achievement motivation
Open communication	Listening and responding, Self-control, interpersonal understanding, developing others

skill on a particular job. It is quite another challenge to determine what makes one individual more responsive to customers, more driven to succeed, and more consistently a top performer. The process of assessing competencies is more than making a simple albeit subjective laundry list. It requires a certain level of training and expertise. Those conducting the

Figure 4–5

**Defining the Competencies: Teamwork and Cooperation
Showing Acceptable-to-Outstanding Range**

1	**Cooperates:** Participates willingly-supports team decisions, is a "good team player," does his/her share of the work.
2	**Shares Information:** Keeps people informed and up-to-date about the group process, shares all relevant or useful information
3 Acceptable	**Expresses Positive Expectations:** Expresses positive expectations of the capabilities of other team members. Speaks of team members, to others within or outside the team, in a supportive manner. Appeals to reason in situations of conflict rather than taking an argumentative position.
4	**Solicits Inputs:** Values the input and expertise of other team members and is willing to learn from co-workers. Encourages all team members to contribute ideas and opinions in team planning sessions or when decisions need to be made ("We haven't heard from Bob yet on this issue").
5	**Encourages Others:** Credits co-workers who have performed well both within the team and outside the team. Encourages team members as they gain new skills and makes them feel like valued members.
6	**Builds Team Spirit:** Takes special actions to promote a friendly climate, good morale and cooperation among team members (plans a party or outing, creates a team T-shirt). Promotes the team's accomplishments and reputation to co-workers outside of the team.
7 Outstanding	**Resolves Conflicts:** Brings conflict (personal, professional) within the team into the open, and encourages or facilitates a beneficial resolution that promotes teamwork. Does not hide conflicts, or avoid the issue, but tries to resolve as quickly as possible to restore team effectiveness.

interviews should be able to effectively probe beneath the surface, and those analyzing the results should be able to convert the interviewers' findings into meaningful competencies.

The ideal place to begin the search for the key competencies is with the exceptional performers themselves. By asking questions about how they approach their jobs or how they solve problems, an experienced interviewer can begin to draw out the key competencies. Take, for example, the issue of customer service: In answering questions about how customer complaints are handled, the superior-performing employee will probably talk about proactively addressing complaints, going beyond the normal expectations, if necessary, to answer them satisfactorily. The average employee, on the other hand, may talk about following established procedures and maintaining company policy—nothing more, nothing less—while the lower-performing employee may place all responsibility and blame with others.

This method of identifying competencies can be applied to teams, job levels or families, or even an entire organization. Holiday Inn, for example, began by interviewing top management to determine the characteristics and behaviors of its future leaders. Then, about thirty outstanding performers from various levels in the organization were interviewed in an effort to determine which of their competencies set them apart from their peers. From these interviews, competency models were developed for four major job levels: executives, managers, professional/technical personnel, and clerical/administrative employees.

LEGO Systems, Inc. took a similar route. First, with the help of employees, the organization's top performers were identified. The toy maker, however, looked at more than just technical skill. After determining that teams made up of highly skilled individuals didn't necessarily work well, it began exploring competencies for team achievement, team orientation, and personal effectiveness. Then, through focus groups and interviews with these top performers, the skills and competencies that made them better performers were isolated. From that, a LEGO team created its competency model.

After identifying the competencies, it is important to test them and determine whether they actually make a difference in performance. Too often, this phase is neglected and just about anything gets called a competency. It is critical in a pay-for-competency system to utilize only *distinguishing* competencies—those that truly separate the best from the rest. Otherwise, the organization winds up paying for new behaviors, but not necessarily new results.

Once the competencies have been identified and tested, they can begin to be linked to compensation. Although they can be incorporated into a variety of pay strategies, they are usually tied—at least initially—to the base salary program. Under such a program, employees are paid up to a target level—usually established by market comparisons—based on their understanding and performance of a job, role, or team function. Employees then move beyond that level through the acquisition of the prescribed competencies. Once competency-based pay is accepted as part of the base pay program, it can then be incorporated into other elements of compensation, such as variable pay.

Competency-based pay, of course, requires more than just identifying competencies and establishing a new pay program. It also must be incorporated into the processes for selecting new employees and assessing employee performance. Unlike traditional employee evaluations, an effective competency-based assessment program emphasizes how employees work rather than merely what they accomplish. And rather than the traditional "judgment by superiors," competency-based assessment often incorporates what is termed a "360-degree" process, which includes review by peers, subordinates, even customers, if service orientation measurements are critical to the competency mix.

Other controls required by a competency-based pay program include an evaluation system that measures jobs or roles, market data for setting pay levels, and a salary administration system flexible enough to track a variety of variables. Because the organization is paying and promoting employees based on the growth of competencies, it also must put in place an extensive training and coaching program.

These additional administrative and human resources requirements may at first deter less aggressive organizations from pursuing a competency-based compensation strategy. Yet, as a growing number of organizations are discovering, the added effort and support required for such a program will more than likely be offset, in short order, by the benefits generated. Indeed, if used effectively, competency-based compensation does far more than merely reward employees for the "added value" they bring to their jobs and roles. It also helps the organization better focus on its core mission and the value of exceptional performance in realizing that mission.

Competency- and skill-based pay certainly aren't for every organization. Yet, for those that are caught in the merit pay conundrum—continually increasing compensation, but getting little in return for the development of new skills or better performance—they offer a positive solution. While not replacing merit increases, they offer a better, more clearly defined process for tying the progress of merit increases to the development of specific skills and competencies.

BROADBANDING: A NEW PAY PLATFORM

While paying people for new skills and competencies can be effective in changing behavior and advancing new goals and business strategies, it is only one step. Other important issues must be faced. If the organization is like most and has reduced staff and cut management levels, it must look for new ways to move people through the organization. The traditional towering career ladders with rungs upon rungs of potential upward movement have, in essence, been pared down to a stepladder. Employees who once could be motivated for an entire career with promises of ever higher positions are getting frustrated as they bump their heads on a very low corporate ceiling or wait much longer for a pay increase. Tom Peters says eloquently what a lot of employees are thinking: "There's not much of a pyramid left to climb. So how will people get their kicks—their bucks, their psychic compensation?"[6]

But the problem isn't limited to motivating employees in an atmosphere of restricted mobility. Even the few organizations that remain fatter than flatter are adopting new organizational values and changing cultures. As these progressive organizations implement teams, expand cross-training, and try to maintain flexibility in the face of change, their traditional pay strategies and delivery systems often become obsolete.

One element of pay that organizations are struggling with is the traditional system of grading. These highly vertical systems with their vast numbers of grades are out of synch with the flatter, flexible, team-oriented cultures that many organizations are moving toward. To counter this growing "disalignment," some are adopting a strategy known as banding or broadbanding, in which numerous grades are replaced by a few relatively broad bands.

Banding is not another pay-for strategy. Rather, it is a platform on which a compensation strategy such as skill- or competency-based pay can be built and effectively operated. An organization might, for example, place all of its professional positions into one band, its management positions into another, its technical positions into another, and its clerical positions into yet another. Rather than climb up through a series of grades, employees might spend most if not all of their careers in a single band, moving laterally, and thus getting more pay as they gain new skills, competencies, or responsibilities, or as they improve their performance. Take, for example, the employee who needs to spend time in a lower-level job to develop a new skill set. Through banding, the worker can be placed in the lower job, yet continue to be paid more, a move considered impossible in traditional pay grade programs. In fact, the compensation concept of broadbanding was taken from radio terminology: Organizations no longer desired "single-frequency" employees. Rather, they wanted employees who could cover a "broad band"—employees who were multiskilled and multi-competencied, employees who, when necessary, could do a variety of tasks.

By deemphasizing titles, grades, job descriptions, and ever-upward movement, broadbanding helps organizations advance the values of group or team performance along with that of the individual. Frequently, for example, both supervisors and their subordinates will be placed in the same band. And, as their duties and roles change, they can very naturally move slightly "back and forth" within the band, without the need for an attention-grabbing promotion or the stigma of a demotion.

Unlike traditional pay grades, bands do not have to be constructed "end-on-end," but can be designed to overlap, adding flexibility to an already flexible pay program. This overlap allows employees to continue to progress within the organization without the elevation to another pay range or job title. At the same time, however, there can be healthy differences between pay levels both within and between bands. Figure 4–6 shows how such overlaps might occur in the banding of three value-adding tiers found in most organizations: professional, management, and leadership.

Broadbanding can be especially useful in the new "boundaryless" organizations and in those team-based organizations that emphasize less specialized, multifocus jobs, and processes that cross departments and require more skills and individual or team authority. Because advancement is not based on continually upward movement to yet another grade, banding also facilitates the growth and development of alternate career tracks. Today, of course, most organizations want to emphasize more than just one behavior or value. The organization that wants not only to weather rapid change, but to stay productive and highly competitive through the change (and what organization doesn't?) may want to develop a more integrated approach that ties pay to the mastery of new skills, the growth of competencies, the assumption of a broader role, and the performance that results.

The one question many organizations struggle with, sometimes to the point of ignoring other, equally critical issues, is how many bands they should create. Unfortunately, there is no single, right answer that would make it easy. (A Hay survey on organizations that had begun broadbanding efforts found that the number of bands ranged from one to eighteen.) The "correct" number for any organization is best ascertained by first determining the number of distinct levels of employee contributions within the organization that actually add value. The number of bands can be determined in a number of ways. In those organizations that are flattening their structure, it might be determined by the number of organizational levels that remain. In other organizations it might be determined by identifying the key areas of accountability, or natural job clusters. One band, for example, might include all support personnel, while another would include all technical staff. In other organizations, the bands might be determined by the key indicators necessary for delivering a service or product.

Once the number of bands are established, individual jobs or roles can be placed and valued within the bands. As with the determination of band numbers, there are a variety of ways to accomplish this. Figure 4–7 shows three typical approaches. The organization that wants to focus primarily on performance may want to use a "performance curve" approach, placing individuals in the band based on their level of performance. The organization that needs to emphasize the acquisition of new skills may determine placement and movement within the band strictly on the acquisition of such skills as determined by training, certification, or demonstration. On the other hand, as the bottom band in Figure 4–7 shows, the organization might also want to incorporate competencies, and thus create a band in which payment up to specific market levels is based on job knowledge and performance, and movement beyond that point is based on the development of critical competencies.

It should be clear from this point that while simple in structure, broadbanding—to be effective—requires attention to numerous details. Take, for example, the labeling of the bands. Although it may at first appear to be a minor task, it is in reality a critical one because of the values such titles imply. A simple numbering approach (Band 1, 2, 3, etc.) should not be used without descriptive labels that convey a clear cultural message within the organization, and should not imply inferior or superior status. Because of the potential confusion new titles may have on customers, it may in some cases be necessary to maintain the traditional external titles in addition to the new—more ambiguous—internal ones.

Effective communications don't end with the creation of titles. Because most workers are unfamiliar with banding, there is sure to be a high degree

Figure 4–6

Positioning the Bands

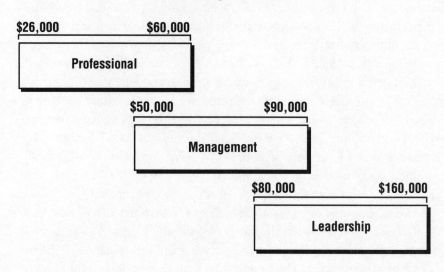

Figure 4–7

Three Approaches to Banding

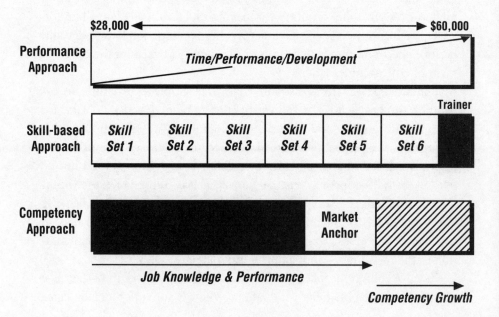

of fear, uncertainty, and misinformation surrounding the creation of such a program. Employees will need to know how their pay is determined, what their real salary opportunity is, and how they can advance. Banding also requires new tools for demonstrating compliance with legislative requirements in such areas as equal opportunity, affirmative action, and disability assistance. An effective salary administration program will continue to be important. Quality market data, based on the measurement of work and roles, will still be needed for establishing benchmarks for pricing bands and the roles within them.

But even more important than these technical and administrative requirements are the requisite intangible supports: a strong performance-based culture, a high level of trust and understanding among employees, and a clear commitment from the organization's leadership.

A number of organizations have attempted broadbanding. Many, like General Electric, which eliminated numerous pay grades in favor of five bands (professional, senior professional, leadership, executive, and senior executive), have reported excellent results with the approach. Others say they have been disappointed. Critics charge that banding is unworkable or overly simplistic—a gimmick, more of smoke and mirrors than substance. In reality, they say, it has nothing over well-designed, traditional pay approaches.

The problem is not in the strategy itself, but how it is perceived and applied. Despite the name and emphasis, broadbanding goes far beyond simply eliminating grades and focusing on paying people rather than jobs. As with the consideration of other pay programs, the organization must first examine its culture, values, and strategies. It must ask itself whether it has the corporate competencies it needs to meet its strategic goals and whether it has or is developing people with the skills and individual competencies to achieve them. Then it can begin to establish a pay program that blends the fundamentals of market pay—essentially pay for the job—with the real contributions or output of individuals, their competencies, and their ability to continue developing.

GE, for example, first determined it had to make major changes in its organizational culture. It effected those changes by defining new values, creating new training and development programs, redefining the role of leadership and management, and truly empowering people to look at ways to simplify processes. Only after those changes were underway did it restructure compensation.

Organizations that have taken a more reactive approach, however, have been less successful. One telecommunications giant, for example, approached banding as little more than a series of "pregnant grades." It collapsed the old grading system without first changing the culture, determining what it was really paying for, or deciding how people would move through the bands. As a result, pay was not linked to other key organizational messages, and employees behaved as they always had. To make matters worse, supervisors, who were given freedom but no structure for moving people through the bands, "broke the bank," exceeding the salary budget.

Just as those organizations that oversimplify the overall strategy of banding are sure to be disappointed, so too are those that mistakenly believe that banding is a work-reducing cure-all for their salary administration and planning worries. True, banding provides a good platform to integrate the market and performance elements of pay. But it is up to the organization to determine the values it should be paying for, the right mix of those values, and how pay is going to be positioned as part of the organization's overall strategy.

Certainly, broadbanding is not for every organization. And in an overly simplified form that merely collapses the traditional grading structure without regard to changing the roles and the organization of work, it is almost guaranteed to deliver less than it promises. Still, a carefully designed program tailored to an organization's individual culture, values, and business strategy can be very effective in helping that organization achieve its goals through the growth and performance of its human resources.

VARIABLE, PERFORMANCE-BASED COMPENSATION

Peel away the design criteria, the mechanics, the technical parameters, and when all is said and done, the pay strategies described thus far focus on two primary issues critical to organizational success—people and how they perform. Yet, while strategies such as skill- and competency-based pay are often vital to the development of new values and behaviors needed in the changing organization, they alone may not make that last most important connection that drives the organization forward—the connection that links the individual and his or her performance to the performance and ultimate success of the organization.

For years such linkage has existed, but only with a few small groups of employees. Senior executives were often given incentives for their roles in leading the organization forward. This came in the form of both annual and long-term incentive programs through which they received cash or stock if they achieved certain individual and organizational goals. Further down the organization, simple individual incentive programs rewarded members of the sales staff for their performance. In some industries, manufacturing, for example, incentive programs were even extended to hourly employees, who were paid on a piecework basis.

Beyond those groups, however, incentives were perceived to be of little value. Employees, traditional business theory said, were merely cogs in a large organizational machine. There was no need to concern them with the bigger performance picture. As long as there were enough of these reliable cogs doing their jobs, things should run smoothly—especially if the cogs were paid a fair and equitable wage or salary that kept them satisfied and secure.

That theory, like so many theories, began to change during the recessionary years of the early 1980s. Struggling to stay ahead of their competitors, many organizations found that they needed cogs who not only were reliable, but also were excellent performers who looked beyond their specific jobs. Faced with declining profits, these organizations also found that they needed to reduce fixed costs, which meant freezing or reducing pay or even eliminating cogs—not a popular move with the security-conscious cogs who had grown to believe they were entitled to a certain level of pay *ad infinitum*.

About the same time, many of these organizations were also discovering that productivity and profits, while important, weren't the only gods to which business must pay homage. More intangible values such as quality, customer service, innovation, flexibility, and cycle time were also becoming critical factors in determining organizational success.

In searching for answers to these fundamental changes in business, organizations "rediscovered" the value of variable, performance-based pay strategies. By moving incentive programs beyond the executive suites and sales departments, organizations found they could begin turning their entitled cogs into empowered people who had a stake in the company. By allowing them to share in the organization's risks and rewards, these "new employees" not only improved their performance, but took on more responsibility for it. By allowing at least a portion of compensation to rise and fall with the fortunes of the organization, the fixed-cost issue, if not eliminated, was at least softened, as was the need to continually cut or add staff.

Despite their obvious allure, performance-based variable pay programs have been slow to gain a foothold in many organizations. In our own survey of more than five hundred companies, we found that while a growing number were considering moving incentive programs deeper into the organization, most have not yet done so. For example, only 19 percent had implemented profit sharing, only 16 percent gainsharing, and only 13 percent had long-term incentives below the executive level. Yet more than 80 percent of those same organizations said they believed that they needed to revamp both their short- and long-term incentive programs.

Why the reluctance? Part of it may be due to the charges by critics that performance-based incentives are ineffective or, as author Alfie Kohn argues, actually do more harm than good. Kohn, in his controversial book, *Punished by Rewards*, makes the case that rewards and punishment are simply two sides of the same coin. Incentives, he claims, discourage risk taking, pit employee against employee, thus destroying teamwork and cooperation, and fail to address many of the issues that are really holding back the organization. "In many workplaces," he writes, "incentive plans are used as a substitute for management: pay is made contingent on performance and everything else is left to take care of itself."[7]

Certainly incentive plans and other performance-based pay programs are no substitute for effective management. Nor are they the right strategy for every employee in every organization. But despite Kohn's claims to the contrary, incentives and other performance-based compensation strategies can be powerful forces in motivating employees and in helping organizations change and succeed.

The key to their success, as with other forms of pay, is alignment. Variable rewards must be tailored to the specific work cultures and values of both the organization and its employees. The traditional incentive programs designed in the 1950s, '60s, and '70s are, unfortunately, often ill-fitted to the needs, values, and structures of business in the 1990s. It's a lesson that even companies with highly successful variable pay programs have had to learn. Consider the case of the Lincoln Electric Company, the nation's largest maker of arc welders and welding supplies, a firm long recognized for its employee incentive program. Lincoln's bonus program,

which was started in 1934, closely links compensation with individual productivity and company profitability. Most line workers, for example, receive
no base wage and are paid only for what they produce. Those who are
highly successful sometimes earn more than $100,000 a year.

Yet recently, the program, which has been studied by the Harvard Business School, not to mention a number of other companies, came under
fire. Rapid growth of Lincoln's business in overseas markets in the 1980s
led to subsequent financial problems that, in turn, resulted in major
losses. Not only did the company's pay-for-performance program not work
in cultures outside of the United States, but its U.S. employees faced a
potential reduction in their bonuses because of problems outside of their
control.

The problem was not that the employee incentive program didn't
work—it did, very effectively—but that its compensation strategies did not
evolve as Lincoln Electric changed and developed into a global player. Lincoln's CEO summed up the problem very succinctly: "We did it too fast,
paid too much; we didn't understand foreign markets and cultures, and
then we got hit by a recession."[8]

Another equally important reason for the failure of some variable pay
programs and the reluctance of organizations to implement them is their
administrative needs: They require highly effective performance management and communications strategies to support them. If, for example, you
are going to link pay to performance, then you'd better have in place effective tools for evaluating that performance. If you are going to require
employees to take on more risk and responsibility for the success of the organization, then you'd better provide them with the information necessary
to make sound, timely decisions.

Initially the employees must be told much more than just how the
program works. They also must know what they—and the organization—
must do to make it work. Once the program is underway, they must
constantly be informed of the progress they are making. They must be told
what is working and what isn't. Communications about performance is
much like the telemetry system of a rocket, which breaks the journey to
the target into small elements and gives constant feedback so that the
rocket will stay on course. Too often, managers are unable or unwilling to
be that open. Indeed, in its purest form, performance-based variable pay is
more about sending messages than about delivering pay. Those messages
must be not only clear, but also consistent with how the overall business

plan is managed and supported. Which is why, in the long run, variable pay programs implemented solely to eliminate fixed costs frequently fail.

Many organizations have begun to expand the use of variable pay programs by simply pushing traditional, executive-type incentive plans deeper into the organization, to directors and managers. Like other variable pay plans, such programs can work, provided the newly eligible members can, through their performance, actually influence the business results that trigger the incentive. If they can't, or if the link between their performance and the results is so tangential or so vague that it can't easily be followed, then chances of the program succeeding will be greatly diminished.

While this expanded use of the traditional management incentive plan has its place, a growing number of organizations are looking at a variety of other, more dynamic approaches. Many are, like sales and management incentives, targeted at small, specific groups of employees or individuals. Others, however, are designed to encompass entire organizations. Among the variable pay strategies whose popularity is growing are:

Profit Sharing.   Perhaps the most common incentive plan in use below the management level, profit sharing has been around in some form or other for years. In its simplest form, all or certain groups of employees share a nondeferred pool created by a percentage of the profits, usually determined by a prearranged formula. While profit-sharing plans can be effective in focusing employees on the financial performance of the organization, they frequently have trouble linking that performance back to the efforts of the individual. Such programs may motivate employees in a general fashion, but they do little to drive performance directly or change the behavior of individuals or teams. They are, however, effective in highly cyclical organizations whose fixed pay is pay generally at or below the market and who want the flexibility of paying above the market in good years while not having to cut staff or costs during difficult years.

Gainsharing.   A variable pay program that began growing in popularity in the 1990s, gainsharing is sometimes confused with profit sharing. In reality, it is quite different. Rather than focus on a flat percentage of profits, gainsharing usually is tied to achievement of very specific goals for productivity, quality improvement, cost effectiveness and the like. If those goals are achieved, then the group shares part of the resulting monetary gains.

Consider the case of a large southern health care organization that, like most health care organizations, was attempting to make its member hospitals more cost effective and more customer focused in order to stay competitive. To help drive these values, the organization created a gainsharing program that had two levels of goals. As Figure 4–8 shows, the main trigger for the plan was a combination financial/quality goal. In order to get any payout, the organization had to achieve a 5 percent net operating margin and maintain accreditation. Fifty percent of the revenues above 5 percent were then put in a pool for employees to share. Sixty-five percent of the pool was then distributed equally to all the employees for achievement of that primary trigger. The other 35 percent, however, was distributed only if employees achieved the second level of goals. These secondary goals, which changed from year to year, tended to focus on quality and customer service.

The advantage of gainsharing plans over their profit-sharing cousins is twofold. First, they are truly self-funding, built on money the organization otherwise would not have saved or earned. Second, the link or line-of-sight between performance and results is much shorter and clearer. If the plan is well designed and communicated, employees can see what changes in behavior and values lead to the expected results. Then, with the right coaching and managing, they can successfully make those changes.

While tremendously attractive in concept, gainsharing is not a simple pay strategy. Organizations must be able not only to measure the gains, but also to determine what role the employees have in achieving those gains. How much of the increase in productivity, for example, was the result of employee behavior, and how much was the result of new technology over which employees had absolutely no control?

Another key issue is the frequency of payouts, which varies from organization to organization, depending in part on the specific business cycle. Many plans pay out annually, while others do it every six months or quarterly. The more frequent the payout, the more organizations must plan for those situations that are beyond the employees' control that could lead to big gains or losses, and that may require adjustments in goals and/or payouts.

Problems frequently arise when plans are overly complex or poorly designed, so that the employees don't see or don't understand the relationship between performance and achievement of goals. Likewise, communications are critical: Participants have to be informed, on an

Figure 4–8

Gainsharing: One Healthcare Organization's Approach

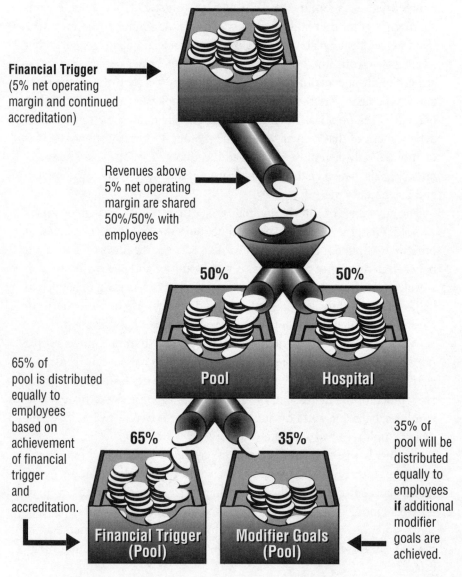

Financial Trigger
(5% net operating
margin and continued
accreditation)

Revenues above
5% net operating
margin are shared
50%/50% with
employees

50%   50%

Pool   **Hospital**

65% of
pool is distributed
equally to
employees
based on
achievement
of financial
trigger
and
accreditation.

65%   35%

Financial Trigger   **Modifier Goals**
(Pool)   **(Pool)**

35% of
pool will be
distributed
equally to
employees
if additional
modifier
goals are
achieved.

ongoing basis, of their progress toward reaching the goals, and what, if any, improvements or changes they need to make in their performance. Management must provide forums and opportunities for employee input so that ideas for improving performance are heard.

Small Group Incentives.   Many organizations, while not ready to expand variable pay to all employees, have begun creating incentive programs for specific career groups, project groups, or teams. Such plans are often project- or venture-driven, with the results based on successful completion of the project or venture. Unlike incentive programs that continue operating from year to year, small group incentives tend to be temporary, lasting only until the group has completed its work or finished its project. While small group incentives are most frequently built around financial goals, such as keeping a project within budget, they are also effective in supporting non-financial issues, such as productivity, quality, timeliness, and customer satisfaction. Typically group members share equally in the payout, although on occasion, rewards may vary depending on the specific level of contribution.

Individual Incentives.   Traditionally, as we've already said, individual incentives were reserved for the senior executives, sales personnel, and on some occasions, hourly workers. Generally, these plans were relatively simple, performance-driven affairs: You received a bonus if you sold a certain number of cars, assembled a certain number of products, or achieved certain financial goals. However, with more organizations flattening their executive and management ranks and expecting more out of their middle managers and professionals, these individual incentive programs are gaining popularity lower in the organization. As with the small group awards, they are being used to drive not only traditional financial goals, but also more "contemporary" values of productivity, customer satisfaction, service, and quality.

This popularization of individual incentives doesn't mean, however, that they can't continue to be used to help drive the performance of the organization's elite—those star performers or top leaders whose individual performance or expertise is critical to the organization's success. To that end, many organizations are creating key contributor plans. These somewhat exclusive plans are usually limited to a few individuals, and are carefully tailored to their individual performance and expertise. Also note that many plans are hybrids, with both individual and small group components. Such a mix can be adjusted from year to year to reflect a change in emphasis or business needs.

Long-term Incentives.   Most of the incentives discussed thus far are considered short-term: Their payout cycles are a year or less, sometimes semiannually or quarterly. At the other end of the spectrum are long-term incentives, which have traditionally been reserved for the organization's executive team and created to increase focus on long-term results.

Although long-term incentives continue to be used primarily in the upper ranks of management and leadership, some organizations are finding that they can be effective at lower levels. Usually these come in the form of all-employee stock plans. By offering the employees a stake—albeit small—in the ownership of the organization, they find they can better focus employees on long-term performance and results. Although these plans are most highly visible in large internationally known companies, such as Pepsico, DuPont, Santa Fe Pacific, and Merck, they are equally effective in smaller organizations.

One such firm is UtiliCorp United, a rapidly growing Kansas City-based utility. In order to create a more participatory, performance-oriented culture, UtiliCorp created an all-employee stock program, the goal of which was 25 percent employee ownership. To whet the interest of its employees, the company offered stock at a 15 percent discount and allowed them to buy shares in amounts of up to 20 percent of their base compensation. The 6 percent company match in the organization's 401(k) program also is awarded in stock, and stock also is included as a plan investment option. Even part of the annual incentive bonus for key employees comes in the form of stock. Company officials say the program has been successful in tying pay to both performance and ownership.

Southwest Airlines took an equally creative approach with its pilots. In return for giving up their raises in the first five years of a ten-year contract, the pilots got options to buy up to 1.4 million shares of stock a year at a relatively low, preestablished rate.[9] Not only was it a good financial move for the company, but it also helped focus a key group of its employees on maintaining peak performance over the long haul.

While such programs can be successful in getting employees at all levels to think more about the company and its overall performance, they can backfire, especially if the stock takes a nosedive, such as it did at Wal-

Mart Stores Inc. Following a two-for-one split in February 1993, stock peaked at $34.125 a share. But by January 1995, it had plummeted to $20.875. Because the company had relied heavily on stock incentives to motivate employees, the nosedive raised serious questions about company morale.[10] Organizations can often avoid such morale-damaging crises by offering variable pay programs that include both short- and long-term incentives.

Although most long-term incentive programs are formed around some type of stock program, other financial rewards also can be used successfully. Employees involved in long-term projects or ventures are sometimes given incentives that operate much like short-term group plans and pay out in cash or a piece of the action (equity). Geologists for oil exploration companies, for example, are sometimes given a percentage of the production from a successful well, while software designers are sometimes given royalties from the sales of their software. Such long-term programs are especially effective in situations where limited funding is available, or where the contribution of the team or individual is extremely critical to the success of the project.

While most long-term incentive programs continue to support financial goals, a growing number are being expanded to cover other elements of performance, such as customer satisfaction and quality improvement. American Express, for example, recently created a program that rewards not only financial performance, but also customer and employee satisfaction. These satisfaction elements, which can impact a reward by as much as 25 percent, are part of a strategy to redirect employees from focusing on short-term financial results, as well as to shift the organization's culture.[11]

Lump-Sum Payments.   One of the most popular incentives, at least with employers, is the lump-sum payment. These periodic, often annual payments given in lieu of part or all of normal base-pay increases, are used to reward those employees who are both high performing and high salaried. By rewarding them through a separate payment, organizations can avoid ratcheting their salaries and benefits higher and higher, and thus limit the need to increase fixed costs. Frequently, however, lump-sum payments offer no real incentive. Rather, they reflect movement toward a leaner, less competitive market position and the need to keep top performers well paid in the process. Needless to say, employees tend to be less than enchanted with such incentives.

Recognition Programs.   Last, and sometimes underestimated in the arsenal of variable reward strategies, are what are commonly referred to as
cash and noncash recognition programs—small, one-time, after-the-fact
awards for exceptional effort or outstanding performance. The size and variety of recognition programs is almost unlimited. They can be as small as
a mention of the person in the company newsletter or on the office bulle-
tin board, or as large as a vacation or several thousand dollars in cash.

Mobil Corporation, for example, created a highly successful program
that included both cash and noncash elements. Noncash awards with a
value of up to $250—anything from a piece of crystal, to dinner, to theater
tickets—were given to both individuals and teams for initiative and creativity. Two types of cash awards, one that ranged from $250 to $2,500,
and another that went up to $5,000—were given for financial results that
impact the oil giant's bottom line. While the program was not cheap, it
was highly cost effective: In the first year alone, the company spent
$32,000 on the two smaller awards but got a $40 million return on its investment. Its ROI on the top award was equally good: $18 million on a
$19,000 investment.[12]

Like many organizations, Mobil discovered that effective recognition
programs have to be carefully designed and administered. (Indeed, an
earlier program had not generated the desired results or motivation.)

As with other variable pay programs, recognition programs must be
aligned with the work culture and business values that they are meant to
support. Organizations that acquire "off-the-shelf" award packages from
services that do little more than provide a catalogue of prizes are often disappointed in the results. To be effective, recognition programs must be
timely and highly visible—almost celebratory in nature. The size of the
awards must also acknowledge the size of the deed. If they are too small,
they may offend winners and trivialize their behavior; too big, and they
may create a sense of unfairness or distort the value of the action for which
they were given.

Unlike the other variable pay programs detailed here, recognition
programs do not change behavior. Highly discretionary, they can have a
negative impact of creating "winners" and "losers" if not carefully administered and clearly communicated. And, while they help keep key performers
on track, they are not likely to motivate an organization's "nonperformers"
to work harder or better. They do, however, recognize outstanding behavior

and send an important message about the value the organization places on that behavior.

Variable pay has come a long way from the piecework of the factory floor, the bonus program of the sales department, and the elite stock plan of the executive suite. Yet, with the variety of variable pay programs available today (not to mention the variations within similar programs) it is essential that organizations take a cautious, educated approach in determining which strategies will suit them best.

In creating any incentive program an organization should follow several critical steps: First it must determine—in the context of its goals and values—what it is trying to accomplish, what behaviors it is trying to change or support, and whether the plan should be short- or long-term, or some sort of a combination.

Second, measurement criteria must be established. These can be objective or subjective, but they must be articulated. The "mix" of the plan—how much of the total compensation is going to be paid out through the variable pay component—must also be determined. The mix should be based on the degree to which the individual or group can drive results. The greater the impact, the more the leverage. The degree of leverage also depends on the pay level of participants. An $80,000-a-year manager, for example, should be able to put a greater percentage of pay at risk than a $25,000-a-year administrative assistant.

The potential range of performance and payout, usually described in terms of threshold, target, and maximum, must also be determined. Because incentives are as much about messages as they are about money, employees must be given a sense of what performance—and payout—they are likely to achieve. That doesn't mean that the goals should be easy, only that they are feasible. One organization we know of, for example, couldn't understand why its incentive program that offered a 15 percent payout for achieving profitability didn't motivate employees. The answer was simple: The firm hadn't made a profit in several years. Participants must also be told what—if any—influence they have in achieving those goals. Otherwise, they will probably assume—correctly—that the program is nothing more than a highly sophisticated mind game.

Indeed, simple or complex, short- or long-term, group or individual, variable pay programs are ultimately about sending messages and changing behavior, about managing people in new and different ways.

TEAM-BASED COMPENSATION

Compaq Computer Corporation is no stranger to productivity-enhancing business strategies. In just three years it doubled the number of computers produced per square foot of factory space and increased by 50 percent the number of PCs produced by workers.[13] Such dramatic improvements are no doubt what led the company to become the industry leader in 1994—two years ahead of the schedule set by Compaq president Eckhard Pfeiffer. Yet even these dramatic results didn't stop Compaq in its quest for more efficient processes. In what more conservative organizations might have termed heresy, it decided to eliminate the traditional assembly line approach in favor of three-person teams or work cells.

While Compaq may be the exception rather than the rule in its "group" approach, it is certainly not the first or last organization to move to teams. As we've already shown in Chapter 2, organizations as diverse as car makers and card manufacturers are embracing their use to improve performance and gain a competitive edge. According to a Hay survey of nearly 250 companies, more than 80 percent said they had created teams to improve productivity, the quality of their product or service, and customer satisfaction. Nearly half said they were also using teams to improve employee satisfaction and morale as well as staffing flexibility.[14]

As these organizations have discovered, the use of teams is an effective strategy for helping them through the change process as well as supporting new values, behaviors, and goals that result from those changes. Some of the most effective change, they have found, comes not through individuals or single departments, but from multidiscipline or cross-functional groups. Unfortunately, creating such an approach is often easier said than done. The team concept, which has been around since early humans discovered the advantages of hunting parties over the lone, club-wielding caveperson, is widely misunderstood and, as a result, misused.

As Jon R. Katzenbach and Douglas K. Smith wrote in *The Wisdom of Teams*, "Extracting team performance is challenging. Long-standing habits of individualism, rampant confusion about teams and teamwork, and seemingly adverse team experience all undercut the possibilities that teams offer at the very moment that team performance has become so critical."[15] So how does one break those individual habits, eliminate the confusion, and turn the effort into a positive experience for the team, its members, and the organization in which it operates? To ask it another way: How does an organization change the behaviors of people who to this point in their careers have been individually focused? And how does it then motivate this group of individuals to achieve the necessary goals?

As with other contemporary organizational efforts, much of the answer lies in the creation of pay strategies that are aligned with and support these new team values—strategies that expand the focus beyond the role and performance of the individual, and at the same time reward people for doing more with less supervision.

Team-based compensation has only recently begun gaining acceptance. Yet as the use of teams continues to grow, so too should the use of pay programs that support them. Hay's survey of more than five hundred companies, for example, found that while only 3 percent had team-pay programs in place before 1992, 9 percent have started them since then, and another 39 percent were considering such plans.[16]

The design of team-based pay strategies, like the design of the structure they support, is not unusually difficult if the designers have a thorough understanding of the concepts of teams—how they are organized, how they function, the dynamics of the members, and what organizational values and goals they can best support. Once that general understanding is in place, work can then begin on determining the appropriate reward architecture.

Teams today come in a variety of shapes and sizes, ranging from two-person work groups to entire organizations (Team Xerox). Yet careful study shows that four general types dominate business today. The first, the *work team*, focuses on how work is being performed. Work teams are made up of cross-trained or cross-functional members who are accountable for a fixed set of activities, usually on a full-time, continuous basis. Hallmark's approach to creating and distributing cards, Chrysler's approach to designing and building a new automobile, even LEGO Systems, Inc.'s approach to packaging its toys are all examples of work teams. Such teams are most effective and usually found in the process work culture or the TQM environment, where resources and efforts are focused on the customer.

A similar approach, popular in time-based cultures, is the *project team*. Like the work team, the project team is a full-time commitment. But unlike the work team, it is temporary, with the members coming together only for the life of the project. Such teams are most often used to design new systems or develop new products, after which they are disbanded, and employees move to new teams or, in some cases, different organizations.

The third type of team, which is frequently utilized by functional organizations today, is the *parallel team*. Unlike work teams, these are organized around tasks, are part-time, and parallel the normal job activities. Such teams also can be cross-functional and interdepartmental, but again they focus on a specific issue or problem: an employee task force or committee, for example, formed to examine a single issue such as productivity.

The fourth general type of team, crucial to the network culture, joint ventures, or strategic alliances, is the *partnership team*. Like the project team, the partnership team comes together full-time for the duration of a single project. But unlike its project cousin which is composed of employees, partnerships usually involve both people within the organization and outsiders—suppliers or contractors, perhaps—hired guns who are brought into the project for their expertise or unusual skills. Work on such teams tends to be either collaborative or individually focused.

Like the cultures described in Chapter 2, these four types of teams have been defined in their pure forms. In reality, of course, multiple types of teams as well as "hybrid" versions are operating in most organizations today. Whether pure or hybrid, however, when it comes to compensation, teams present a unique challenge for managers and executives.

The general architecture of team-based pay is shown in Figure 4–9. Of the four types, the parallel teams are the simplest to align with compensation, although even here a number of issues must be addressed. Because the team assignment is parallel to the regular work assignment, it is critical that any reward not create conflict between the dual responsibilities. For example, a simple, well-intentioned incentive program might focus team members so intently on the goals of the team that they neglect the performance of their regular roles.

To avoid such conflict, rewards for parallel team members should be based not only on their contributions to the team—as assessed formally or informally by other team members—and team results, but also on their overall job performance. Such rewards should usually be given after the fact, rather than established beforehand as incentives. For that reason, one-time recognition awards are perhaps the most effective means of compensating parallel team performance.

Reward strategies to support work and project teams tend to be bigger and more complex than those that support parallel teams. In the case of the work team approach, employees are being asked to learn new skills, be more flexible, assume new roles, and take on some of the management

Figure 4–9

Team Pay Architecture

Parallel	Work	Program/Project	Partnership
• Merit increases • Recognition awards (cash/noncash) • Performance appraisal • Predefined incentives	• Skill-based pay • Competencies • Peer evaluations • Gainsharing	• Proficiencies • Competencies • Recognition awards • 360-degree review • Phantom Stock • Profit sharing	• Recognition awards • Venture profit sharing

roles—scheduling and coordinating work activities, for example—that previously were handled by designated supervisors. As a result, new methods are needed for comparing work, for determining base salaries and increases, for promoting the development of new skills and competencies, and assessing performance.

Many of these new team issues can be addressed through the use of one or more of the performance-based pay strategies already discussed. For example, in addition to sharing in team rewards, an individual's pay might be determined by the new skills and competencies that he or she needs in the team setting. Roles or jobs themselves might be incorporated into a broadbanding approach. A "360-degree" evaluation process involving peers, and perhaps customers, might be implemented to assess performance. Yet as the team matures and grows, as the roles are defined and the skills and competencies necessary for success are acquired, the focus of the reward strategies must broaden to include the ultimate purpose of the team—mutual accountability for its results. To that end, the individual pay strategies must be supplemented and balanced with team rewards that are established before the fact and based on collective results. Such performance-based incentives might take the form of gainsharing, profit sharing, or stock options, and be measured through predetermined milestones and result expectations, such as getting the assignment done on time and under budget. (Whatever incentives are used in both project and work teams, they should be based on operational measures under the control of—and within somewhat clear sight of—the team.)

In developing a total compensation program for project teams, other issues also must be considered. Perhaps the most critical of these is the long-term role of the team members—whether they are involved in such project work regularly or whether it is a one-time, special assignment. Team members such as system experts and product development staff, for whom project work is the norm, should continue being rewarded primarily through the use of base salaries and merit increases. As with work groups, evaluations might be sought from other team members as well as both "internal" and "external" customers. Additional rewards for exceptional work on a specific project can come in the form of cash or noncash recognition awards, or in the case of project development, a piece of the action in the form of royalties or profits.

If, however, an employee is being pulled off his or her regular job to be assigned temporarily, yet full-time, to a project, a separate incentive program for that particular project might be appropriate.

Because of their uniqueness, partnership teams tend to require more complex compensation solutions than the other types of teams, usually some form of a hybrid reward strategy. Internal members—the employees—may, for example, continue to receive their standard base and merit pay for their normal job or role. The outside members, on the other hand, may be paid solely for the level of expertise they bring to the project. Journeyman-level outside members may be paid at a set rate lower than that of the internal members, while the outside "star" experts may be paid at carefully negotiated rates that far exceed the highest-paid internal team member and include some sort of predetermined performance incentive. The entire team might also be eligible for an after-the-fact reward, based on the overall success of the venture.

One issue that invariably arises when a limited group of employees is given an added incentive is that of fairness. Why, some of the organizational "have-nots" are bound to ask, weren't they included in the program? After all, they too worked hard and performed well. Why weren't they given the same opportunity to make more money? It is a good question, one that is best answered when the "increased opportunity" is linked to an "increased risk." In other words, individuals who are given the opportunity to earn more than their peers should also have more of their pay at risk. This can be achieved by limiting their base pay to levels below those of their nonparticipating peers. Thus, while they have the opportunity to earn more than their peers, should they achieve the incentive goals, they also run the risk of earning less than their peers, should they fail to meet those goals.

The use of teams and team-based compensation will no doubt continue to gain popularity, as organizations better understand the value they can add. A word of caution, however: Organizations should not rush to redesign compensation so that it totally focuses on team performance. Team pay, like other contemporary compensation strategies, must be carefully aligned with the organization's culture, and integrated with other pay strategies into a balanced, total compensation package. And finding the best possible balance between individual and team rewards is a critical, but certainly not foolproof, step in the process. Ultimately the question that must be addressed is this: What message best conveys your organization's culture and values? Is your strategy one that can win through high level individual performance, or is winning much more dependent on a full team effort?

ALIGNING AND MIXING THE ELEMENTS

Whether the emphasis is on teams or individuals, it is clear that pay strategies, like the business strategies they support, are changing dramatically. Unfortunately, the variety of pay programs has rendered the one-size-fits-all solutions obsolete, and created a high degree of confusion.

Much of that confusion can be eliminated, however, if the organization's managers and leaders understand five basic tenets of dynamic compensation. These are:

1. Pay is first and foremost a people issue. It is about motivating them. It is about reshaping and refocusing their behaviors and accepting new values.
2. Pay is a major organizational communications tool. It is perhaps the most direct way that an organization has of communicating with its employees.

3. No single pay strategy is right for everyone. Different organizations, as well as different employee groups in the same organization, may require different strategies.
4. Pay must support—not lead—the organization's vision, values, and business strategies.
5. To achieve points 1 through 4, pay must be aligned with the organization's work cultures.

Achieving this last but most critical step is the subject of the next chapter.

5

Aligning Cultures and Compensation

Having sorted out the evolving work cultures, and having identified the variety of dynamic pay strategies that can support those cultures, a natural reaction is to quickly seek the right match for your organization. Simply select your work culture from one column and a comparable pay strategy from another, and you should—or so it may appear—achieve that all-important alignment that we have been emphasizing since the beginning of the book.

Such a simple approach might have worked well in the one-size-fits-all organizational world of the past. But, just as work cultures and compensation programs have become more dynamic, so too have the processes that are needed to align the two. True, each culture lends itself to some of the general compensation strategies we have detailed—strategies that support certain behaviors, values, and employment relationships. Yet chances are your organization may have several cultures at work within it, and most, if not all, of those cultures are not pure, but some sort of hybrid.

To further complicate the equation, each of those unique hybrids may have its own priorities, behaviors, values, and employee relationships. You may, for example, have an overriding goal of improving quality and cost effectiveness. Yet to achieve those goals, you also need to increase teamwork

123

while expanding the skills and competencies of the individual team members. And let's not overlook the need to increase the feeling of ownership among managers and the feeling of involvement among the employees below them.

Nor are your cultures static. They are continually evolving. They may be shifting from functional to process, or from time-based to network. Frequently that movement may be barely perceptible, a natural and perhaps unconscious shift in reaction to the changing business climate, market dynamics, or competitive forces. In other cases the shift may be dramatic, decisive, and revolutionary. When CEO Jack Welch transformed General Electric from a highly institutionalized, functional giant into a leaner, more agile, faster, time-based organization, he took just such an approach. Using a number of organizational tools, including compensation, he drove home his message of speed, simplicity, and self-confidence—quickly changing the culture of the organization, the behavior and values of its employees, and the future of the business.

But whether change happens in tiny increments or huge strides, when it comes to the issue of compensation, what used to be a simple alignment issue has turned into a complex organizational puzzle that can overwhelm even the most talented executive or manager. Instead of a single dimension you are suddenly looking at several, including:

- the culture or cultures, and how they are evolving and hybridizing
- the individual employees, how they are changing, and whether their values and behaviors fit the cultures
- the changing roles of the various employee groups (managerial, professional, technical, clerical, hourly) within those cultures
- the mix of compensation elements needed to support the values, behaviors, and outcomes for each of those employee groups in advancing the core competencies of the business and its commercial success

A NEW EMPHASIS ON DELIVERY

For most of us, solving this multidimensional puzzle would be challenge enough. But it doesn't end there. There is another important issue that, although we have discussed it at some length, is still often overlooked in the evolving compensation equation. That issue is determining *where* changes should be made within the reward program.

In the past, changes to compensation programs were usually made in two of the three primary components that make up such systems: the *pricing* component—how jobs or roles are priced, both internally and within the marketplace, and the *work comparison* component, which defines the relative value of different kinds or types of work. The third component, the *delivery* of that pay—the actual strategies for paying people—was seldom modified.

Today, however, the emphasis has done a 180-degree shift. While there may continue to be refinements in both work comparisons and pricing, the major emphasis must be on the primary rules, guidelines, and strategies for how pay is delivered. As we detailed in the last chapter, a seemingly endless number of new pay strategies—everything from pay for competencies to broadbanding—have evolved during the past few years. Rather than merely reprice or revaluate jobs based on the latest survey data, organizations are now also facing the challenge of creating entirely new compensation programs that not only blend a variety of base and variable pay but also look at both team and individual rewards.

THE APPROACH: DESCENDING FROM
FIFTY THOUSAND FEET TO GROUND ZERO

With all these factors to consider, the issue for many organizations quickly shifts from the more theoretical question of what the appropriate compensation strategies should be to the much more practical ones of how to proceed with changing the strategies—where to actually begin aligning pay with the new or changing cultures.

Unless radical, revolutionary change is required, organizations should change their compensation strategies in phases rather than blowing up the old system and building a new program organization-wide from the ground up. In theory, there are a number of potential entry points for beginning the alignment process. An organization might start with a certain employee group—managers, perhaps, or professionals. Or it could begin with a specific element of compensation, base pay, for example, or variable pay.

That is not to say that organizations should ignore the development of an overriding compensation philosophy, based on their culture, vision, and business goals. That certainly should be one of the initial steps in shifting compensation strategies, one that should have begun to take place in the assessment phase of the change process. But after the organization has formulated this high-altitude vision (which should of course be an integral part of its overall organizational vision), it must rapidly descend to ground level, implementing changes that will—with minimal disruption—support that vision and the changing culture.

The speed with which organizations should shift their compensation strategies depends of course on the amount of change required and the degree to which the change is critical to their success—or in some cases survival. Organizations that are highly successful and are proactively changing to stay ahead of the competition can usually take more time than those facing major crises. One large manufacturing organization we worked with, for example, which was rapidly expanding and acquiring new businesses, put together a three-to-five-year plan for shifting and combining its cultures, reengineering work, and aligning pay and its other human resource processes. Yet many of the health care organizations we assist feel they must change everything—including compensation—in a matter of months. Given the highly competitive, frequently hostile health care market, it often is a matter of survival.

The best approach, if possible, is a proactive, yet measured one. While most organizations want rapid change, they must be careful not to place themselves in situations in which they must fight a war on numerous fronts. Rather, they should start with the most basic elements and build on these as change becomes an accepted part of the organization's new world order. Whatever the speed or scope of the change, whatever the compensation strategy, all organizations should accept one overriding tenet in developing a new compensation strategy: The approach must be dynamic. Today's compensation strategies must be flexible enough to move and evolve with other organizational changes.

BEGINNING WHERE THE PAIN IS GREATEST

In changing their reward programs, organizations are best served by first identifying those areas of their compensation programs where the pain is greatest—areas in which there are problems that often signal a serious lack of alignment and send out the wrong messages for the new business realities. In searching for this pain, organizations should examine the primary elements that make up their total compensation program: base salaries, variable pay, benefits and perquisites, and "ownership"—forms of pay, such as stock programs, that either put employees in the position of actually being owners or at least simulate ownership.

Organizations may already incorporate all of these elements into their current pay programs. But the strategies, while perfectly good, may no longer support their cultures and values, reinforce the desired employee behaviors, or support achievement of the necessary business goals. An organization may, for example, have a traditional pay program that, through solid base salaries and steady merit increases, continues to reward individuals for doing very specific jobs and being very reliable. Yet the organization may have begun shifting to a process culture, forming cross-functional teams, and replacing the old goal of reliability with a drive to improve customer service and increase quality. Or an organization that is rapidly assuming a time-based culture—one in which employees are constantly shifting from team to team or even from business unit to business unit—may have maintained a highly inflexible benefits program that plays havoc with shifts in assignments. In both cases, the "old" elements of pay, while perfectly good in the right setting, no longer fit with the organizations' changing cultures.

There may be other programs that are properly aligned, but are "broken" and operate poorly. They may be cumbersome, bureaucratic, rigid, or overly stylized, and thus not adaptable to the new realities of the organization. An organization, for example, may continue utilizing a long-standing profit-sharing program that, although it continues to reward the employees based on the performance of the business, in no way links *their* performance with that of the organization. Such an organization would probably be wise to replace the old program with a new incentive plan—perhaps a gainsharing program—in which employees could more directly see how their efforts impact the overall performance.

Frequently the pain is caused by a combination of these two factors. Many programs are neither aligned nor functioning properly. The breakdown in the program—its rigidity or inefficiency, for example, which may have existed for some time—is exacerbated when the culture starts to shift and the program is thrown further out of alignment. From these critical pain points, organizations can begin developing and expanding effective compensation programs that are either better aligned with their current cultures, or that will help them evolve their cultures to better support their goals and values.

Consider, for example, UtiliCorp United, the midwestern regional utility that wanted to move rapidly toward becoming the first nationwide energy company. In making that strategic shift, it found it needed a new approach to executive leadership, and formed a new executive team. While each of the members filled key, individual roles—some line, some staff, some a combination—they all shared responsibility for the general management of the entire enterprise.

The resulting new culture demanded teamwork, a focus on growth, and shared accountability for improving the operation of the various affiliated companies. These new team values, competencies, and behaviors, however, clashed dramatically with the established compensation program, which primarily rewarded the individual. Base salaries were tied to individual jobs; annual incentives were MBO-driven; long-term incentives were limited to simple stock options.

To eliminate that conflict and realign the compensation with the new culture and business goals, a new program was created. The organization adopted a banding approach to base salaries and tied increases to the growth of team competencies. It also created an annual cash incentive program with stock ownership targets, which was based on operating results. If incentive goals were reached, participants were given the option of taking part of the award in company stock. Finally, utilizing restricted stock, a long-term incentive program was developed, the goal of which was to beat the three-year performance results of competitors.

The resulting messages were clear: Work as a team and increase your effectiveness. Do all that and it is possible to improve each operation in order to create the most efficient company possible. Beat the competition in earnings and returns to generate cash for growth. And finally, view this as a long-term enterprise in which you have a significant stake.

This new approach worked so well at the executive level that UtiliCorp quickly extended it to the next levels of managers, who were even more functional in their outlook, performance, and operating paradigms. It also created an annual incentive program that more than 80 percent of the company's nonunion employees participate in. For the majority of employees, payouts are determined largely upon achievement of personal, nonfinancial goals, such as customer service or increased efficiency. Today, as the industry moves toward deregulation amid intensifying competition, UtiliCorp is rapidly evolving into an aggressive market-oriented international player.

In the remainder of this chapter, we will examine—by culture and employee group—how these and other compensation strategies detailed in the previous chapter can best be utilized and integrated to limit or target the pain of change and help your organization maximize the results you desire in the shortest time possible.

As we move through the various cultures, you will see not only how the pay strategies change, but also how the variety and number of compensation strategies utilized within the organization, the percentage and level of employees who are involved, and the measures of success all should vary. Through these differences, some of which are summarized in Figures 5–1 and 5–2, you will begin to understand how compensation can be used to obtain a high degree of integration and alignment in your current cultures, as well as how it can be used to move your organization to the desired cultures of the future.

FUNCTIONAL COMPENSATION: AN EMPHASIS ON THE INDIVIDUAL

Just because the functional culture is older, more traditional, and perhaps less dynamic than some of its more recently evolved cousins doesn't mean it should be neglected in a discussion of compensation. Despite the movement away from purely functional cultures, most organizations continue to have functional elements that are critical to their success. And for good reason: The television commercial of Saturn automobiles notwithstanding, not every organization is willing—or should be willing—to empower its employees to shut down something as important as the assembly line. Nor does every department of every organization need self-directed work teams. And even for those organizations that are making dramatic shifts away from a functional culture, it remains an important entry point for understanding the alignment of pay and how it must evolve along with the culture.

As we have already discussed, the purpose of the functional culture, simply stated, is to ensure the reliable delivery of a product or service through the technology a company possesses or manages. To minimize mistakes, tasks are broken down into their lowest common denominator, their simplest form. The individuals who perform those tasks focus on narrowly defined functions that require an equally narrowly defined—albeit deep—set of skills. These individuals are rewarded for their reliable performance over time, and for improving their skills and increasing their

Figure 5-1

Compensation Approaches to Work Cultures

Compensation Elements	Work Cultures			
	Functional	Process	Time-based	Network
Base Salary	Standard job grades Moderate variability in base pay	Broader salary bands Low to moderate variability in base pay	Very broad salary bands High variability in base pay	One salary band High variability in base pay
Individual Incentives	Limited use of incentives Paid annually	Wide use of incentives Interim payments	Moderate use of incentives Paid after program success	Low to moderate use of incentives Paid after phase of venture completion
Team-based Pay	Recognition for exceptional success	Gainsharing Group/team incentives	Program profit sharing	Venture profit sharing
Other Compensation Elements	Pay for competencies Pay for skills	Pay for competencies Pay for skills	Pay for competencies	(Critical competency for individuals gives them entree to venture team and sharing in venture profit)

Figure 5–2

Incentive Approaches to Work Cultures

Work Cultures	Functional	Process	Time-based	Network
% Eligible	• 20% of employee's or less	• 80%–100% of employee's	• 60%–80% of employee's	• 20%–40% of employee's
Target Payout to	• 60%–80% of eligibles	• 80%–100% of eligibles (when available)	• 40%–60% of eligibles	• 20%–40% of eligibles
Target Payout Level	• 25%–40% of base	• 10%–25% of base	• 40%–60% of base	• 60% or more of base
Payout Timing	• Annually	• Quarterly	• Ad hoc + post project completion	• Post phase or venture completion

experience in their functional specialty. This increase in skill and experience adds real value to the organization, ultimately generating greater reliability, efficiency, and effectiveness.

The individual's contribution to the overall success of the organization, at the hourly and exempt level especially, is of secondary or minimal importance, as is the expectation that they fully understand the overall process to which their specific function belongs.

Functional compensation programs have traditionally championed these narrow, individual goals. The major element of compensation is the base salary, which integrates the variety of functional specialties through numerous, and narrow pay grades. People advance—move upward—through these grades, based on their level of experience and the improvement or acquisition of needed skills. These functional specialties are calibrated through specific work measurement systems, and internal equity becomes a major priority in establishing pay levels.

At the nonexempt or hourly levels, efficiency and productivity are the main goals—how the employee, through his or her specific skill and function, utilizes the organization's materials and assets. At the exempt level, the priorities shift to the development of excellence and professionalism in key functional areas that are the primary drivers of the organization. Exempt employees in a functional organization climb (note the emphasis on upward movement) career ladders by acquiring individual experience and technical expertise in one or more of these key areas. If it is a consumer product manufacturer, that may be excellence in marketing. If it is a technology company, the focus of excellence may be in engineering or product development. Developing excellence in one of those areas and sustaining it over time is rewarded by a new title, a merit increase, a bigger base salary, and frequently more individual responsibility in order to exploit these skills across a broad array of issues.

Variable pay is usually little used at the hourly or exempt level of the functional organization. Some hourly employees, those on the manufacturing floor, for example, may be paid for piecework in order to achieve the added goals of productivity and efficiency. Exempt employees, however, are often out of luck when it comes to incentives or other forms of variable pay. Too far from the bottom of the organization for their individual performance to be tied to productivity and efficiency, too far from the top to have their performance linked to that of the organization's total success, they are in what could be viewed as a sort of organizational limbo.

Indeed, at both the hourly and exempt levels the basic philosophy of the functional employee is very simple: "If I do my job well, I will get a promotion. And with that promotion will come a bigger salary." How well the company is doing is of secondary importance (although as we have already noted, individual or work group incentives can play a role in improving operations or specific areas of contributions—improving productivity in a department or within a work group, for example, or reducing waste). In any other work culture, such a narrow focus would be viewed as selfish and self-centered. In the functional culture it is not only expected, it is rewarded. The exception is at the very top of the organization, where the emphasis finally shifts from the performance of the individual to that of the organization. These key executives must be primarily concerned not with their own performance, but with maximizing the value of the existing business and its investments and the utilization of its assets.

To encourage these goals, these individuals (usually the top 20 percent of the organization, according to our research) are eligible for some sort of incentive plan in addition to their base salaries. Typically, these plans are a combination of annual and long-term incentives linked to company growth or stock performance. While eligibility in such plans is highly restricted, the odds of receiving a payout tend to be high, with up to 80 percent typically achieving some sort of reward. The reason for this high success rate is relatively simple: With the planning and reliability of the functional organization comes a certain degree of predictability. And that is what the incentive, after all, really rewards. Follow the business plan, it says, and you will get the desired results; get the results, and you will receive a payout. Those payouts tend to be relatively robust in size, with many earning up to 40 percent of their base salary in variable pay of one form or another.

One industry that has seen an explosion in the use of incentives such as these is health care, which finds itself scrambling for new organizational approaches in the face of dramatic market changes. Take, for example, the University of Pennsylvania Health Systems. Although a leader in research, teaching, and clinical excellence, UPHS found that to remain competitive it needed to expand into new markets and position itself for the onslaught of managed care.

To achieve these new goals, UPHS, under the direction of Dr. William Kelley, determined that it would have to change the priorities of its leaders. To that end, a compensation program was developed that included a competitive base salary along with lucrative incentives. The new compensation plan focused executives on market share growth and operating cash flow. It focused medical leaders on the contributions of their areas to the overall health system, and on recruiting world-class talent. Research leaders were encouraged to obtain grants as well, helping the system achieve a high ranking with the National Institutes of Health.

While initially a foreign concept to this culture, the incentives quickly reinforced the importance of the functional contribution of each area along with the positioning of the total organization. Not only do the various "functional" leaders share a commitment to improving the organization's position, but many who were initially skeptical of the use of incentives have become true believers. UPHS's new program has been very effective. It has helped the organization dramatically improve its financial performance, increase its market share, and enhance its community image. It also has played a role in improving the quality of clinical services, as well as helping the organization raise its National Institutes of Health ranking in terms of research dollars received from sixth to fourth in the country.

The traditional belief that incentives should only be used at the top of the organization is also being challenged as functional organizations try to shake loose some of their rigid, confining, techno-centered values and become more humanistic. To create a sense of ownership or organizational involvement often missing in such organizations, some have implemented organization-wide profit or gainsharing programs. Traditional gainsharing programs, which are typically linked to internal goals of cutting costs and improving efficiency, can be effective at the hourly and exempt levels of the functional organization—but only if they are designed in a manner that allows the employees to see directly how their actions can impact the program's goals.

PROCESS COMPENSATION: FOCUS ON TEAMS, CUSTOMERS

As its name implies, in the process culture, the importance begins to shift from the individual's job and efforts toward the processes of groups and teams. This movement is caused by an equally dramatic shift in the focus of business strategies from internal to external. No longer are the organization and its employees concerned only with how well it—and they—perform in terms of their own internal measures such as productivity and cost effectiveness. As their markets have expanded and their competition has intensified, organizations have had to reckon with powerful new outside forces—quality and customers. And they have also discovered that the most effective way to continually improve quality and satisfy the customer is through processes that are carried out by teams who bring the organization close to the customer. Such teams make the organization more customer friendly and assure an immediate response to their needs.

To that end, quality, customer satisfaction, and teamwork are the primary drivers of compensation in a process organization. Generally speaking, people in process organizations are paid for their team's contribution to the system, not their individual results.

The shift away from internal, individual priorities begins, for both hourly and exempt employees, with base salary. While individual skills are, of course, still important, there also is a need to begin developing team skills and relationships, as well as team loyalty to the customer. Thus a balance must be struck between the individual and the team. To achieve that balance, wider salary ranges broad enough to incorporate entire teams should be established. They must be wide enough to recognize the natural and obvious differences in work and jobs, while at the same time minimizing the distinctive specializations within a team.

Salary, especially at the lower end of the bands, is based on the development of individual skills. After employees learn the primary skills necessary for their work and the crossover skills that they need as team members, compensation levels are determined more by the development of team competencies—behaviors and characteristics that lead to effective team performance. Development of these competencies is based on group—not individual—behavior. If a team is highly effective, then the pay of everyone on the team is raised. Rating team performance is, of course, critical. And given the customer service goals of most of these teams, customer input is often an important part of the performance assessment process.

At the exempt level there also may be some reward for the development of individual competencies. Here, however, compensation goes beyond rewarding externally driven individual and team performance and includes the development of future leaders in major aspects of the organization, such as finance, marketing, human resources, and operations. In finance, for example, the issue becomes not simply how the employee can help his or her team to serve the customers better, but rather what they can do to help the entire organization serve its customers. In other words, the team concept is elevated to another, higher, level.

While base salary remains an important part of the pay structure in a process culture, variable pay, especially in the form of incentives, frequently begins to take on a much broader and important role. The reason is simple: Unlike the functional organization, in which only a few—primarily those at the top—can influence organizational performance in a measurable way, all the members of a process organization are expected to play a measurable role.

Take, for example, a retail operation. Traditionally, only the store manager would be eligible for an incentive. But when that store moves from functional to process culture (and move it must if it expects to survive today), *everyone*—from the store manager to the showroom clerks—is considered a critical link in the chain that leads to customer satisfaction. Incentive programs can be utilized to show the importance of that linkage. The manager may continue to be rewarded based on the store's financial performance, while the clerks are rewarded based on customer service measures, such as the number of complaints. The only exceptions are the employees who have not been with the organization long enough to be considered truly part of the team.

In other highly process-sensitive organizations, the link to customers may be even tighter, with employees working on-site with the customers and fully integrated into their supply chain. When Boeing Company designed its state-of-the-art 777 passenger jet, for example, airline customers actually sat in on the planning sessions with members of the design team.

Despite the need for total organizational participation from all employees, the use of incentives in process organizations to achieve such behavior remains a very delicate issue. While they can be very effective, incentives shouldn't be overemphasized. After all, the focus of the process organization is not only on the final destination—financial results and market-share growth—but also on the journey that takes it there—how it improves quality and satisfies the customer along the way. Effective incentive plans, then, must balance the process and the final results—results that are expressed first in terms of the customer, and secondarily in terms of the company.

A number of organizations we have worked with have created incentive programs tied to measures of quality and customer satisfaction. One health care organization, for example, developed a gainsharing program with quality and customer satisfaction "triggers." If the organization didn't meet its goals in these areas, no incentive was paid out, no matter how well the organization did financially. And a metropolitan transit authority we worked with created an incentive program that only paid at maximum levels when ridership reached certain levels.

Those process organizations that choose to use incentives tend to develop broad, inclusive plans, with relatively small, easy-to-achieve payouts and short cycles—usually quarterly. Typically, 80 percent or more of the employees in process organizations are eligible to participate in some form of incentive programs. The average payout is 10 percent to 25 percent of base salary, with about 80 percent receiving some sort of payout.

In the lower levels of the process organization, incentives should be tied closely to quality and/or customer service measures. At the hourly level, the measures should be linked to the performance of the team or unit in satisfying the customer, and the measures should be very specific—a certain on-time delivery goal, for example, a certain rate of returns, or specific quality or financial measures.

Incentives at the exempt level should also be tied to customer satisfaction, and should be expanded to include internal as well as external customers. The issue here is more complex, longer-term service and quality goals, but nonetheless is still customer-centered.

Incentive programs in process organizations can assume a variety of forms. Frequently, organizations create gainsharing programs that are tied to organizational and/or unit results. Such programs can be effective, however, only if they go beyond the traditional approach, which primarily rewards cutting expenses. To truly support the behavior and values of a successful process organization, gainsharing—or any other incentive, for that matter—must, like the health care organization mentioned above, emphasize quality and customer measures first. Financial performance, while of course important, nonetheless becomes secondary—a by-product of these nonfinancial, incremental operational improvements. By creating an incentive program that more closely links rewards to the necessary employee behavior, be it reducing customer returns or increasing on-time deliveries, the organization can create value that ultimately leads to financial gains.

Gainsharing programs, while popular, tend to be broad in scope and measures, and may not be useful in encouraging specific customer-centered behavior. Other small group incentive strategies may be more effective. While such programs traditionally have been tied to financial results, more and more organizations have discovered their value in driving quality and customer satisfaction. In a Hay/Conference Board study of large U.S. companies, for example, more than 50 percent of the eighty-six organizations responding found that short-term incentives were effective in advancing Total Quality Management. Among the measures that organizations reported successfully using in such programs were customer satisfaction, reduced errors and cycle times, and team performance.[1]

Eaton Corp. used such measures when it implemented an all-employee incentive plan in one of its divisions in an effort to improve customer satisfaction. The plan, funded by the overall financial performance of the division, based rewards on on-time delivery to customers, average sales per employee, and return rates on products shipped. The ability to meet customer requests was directly related to profitability and sales, since there were other vendors who could quickly meet the customer needs if the Eaton division couldn't. The average-sale-per-employee goal emphasized the need for employees to be more efficient with what they had to work with and reinforced the importance of working not as individuals, but as members of multiskilled teams. Lastly, returns involved costly re-inventory and shipping which, when lowered, boosted the bottom line. In effect, the measures improved customer relations while at the same time improving the financial performance of the division.

As an organization moves toward a process culture, its executive compensation strategies also must shift. Not only should a greater portion of compensation be tied to performance, but it should also be tied to nonfinancial measures such as quality improvement and customer service, as well as to financial performance goals.

Rather than look at measures of customer satisfaction, however, the executive team—which typically includes a greater number and broader spectrum of individuals than in the functional organization—is expected to concentrate on the broader issue of long-term market satisfaction. Executives are expected to expand the customer base and increase market penetration of current products, ultimately developing a rock-solid organizational platform from which to successfully launch new products or develop new markets. Thus executives in the process organization are frequently eligible for a mix of both annual and long-term incentives—the shorter-term based on the more immediate goals of the organization, the longer-term tied to the organization's continued success over time.

In essence, the executive team in a process culture is responsible for developing and maintaining an organization in which high quality and customer service are a given, no matter what new product or service is created. They want to create an automatic acceptance of their products or services, such as Mercedes Benz has with cars and trucks, and Sony has with personal electronic products. At that point, quality becomes a true corporate competency that is attached to all new products or services.

TIME-BASED REWARDS:
AN EMPHASIS ON PROJECTS, GROUP EFFORTS

If "The customer is always right" is the motto of the process organization, then "Do it faster, do it better" is the mantra of the time-based organizations. The overriding strategy of the time-based organization is—at the right time and with the right people—to create project teams that can develop, build, and/or market new products and services, reengineer costs out of existing products and services, and continually decrease cycle time. These organizations want to lead the market in existing products and be the first in creating new markets.

Compensation programs in the time-based organization must reinforce these business strategies. Because the project groups are made up of highly skilled specialists, compensation strategies must reward the development of individual skills and specialties. Because the efforts of the project group are critical, programs also must reward the development of team competencies. Because the outcomes of the project groups (which can range from a small group to an entire business) are critical, compensation must emphasize results, primarily at the project level. And, because most of the project teams are at best temporary—lasting from a few months to perhaps a year or two—compensation programs must reward mobility, flexibility, and more than a little risk taking. It is important to note that such values, although concentrated at the project level, can permeate a whole company. Such was the case, for example, at General Electric, where a new focus at the project level helped drive Jack Welch's broader organizational vision.

As a result of this wide range of goals, dynamics, and values, a complex compensation strategy is often required. Even within the same organization, different markets and different business units may have different strategic needs that require different compensation programs. The competencies needed by one project team or group, for instance, may be totally incompatible with those needed by another.

As with process organizations, base pay in the time-based organization, while important, is not the be-all, end-all of the functional organization. Because of the constraints of time and the need for flexibility, both work comparison and pay delivery need to be loosened. Granted, there is a need for personal initiative and specialization. But time is of the essence in all aspects of the business—including administering the compensation program. There's just not enough time for a lot of highly structured pay plans.

Because there is a continuous need to move people around the organization and encourage them to develop different skills and competencies, the base pay strategy must provide a high degree of flexibility and maneuverability. It must encourage people to develop a certain level of specialization, but at the same time not restrict them should the need arise to shift or expand the focus of that specialization. After all, the last thing a time-based organization wants is for its employees to balk at taking a new assignment or learning new skills or competencies because they are afraid it might negatively impact their title, grade, or pay.

A competency-based broadbanding platform works well in such situations because it can address both of these seemingly conflicting issues. By drastically reducing the number of bands, the issue of constantly changing and limiting titles and grades can be eliminated, along with the perception that the only good movement is vertical. At the same time, by tying movement through the bands to the acquisition of new competencies, a premium is placed on professional growth and the continued expansion of skills and competencies that contribute to the organization's success. And, with the emphasis on speed and the effective use of assets, this balanced approach that rewards both current performance and long-term performance potential is critical. In a real sense, the improving asset value of employees to do more through expanding competencies that add value to the organization is the foundation for reward and recognition in the time-based culture.

A banding approach also provides the flexibility and latitude necessary to address a wide variety of project groups within the same organization. By creating five or six bands that cover the organization from top to bottom, and then giving managers the latitude and authority to make critical decisions about the placement and movement of people within those ranges, the organization can maintain a high degree of fairness in its compensation program despite a wide range of individuals and groups in an equally wide range of situations. Because there are different sets of rules for different employee groups in the time-based culture, the issue of "fairness of contribution to the enterprise" replaces the concept of internal equity that is found to a large extent in functional organizations, and to a smaller extent in process organizations.

Perhaps the best documented banding program is that created by General Electric, which collapsed twenty-seven levels and grades into just five bands. Based on competency growth, and with an eye toward the market, people move through the bands based on their demonstrated utilization of competencies. This demonstration is assessed via a 360-degree appraisal in which supervisors, peers, subordinates, customers, and the employees themselves rate their competencies and performance. GE's program has been very successful. It has helped the organization successfully transform its culture, shifting importance away from individual organizational rank to the value employees actually create.

Because of the high-velocity nature of many assignments in a time-based organization, the issue of risk—the overriding fear that "once it's finished, so am I"—must also be addressed through the compensation program. If there is a risk that an employee will work his or her way out of a job, then there should be an equivalent reward for assuming that risk. What employees come to realize, however, is that their best security lies in developing the greatest level of competencies possible and then being able to apply these in the broadest possible range of situations.

Much of the risk can also be addressed through a variety of variable pay programs. Typically in time-based organizations, 60 percent to 80 percent of the employees are eligible for incentive programs. Eligibility, however, is not determined by the level within the organization as it is in the functional organization. Rather, it is established by the nature of the role and contribution to the organization, or project. Those people who are critical to the success of the organization—be they high- or low-level employees—tend to be eligible for some form of incentive.

Of those who are eligible, however, only 20 percent to 40 percent typically receive a payout. The reason for these apparent long odds is simple. Unlike the process organization, where success, especially at lower levels of the organization, is frequently measured in relatively small, achievable, and continuous increments, the time-based organization is looking for success in terms of major, high-impact winners. Thus, the odds of success, along with the stakes, are greater.

Yet the payout, should the odds be achieved, also tends to be much larger—typically between 40 percent and 60 percent of base salary. That payout, however, unlike that in the process organization, is frequently a one-time event that comes only after completion of a successful project. In these situations, the distribution of stock can add to the potential value of the incentive and increase the retention of these key resources.

While the payout may be determined by the overall team performance, it should not necessarily be shared equally. Rather, the distribution should be based on who did the most for the project or enterprise. As with high-performing teams in the world of professional sports, those whose performance counts most—the stars or most valuable players—should be rewarded the most. Again, this dynamic reinforces the desire for people to develop their competencies and find ways in which to utilize them to the greatest degree possible.

As in the functional and process organizations, the goals at the executive level of the time-based organization naturally shift more toward the overall success of the organization. Because of the variety of business units that are frequently found in time-based cultures, performance at the business unit level also is an important concern of executives. Since the overall goal of the time-based unit is to create and capture markets and move them to the highest profitability possible in the shortest length of time, the measures of success of executives are determined by market share, economic value added, and cash flow. This last element is critical because of the operating leverage it creates for continued expansion.

NETWORK PAY: REWARDING RISK, ACKNOWLEDGING INDEPENDENCE

It should be clear at this point that many of the shifts in compensation strategies and cultures that are necessary to maintain alignment with changing cultures—especially as an organization moves from functional to process or time-based—are important, but subtle.

In both the process and time-based organizations, for example, there is a shift away from a reliance primarily on base salaries, and a greater percentage of compensation is variable, tied to performance. In both time-based and process organizations, the development of reliable technical skills takes a back seat to the development of individual and team competencies—the ability to deal with customers, for example, or the ability to negotiate and facilitate in a team setting. And in both cultures, narrow, highly defined pay grades tend to fade, replaced by broader, flexible bands.

As organizations move beyond these two new cultures, however, and begin embracing elements of the network culture, we find they have to make far more dramatic changes to maintain the culture/compensation alignment. For starters, issues such as security and the development of new skills and competencies are no longer relevant. From the hourly to the executive level, network organizations are made up of people who are already trained, already highly competent. They are, by their nature, risk takers and organizational gypsies. They live for the challenge, the independence.

As a result of these very different values, different pay strategies are in order. Except at the bottom of the organization, where the hourly workers— or "extras"—are paid a "scale" wage based on the market rates, there is little need for traditional pricing measures. As a result, the level of compensation tends to be negotiated, especially at the exempt and executive level, with a large proportion delivered in some form of variable pay that is tied to the success of the venture or project.

At the executive level are the producers and directors, who are highly paid for their competency and ability to make deals, build relationships, and successfully lead the project. Frequently, these individuals, along with the venture's star contributors, are paid a star-level base salary plus a large, long-term incentive based on the success of the venture. This might come in the form of equity in the outcome of the venture or project—a share of the profits, royalties, or stock.

At the exempt level, pay is more structured. Here, depending on the type of organization, the professionals, the craftspersons, the highly skilled technicians, the journeymen if you will, support the achievement of the venture. A negotiated base salary—tied to some extent to market measures—rewards them for the skills and competencies that they bring to the venture, while an aggressive incentive plan rewards them for their contribution to the project.

Outside of the hourly employees who tend to make up a large part of a network organization, almost everyone is usually eligible for some type of incentive. (Even the hourly employees—the support staff—may be given an occasional discretionary bonus.) Typically, 20 to 40 percent of the network employees are eligible for an incentive, and about that same percentage receive some payout. But that payout can be high, averaging 60 percent or more of the employee's base pay.

Perhaps the best example of effective network compensation strategies can be found in the movie industry. The producers who bring the film projects together typically receive a big fee or salary as well a major "piece of the action," and may retain the right to the product and its long-term distribution. The stars are paid a negotiated rate based on their stature in the industry. They may also receive royalties or residuals based upon the success of the film. The supporting cast is paid accordingly, and the "trades" people are paid at scale for the duration of the project.

But even the movie industry's pay paradigm may be changing. Dream-Works SKG, the multimedia company founded by Steven Spielberg, Jeffrey Katzenberg, and David Geffen, reportedly was considering splitting equity with all employees, including secretaries, and offering a share of gross movie revenue to the artists, writers, and animators.[2]

A FOOT IN BOTH CAMPS: SHIFTING CULTURES

While a few industries thrive on the network culture, most organizations today are a long way from embracing what they would no doubt view as a radical culture shift. Nor should they want to. While most organizations have begun shedding their purely functional roots, they are still feeling their way through the cultural evolution. There are exceptions, of course: the GEs and Chryslers of the world, for whom radical change was key to their success and global growth, and the recent arrivals, those organizations and industries born into the age of change, such as high-tech firms and information/entertainment giants. But for the most part, organizations are pushing—or being pushed—ahead cautiously, developing pockets of new cultures within the old structures. Take the airlines, for example. Still functional in aspects such as scheduling, maintenance, and pilot training, they nonetheless have had to embrace process values of customer service and quality to remain competitive.

While the balance that these organizations must strike as they slowly traverse the tightrope of change is never easy, it can be rendered less difficult and less painful through the alignment of dynamic compensation strategies. The key is at all times to keep a foot in both camps—where you are today, and where you want to be tomorrow. By moving carefully, implementing dynamic pay processes in a targeted manner, organizations can strike the appropriate balance, continually advancing, yet never leaving employees ungrounded. One organization might start with its base pay program, another with its incentive plan. It all depends on where the pain is, where the need for alignment is most critical.

ONLY THE BEGINNING: LOOKING AHEAD TO OTHER CHANGES

Although critical, the alignment of pay is only one small part of successful cultural change. A wide range of related issues must also be addressed, including leadership and how it is rewarded, all the elements of the human relations paradigm—everything from selection and assessment to communications and administration, and those often overlooked yet important noncash elements of compensation.

The next chapter begins exploring these related issues with a discussion of the changing, yet important role of benefits and perquisites.

6
Benefits in the Changing Organization

W hat's your salary? How much do you make? What are you paid? When the subject of compensation is discussed, most people speak in terms of direct monetary gains—the money they receive for the work they do, their base salary, and perhaps any bonus or incentive they receive. Yet in virtually all organizations, the total compensation paid to employees is, of course, much more than that. What is frequently overlooked in the equation is the major noncash element, an element that is critical to the design of an effective dynamic reward strategy: benefits and perquisites.

Like their cash counterparts, today's benefits packages can provide organizations with a high level of support as they evolve and undertake major change initiatives. They can help motivate performance, support behavioral change, reinforce new values and business goals, and reflect and fortify the organization's evolving culture. As they grow increasingly flexible, benefits can also be used to support workplace diversity and eliminate barriers to performance and productivity. Finally, as personal and professional values—especially those of younger generations of workers— continue to shift, benefits provide a powerful alternative and supplement to the more traditional pay programs. The young, single-parent employee, for example, may be motivated more by an on-site child care program or the option of a flexible work schedule than by a few more taxable dollars in each paycheck.

To maximize their value, noncash reward strategies, as with cash programs, should be carefully aligned with the organization's changing business goals, strategies, and work cultures. The first step in that alignment is understanding how benefits, like other aspects of the organization, have themselves evolved.

MOVING FROM THE FRINGE TO THE FOREFRONT

Employee benefits gained widespread popularity only in the years following World War II. Initially, they amounted to a tiny percentage of the organization's overall expenses and were not considered part of compensation. The fact that they were commonly referred to as "fringe" benefits says much about how they were perceived: as something extra perhaps, or a freebie, but certainly not an element of pay.

About ten to fifteen years ago, however, the importance of benefits began to change dramatically. This shift in large measure was triggered by rapidly rising health care costs, which since that time have increased from about 4 percent of total compensation costs to 11 percent today. Benefits also have been influenced by the massive changes in retirement programs. These changes, some of which were brought about by a toughening of the tax code, have forced employers and employees to reevaluate their retirement programs and frequently create supplemental programs.

As a result of these and other changes, benefits today are a costly part of doing business. In fact, Hay research shows that, on average, benefits today represent more than 25 percent of total payroll costs.[1] In some specific industries, however, benefits account for more than 40 percent of compensation costs.

As the costs of benefits began rising sharply, organizations suddenly began paying much closer attention to them. Employers began communicating to their workforces the seriousness and magnitude of the issue. Benefits, employees were told, could no longer be viewed as merely a gift from a benevolent organization, but had to be considered a valuable and costly part of their compensation package—a "hidden" or "second" paycheck.

At first, this new message no doubt sounded much like "management-speak" to employees. After all, employees never actually saw this so-called "hidden paycheck." The impact—positive or negative—on their pocket-books was nonexistent. Or so they thought. Then one day they were asked to begin sharing or dramatically increasing their share of the cost of health care benefits. Suddenly, the new message about benefits began to hit home. Any lingering doubts about the cost of benefits vanished when these new employee-borne costs began to chew away at—or in some cases actu-ally exceed—annual merit increases. This phenomenon became increas-ingly common as annual merit increases dropped from their 10 to 12 percent levels of a decade ago to today's average of about 4 percent. Al-though it may not have been stated as such, a few unfortunate employees found that, through the changing balance of benefits and cash compensa-tion, they had actually experienced a cut in pay.

This tenuous relationship between cash compensation and benefits programs has become even more complicated and muddled as organiza-tions begin moving away from an emphasis on base pay toward a compensation mix that includes more performance-based, variable pay. Be-cause many benefits—pension plans, for example—are tied directly to base pay levels, changing any part of the mix may, in effect, reduce ben-efits. For this reason it is critical that benefits be considered in the context of total remuneration; before employers change any component of the total remuneration package, they should look at the impact that it has on all the other pieces.

UNDERSTANDING THE PIECES
OF TODAY'S BENEFITS PROGRAM

Benefits programs not only cost more and play an increasingly important role within the organization today, but the services they provide have also evolved from a few basic staples—health care, life insurance, vacations, and pension plans—into a smorgasbord that conceivably covers everything from child care to commuting assistance. Just how much the elements of benefits programs have evolved can be seen in the results of Hay's annual benefits survey, a comprehensive study that identifies developing trends across a variety of industries.

Health Care.   In the wake of continuing market-driven reforms, managed care, including preferred provider organizations (PPOs), health mainte-nance organizations (HMOs), and point-of-service (POS) care, continues to gain popularity, replacing the fee-for-service plans that were once the norm. As Figure 6–1 shows, more than half of the organizations Hay surveyed offer some form of managed care as their primary plan, compared with only 31 percent four years earlier.

According to Hay research, only 35 percent of organizations continue to fully fund health care insurance for employees, and only 18 percent fully fund dependent coverage. The vast majority of employees pay, on average, 18 percent of the cost of their coverage and 25 percent of the cost of dependent coverage. At the same time, a growing number of organizations are increasing the deductibles and reducing the coinsurance levels for out-of-network benefits. Traditionally, after the deductible level was reached, employees had to pay 20 percent of the benefits. The other 80 percent was covered by the insurance carrier. Today, however, in order to keep costs down, many organizations require employees to pay 30 percent or more of the fees.

Figure 6–1

Design of Primary Medical Plan Is Moving Away from Fee-for-Service and Toward Managed Care

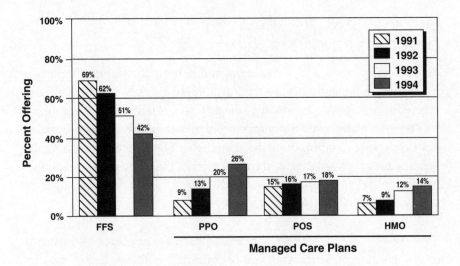

Source: 1994 Hay/Huggins Benefits Database

Increasing the deductibles and the employees' share of the costs aren't the only strategies organizations are adopting in an effort to reduce health care expenses. With the increased emphasis on "wellness," many organizations have begun educational programs that may include monthly newsletters, courses in weight reduction, smoking cessation programs, and health club memberships.

How well these programs work remains debatable. Results are often difficult to measure, and such programs obviously don't work with all employees. Still, after implementing such programs, a number of organizations—including our own—have seen a significant improvement in the way people use their health care plans and an overall flattening of health care costs. Johnson and Johnson, for example, estimates that its $4.5 million-a-year wellness plan, which earned it the C. Everett Koop National Health Award, saves the company $13 million a year. Studies by the huge manufacturer of health care products and the University of Michigan have also revealed some other interesting numbers: Quit smoking or lower your cholesterol and you save the company a little more than a grand a year; exercise and you'll save it $260; lose weight, and you save it $177.[2]

Prescription drug cards and mail order programs also continue to increase in popularity, with more than half of the organizations surveyed offering them, typically with $5 copayments. Figure 6–2 shows in detail how health care plans have changed since 1990.

Retirement Benefits.   Defined benefit pension plans, which provide a fixed pension at retirement, continue to be used by most organizations. But due to a number of factors such as the aging of the baby-boomer generation and a lackluster performance by the stock markets, their costs are rising sharply. As a result, most organizations are taking a hard look at such programs, and often are eliminating expensive features such as cost-of-living adjustments for retirees.

To supplement—or in some cases replace—such plans, many organizations are offering a variety of more portable, defined contribution plans and capital accumulation options, including 401(k) plans, profit sharing, employee stock ownership plans, and tax-shelter annuities. Of the organizations Hay surveyed, 71 percent offer 401(k) plans; 58 percent of those provide employer-matching contributions and 75 percent offer four or more investment choices for participants. Such programs cost far less than defined benefit plans and are also highly popular with employees, who like

Figure 6–2

Prevalence of Health Care Plans

Type of Plan	Percentage		
	<u>1994</u>	<u>1992</u>	<u>1990</u>
Medical coverage			
Employee coverage fully			
employer-paid	35	39	49
Family coverage fully employer-paid	16	19	25
Hospital and surgical plan design			
Hospital and surgical at			
100% of R&C*	38	33	33
Hospital only at 100% of R&C	8	10	14
Hospital and surgical at less than			
100% of R&C	53	57	53
Flat dollar deductible	64	76	83
$100 or less	20	30	38
$101–$199	14	16	20
$200	31	29	26
Greater than $200	35	25	16
Well-baby care	69	54	45
Routine office visits	68	51	39
Offer HMO option	67	67	72
Offer choice of indemnity			
(non-HMO/PPO/POS plans)	33	29	23
Offer PPO	53	49	40
Offer POS	42	32	—
Medical coverage offered to:			
Normal retirees	56	57	63
Employee coverage			
fully employer-paid	36	41	46
Early retirees	60	61	65
Other coverages			
Dental	95	95	91
Vision	39	35	29

*Reasonable and customary charges.

their flexibility as well as the variety of investment choices they offer, including the provision most have for offering loans to participants.

Life Insurance and Disability Plans.   Group life insurance and disability programs continue to be mainstays of most benefit programs, with 99 percent of those organizations surveyed providing basic group life insurance, and 97 percent long-term disability income. The typical basic life plan provides coverage of one to two times base salary, with maximum coverage of between $50,000 and $500,000. The costs of such policies are primarily paid by the employers. At the same time, a growing number of organizations—72 percent of those surveyed—offer supplemental life insurance programs, most of which are paid by employees.

A few organizations have also begun offering policies that include "living benefits" clauses. Such clauses allow terminally ill employees to withdraw some or all of their life insurance proceeds to help pay medical bills. A number of organizations also are moving to better manage the expense of both work- and nonwork-related disability cases, quickly providing help and rehabilitation as soon as the individual is injured.

Holiday and Vacation Policies.   Among the most stable benefits provided by employers, holiday and vacation policies are also some of the most costly. Except for a slow but steady increase in the number of holidays and vacation days employers provide, most policies haven't changed much over the past decade. The organizations surveyed by Hay grant, on average, ten holidays annually, with two thirds providing at least one floating day. The typical vacation policy allows two weeks off after one year of service, and increases by one week every five or ten years to a maximum of five weeks after twenty-five years. Almost two thirds of the organizations surveyed compensate employees for unused vacation time, most allowing them to carry the time to the next year.

A few organizations have begun rolling traditional vacation days, personal days, sick days, and holidays into a single bank of days that can be used by employees as they see fit. These paid time off (PTO) plans are especially popular in health care organizations, which require a high degree of employee flexibility to meet continually changing staffing needs. But they also are gaining popularity in other industries, where freedom and flexibility have become staples of the work culture. Nike Inc., for example, has a generous policy that provides from three to seven weeks of time annually—time that can be carried over at the end of the year if not used.[3] Such policies are especially attractive to those employees who seldom use or abuse traditional sick leave, as well as working parents who appreciate the flexibility of being able to take time off for pressing family matters, such as caring for a sick child.

Other Benefits.   In addition to making changes in traditional benefits programs, many organizations also are adding a variety of new benefits. These new offerings are, for the most part, based on changes in employee needs, desires, and values. With more families depending on the income of both parents, and the presence of more single-parent families, a number of organizations have begun offering more family-oriented benefits such as child care and dependent care days. Figure 6–3 shows the growing use of these and other family-oriented benefits including flexible hours, job sharing, and employee assistance programs.

Figure 6–3

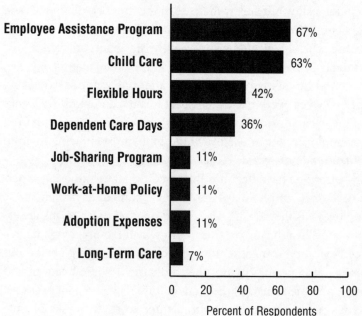

Design of Family-Oriented Benefits

Other programs that make life easier for today's often harried employees also are gaining popularity. Figure 6–4 shows the prevalence of a full range of benefits now available in many organizations.

MORE FLEXIBILITY AND CHOICE AMONG PLANS

Organizations are not only offering a wider range of benefits, but in many cases are also giving their employees more choice in determining which benefits they want. About 20 percent of the companies Hay surveyed offer full cafeteria plans in which employees can choose from a variety of benefit options. Most of these provide a basic set of benefits, along with a certain number of options from which employees can select optional or additional coverage.

Far more popular, however, are less-comprehensive plans that offer a variety of health care options or flexible spending accounts in which pretax dollars can be set aside to cover health care costs, including unreimbursed medical expenses, or dependent day care expenses. Figure 6–5 shows the growth in these plans since 1990.

This growth in the scope and variety of benefits provides employers with a seemingly endless number of options. But not all of these options are effective with all employee groups or in all organizations. Indeed, some can even clash with the organization's goals, values, and overriding business strategy. Designing a benefits program that addresses these issues is in many ways very similar to designing any other element of compensation. It certainly requires an understanding of the full range of benefits that the organization is considering. But beyond that, it demands an understanding of the organization, its values, its business goals and strategies, and the changes that it is going through. It also requires an understanding of the work cultures that are in place in the organization and how they are evolving. While benefits do not differ greatly from culture to culture—except in the network organizations—there are, as Figure 6–6 shows, some subtle differences that should be acknowledged.

FUNCTIONAL BENEFITS: AN EMPHASIS ON LONGEVITY, SECURITY

The benefits in a functional culture typically reflect the values of longevity and security that are common to such organizations. Employees in

Figure 6–4

Benefits Prevalence

Benefit	Percentage		
	1994	**1992**	**1990**
Long-term care	7	5	3
Living benefits	13	6	—
Waiver of health care coverage	19	19	—
Earned time-off policy	14	10	10
Dependent care days	36	20	—
Work-at-home policy	11	14	14
Job-sharing program	11	—	—
Flexible hours	42	36	38
Adoption expenses	11	10	8
Child care	63	59	55
Employer discounts	38	38	45
Credit union	66	62	62
Employee assistance program	67	64	61
Tuition reimbursement	92	90	90
On-site cafeteria	47	50	52
Smoking policy	97	93	86
Drug testing	55	50	40
AIDS policy	23	25	29
Health promotion	76	79	80
On-site medical clinic	29	30	—
New retirement plan	41	29	—
Commuting assistance	24	20	36
Special inducement for early retirement	15	17	—
Casual dress days	61	—	—
Employee benefit communication programs	95	—	69

Source: 1994 Hay/Huggins Benefits Database

Figure 6–5

Prevalence of Flexible Benefits Programs

	Percentage		
	<u>1994</u>	<u>1992</u>	<u>1990</u>
Flexible benefits program	80	75	62
Flexible spending account	75	70	57
• Health care premiums	84	87	70
• Unreimbursed medical expenses	77	71	64
• Dependent care expenses	84	79	80
Full cafeteria plan	20	15	14
Choice of indemnity plan	31	29	23

Source: 1994 Hay/Huggins Benefits Database

Figure 6–6

Work Cultures and Benefit Program Designs

Benefits	Functional	Process	Time-based	Network
Retirement	Career-based, service related	Profit-sharing emphasis	Emphasis on profit, portability, and short service	Little, if any
Health	Uniform with some flexibility/choice Low cost sharing	Uniform with some flexibility/choice Low-medium cost sharing	Flexible, tailored to individual Medium-high cost sharing	Flexible, tailored to individual High cost sharing
Life	High, uniform benefit	Medium, optional coverage available	Minimum level, employee options	Minimum level, employee options
Retiree Medical & Life	Yes	Varies	No	No
Short & Long Term Disability	High benefit, comprehensive	Medium benefit, comprehensive	Minimum benefit, optional coverage available	Minimum benefit, optional coverage available
Vacation	High, service based	Medium, service based	Low, service or position based	Low, position based
Holiday	High-fixed	High-fixed	Medium-flexible	Basic only

functional organizations tend to be career-focused individuals who stay with the same company for a long time. To that end, retirement programs are typically geared toward more traditional pension and defined benefit plans that provide the best payouts over the long term. These plans tend to be tied closely to base salaries, but are fairly standardized throughout the organization, except perhaps at the executive level. Given the paternalistic nature of most functional organizations, the employer tends to fund a major portion of these, as well as other benefits.

This same paternalistic influence and emphasis on security and stability are also seen in health care benefits, which tend to provide few options, but are highly comprehensive and in large part employer-funded. That is not to say, however, that there should be no flexibility or options. Even the functional organization today needs to provide some individual choices. Typically, employees—especially those in dual income families—want to have the option of taking the health care insurance. They also prefer the option of purchasing additional life insurance. When it comes to health care plans, functional organizations also sometimes try to help lower-paid employees by "leveling the playing field" through plans in which the employees' contributions vary depending on the size of their base salary.

Life insurance is another benefits mainstay of the functional organization. Again emphasizing paternalism, security, and longevity, these insurance policies tend to provide a fairly high level of coverage. Such policies also are fairly uniform throughout the organization, with most employees receiving the same multiple of their pay in benefits. Many functional organizations also continue to provide health care and life insurance to retirees, although such benefits have been dramatically reduced in recent years.

Functional organizations also tend to have rich disability benefits—comprehensive packages that include attractive short- and long-term coverage, as well as a generous number of sick days. They also usually provide time-in-service-based vacation policies.

While functional organizations are beginning to provide employees at least a few benefit options, especially in the area of health care, most continue to offer more traditional, basic programs that are relatively rigid and limited in the variety of benefits that are offered. Most, for example, still do not offer contemporary benefits such as flextime and child care. Typically, a functional program will include a rich defined benefits plan, perhaps a 401(k) plan added within the past five years, a medical plan with a couple of HMO options, and finally, fairly rich life insurance benefits—commonly two times the employee's salary—and a substantial long-term disability plan.

PROCESS BENEFITS: EMPHASIZING PRODUCTIVITY, PROFITABILITY

As we move toward the process culture, and the values of both the organization and its people begin to shift, we see a shift in the benefit requirements. Certainly there is still a need to emphasize security— employees may not be as focused on the long-term as their functional peers, but they remain career-oriented nonetheless. As we have already shown, however, the individual orientation of the functional organization takes a backseat to the performance of the group or team in the process organization. Rather than emphasizing "how well *I* do my job," the focus turns to "how efficiently and effectively can *we*, as a group, enhance productivity and, ultimately, profitability."

This increased emphasis on teams and the sharing of responsibility with employees is often reflected in benefit plans. Effective retirement programs, for example, often come as some form of profit-sharing plans, which, although continuing to stress a fairly high level of long-term security, are nonetheless tied to organizational performance.

Health care benefits in process cultures also reflect the shift away from the rigid, paternalistic values of the functional organizations. They tend to provide more options to employees—both an HMO and a PPO plan perhaps—or even allow people to opt out of the program if they feel it is unnecessary. At the same time, however, process organizations tend to share more of the costs of the program with the employees.

Like health benefits, life insurance in the process organization begins to gain a measure of flexibility. But while there are more options, the amount of insurance provided by the employer tends to drop, since such benefits, although relatively inexpensive, are heavily taxed over certain levels.

As organizations begin to move from functional to process and time-based, health care and life insurance benefits for retirees tend to disappear. After all, with the emphasis moving from longevity and security to shorter-term if not periodic employee/employer relationships, far fewer individuals stay around long enough to be eligible for such benefits. Emphasizing such benefits would in fact send out a message that is quite different from the values and behaviors the organization wants to foster. At the same time, however, eliminating such benefits raises a significant social issue regarding how people will provide for their health care during retirement.

Disability benefits in the process organization tend to be somewhat similar to those in the functional organization, although here again, as organizations move across cultures, they tend to be less comprehensive and require more employee funding. Process organizations also tend to begin offering some of the more contemporary, family-oriented benefits such as flextime, child care, and elder care.

TIME-BASED BENEFITS: PORTABILITY AND FLEXIBILITY

Like the process organization, time-based cultures also emphasize group efforts, productivity, and profitability. But here, longevity tends to become a nonissue, replaced by portability. Unlike functional employees who are wedded to a specific job, or process employees who are tied somewhat permanently to a team, time-based employees tend to move around a lot. Sometimes that movement is from team to team. Oftentimes it is from one business unit to another. And frequently, it means jumping from organization to organization. To that end, benefit programs have to be highly flexible and portable.

Retirement programs tend to focus, as they do in process cultures, on performance and profitability. But they also must emphasize even more flexibility and portability. After all, when it comes time for employees to move on to other organizations, they want to be able to take their nest eggs with them. As in the process culture, a profit-sharing program may be highly effective, but only if it is designed with a tighter vesting schedule (five as opposed to seven years), so that people who want to move on in a few years can do so and still reap the benefits of the program.

Health care benefits and life insurance in the time-based organization also reflect the more temporary nature of the culture and the short-term nature of many assignments. These plans tend to be very flexible, with a lot of choice built in, as well as the option not to participate. As organizations move toward time-based cultures, the employee share of the costs continues to increase. Employees can also be expected to share the cost of the disability plans in the time-based organizations. While vacation policies often remain relatively traditional, some organizations have started replacing them with more flexible, paid time off (PTO) programs.

NETWORK BENEFITS: FEWER, BUT MORE FLEXIBLE

Like the other compensation elements, benefits in the network organization tend to be very dissimilar to those in other cultures. Generally there are far fewer benefits, those that do exist are highly flexible, and the employees' share of the costs is much greater. Take retirement for example. People attracted to networks tend to be free agents and risk takers. They really aren't interested in a company retirement program, however grandiose. Besides, they probably won't be around long enough to become vested, unless vesting is immediate. They are quite satisfied to create and maintain their own retirement programs. They are, after all, entrepreneurs. So instead of putting money into a retirement program, most network organizations put it into their cash compensation programs—often in the form of premium base salaries.

Network organizations take a similar approach toward health care and life insurance. Many offer highly individualized programs with tremendous flexibility. Employees, if they choose to participate, are responsible for a large share of the costs—typically 50 percent or more. Many employees, however, assume their role with the network is only temporary and choose to purchase their own policies instead. The cost of funding and self-administering their own health care and life insurance is clearly preferable to the hassles and uncertainty of periodically being forced to jump from one policy to another as they switch organizations.

Vacation policies in network organizations tend to shift from service-based to position-based, with the number of days determined by the employee's job or position with the organization. Many network employees receive basic holidays, but not the additional frills, such as personal days, that employees in other cultures tend to expect. Their time off, after all, comes between jobs.

NARROWING THE ORGANIZATION'S
OPTIONS: SEVEN KEY QUESTIONS

In designing a benefits package that is tailored to its goals, values, and work cultures and yet is not loaded down with unnecessary and costly bells and whistles, an organization must establish some specific parameters around what it can and cannot deliver. It must look at its true benefit needs, its limitations in funding and administering a benefits program, and how best to integrate benefits with the rest of the compensation elements. This can be done by first answering a series of questions.

1. *What are the messages that the organization is trying to convey?* The message may be one of paternalistic, long-term security. It may be one of partnership—of shared responsibility. It may be a message of flexibility: You perform well, and we'll go out of our way to meet your benefit needs.

Consider the organization that is moving from a functional to process culture and wants to create customer service groups. In determining its approach to benefits, it first must make some decisions about what messages those benefits communicate to employees. Take its retirement program, for example: The old program that was funded in part through profit sharing based on company-wide financial results—results that had little real link to employee efforts—will certainly not reinforce the new value of team performance. Instead, the organization should consider a funding element that is tied to team or group success. That could be something as simple as tying the profit sharing to team or division results, or something as creative as a new 401(k) plan in which matching contributions are tied to certain financial, quality, or customer service measures.

At the same time, the organization probably will want to scrap that part of its traditionally defined benefits plan based on years of service. After all, the new message is one of productivity, not of longevity. Certainly employees are welcome to stay with the organization—as long as they continue to produce more and more. At the same time, they should also have the incentive to move on if they wish, or if they no longer add value to the organization. In such a case, a plan should be developed that the employees perceive is not only a sound investment as long as they are part of the organization, but also one they can take with them should they choose to leave.

2. *How much variability and flexibility does the organization want to allow in its program?* Organizations with a highly diverse workforce and a variety of work cultures will need highly flexible programs that offer a wide range of options. Organizations with a single culture and a homogeneous workforce will probably be just as well served by less-complex programs with far fewer options.

While a more flexible plan, if well designed, may provide an organization with a certain amount of savings, it is important that employees understand that choice—not cost—is the primary driver. They should make decisions on which health care plan is right for them based on how it is designed and what it offers, not merely what it costs them.

3. *What is the organization able or willing to spend?* As the cost of benefits rises, what used to be a nonissue has been transformed into a major concern, even for large, highly successful, paternalistic organizations. Most organizations, for example, would like to provide health insurance for their employees. Yet not only do health care costs continue to climb, but they are outside the control of the organization. In fact, employees generally have more control over costs than their employers do.

To effectively address the cost issue, organizations must go into partnership with their employees. They may decide to pay a healthy percentage of the costs, while making it clear that the employees' contributions will be adjusted upwards should there be a continued rise in those costs. At the same time, they must provide employees with a variety of options for keeping costs down.

General Mills, for example, several years ago began offering voluntary "health appraisals"—forms employees filled out which helped them determine how healthy they were. Initially, if employees filled out the form, their health care contributions were automatically reduced by $10 each month. The second year, the company raised employee contributions significantly, while at the same time offering them another opportunity to further reduce their costs. Employees who were among the 80 percent of the population that incurred less than 20 percent of the health care claim costs received a $40-a-month reduction of their health care costs. Ultimately, the new program not only reduced company costs, but it also helped educate employees about the importance of maintaining healthy lifestyles, and about their opportunity individually to benefit directly through lower contributions when their personal use of the plan was minimal in the prior year.

4. *How can the organization make its programs more tax efficient?* The continually changing tax code has had a major impact on the design of benefit plans today. Understanding implications of the tax code and determining how to make benefits "tax-friendly" are critical steps in the design process. Obviously, the more tax efficient the program, the more it will be seen as a true benefit by today's savvy employees.

5. *What are the organization's administrative constraints?* The increased complexity of today's benefits programs has created administrative

nightmares for many organizations. Administering a multioption program to a highly diverse workforce located at a variety of work sites in far-ranging regions or even countries can be a daunting and costly task—even for a highly sophisticated benefits staff. Some organizations have met the problem head-on, expanding staff or implementing the latest software programs to track benefits. Others have passed on much of the adminis-trative tasks to outside experts. All of these approaches have merits. In deciding which to use, organizations must balance the complexity of their benefits program with their ability to administer it effectively. They need to determine whether they have—or can acquire—the staff, expertise, and technology to effectively support their plan, or whether they would be better off outsourcing most, if not all, of the program's administration.

6. *How is the organization going to link benefits with the other elements of compensation, including base and variable pay?* With the cost of benefits continuing to climb along with their acceptance as a legitimate piece of the pay package, organizations—even small, single-culture ones—are best served by adopting a total remuneration philosophy that balances the full range of compensation strategies. While not as strong a behavior modifier as cash compensation, benefits are nonetheless effective in supporting change, and should, in many cases, be tied to performance.

7. *How is the organization going to communicate the plan?* One of the most critical elements of a successful benefits program is an ongoing com-munications plan. It must not only explain how the benefits work, but also why they were designed the way they were, and how they are tied to the organization's broader vision and mission. Always a necessary element of an effective benefits program, communication has become even more im-portant as benefits have become more complex.

But like the benefits themselves, communications have evolved. No longer can the organization rely on an "official" plan document, a section in the employee handbook, and perhaps a short introduction to new em-ployees to communicate benefits. Given the array of choices many employees have, they need ongoing and, at times, instantaneous access to data that will help them make informed decisions. That access may be pro-vided through a variety of sources—from someone in the human resources department dedicated to answering questions to an interactive software program that will allow employees to "model" a variety of options to see which is best for them, or even let them modify their investment options. For those organizations that have neither the commitment nor the resources to communicate effectively on an ongoing basis, the options are relatively few. They should, to the greatest extent possible, keep their benefit plans simple.

Perhaps most important, organizations need to keep their employees apprised of the changing costs of benefits. Many organizations, including our own, regularly inform employees of the value of their benefits, and how that is linked to their total compensation. See Figure 6–7.

TAKING A HUMANISTIC, "OUTSIDE-THE-BOX" APPROACH

As organizations gain a better understanding of their current cultures and determine what cultural makeup they need in the future, the answers to many of these questions often become clear. Armed with these solutions and a thorough understanding of today's benefit options, they can then begin to make some sound design decisions.

But it is only a beginning. To create effective benefits programs, organizations must look beyond the usual options. They must "get out of the box," and take creative approaches tailored to the needs of their people and the cultures in which they live and work. If, for example, an organization is an extremely stressful place to work, and its benefits expenses for psychiatric counseling and Prozac prescriptions are going through the roof, it should explore ways of reducing stress in the workplace and create programs to help people deal with that stress. That may mean starting an employee assistance program with confidential counseling, or perhaps workshops on stress reduction and time management.

At the same time, of course, organizations must continue to examine their cultures, identify what they are, and then make sure that all of their benefits are aligned. If the organization wants a mobile, flexible workforce, then it should design plans that allow people to leave the company without a major loss of investment. If it wants employees to stay for the long haul, then it should design benefits that promote security and longevity. By taking this humanistic approach and tying it to the organization's cultures, the issue of cost will often take care of itself.

Reuters America, Inc. discovered just how important this cost-culture link can be when it decided to change its benefits program in an effort to limit future cost increases. Even though a committee had only months

Figure 6–7

**Example of Employee Benefits Statement
Showing Total Value of Benefits**

Value of Your Benefits

You and your family are provided the security and protection of the benefits described in this report. The value of these benefits represents significant additional compensation to you—most of which is tax-free.

Your base annual salary
    as of 10/1/95 .... $50,000

Your bonus opportunity $15,000

Hay's estimated annual cost for your benefits $11,962

Your annual total compensation as of 10/1/95 .... $76,962

Additional benefits of significant value which are not included in the Hay cost of benefits are:

- 15 FY94 Vacation
  Days Eligibility

- 10 Holidays

- Military Leave
  of Absence

- Worker's Compensation

- Bereavement Leave

- Jury Duty Pay

- Tuition Reimbursement

- Reserve Training Duty Leave

- Unemployment Insurance

- Long Term Care

The following dates were used in calculating your benefits:

Birth Date 06/08/49

Employment Date 10/16/91

earlier designed a sound, new point-of-service plan, the organization's new vision and culture required that before the program could be changed, the employees themselves had to be asked what changes they would like. As daunting as the task appeared, a series of focus groups were held, during which the various options were explained. Through these focus groups it became clear that employees wanted quality health care, flexibility, and choice—although not full responsibility for making that choice. Most importantly, they didn't want to spend half of their paychecks for these benefits.

Using their suggestions, a flexible new plan was developed. But before it was rolled out, it was again presented to employees—this time to a group of what were perceived as the organization's "toughest customers." Tough though they were, the group didn't shoot the plan down, but instead provided some excellent suggestions for how it should be further modified and then communicated to employees. The result was a presold, employee-friendly plan that not only reduced costs by 15 percent the first year, but also reinforced the organization's new culture and vision of high employee involvement.

THE FUTURE: MORE TWEAKING, MORE TAILORING

Of course, even the most effective of today's benefits programs doesn't end with its successful implementation. Given the nature of change in the organization, programs have to be continually monitored and fine-tuned. For example, we review most client health care programs on a quarterly basis, and recommend—at minimum—an annual review.

Because of the close ties with the other elements of compensation, any changes in benefits must be considered in the context of the total remuneration strategy—just as any changes in the cash elements of the program must be considered in terms of how they impact benefits. The somewhat "fuzzy" line that separates cash and noncash compensation will probably grow even less defined in the near future, as benefits become even more flexible and individually tailored.

As work cultures continue to shift, and long-term employment continues to erode, benefits may eventually become so flexible that many of us will have our own portable plans. As we move from employer to employer, from organization to organization, we will maintain our own unique plan, modifying it as our lifestyle and career changes.

Such programs are already being used in some places. In the higher levels of financial organizations in Australia, for example, employees are often provided an overall total remuneration package, and then have complete control—and responsibility—for selecting and funding benefits.

What the benefits plan of the future will look like will, no doubt, depend on how organizations continue to evolve. Given the current emphasis on family and flexibility, however, we believe there will continue to be an increased use of flextime, job sharing, even the use of virtual offices—a concept that already has taken hold in a number of industries, including our own.

Changes in lifestyles also are leading to shifts in benefits. As Boomers—and their parents—continue to age, for example, we can expect to see more organizations offering elder care. And, as the very concept of the family continues to shift, we can expect to see more benefits offered to domestic partners of both the same and opposite sex.

Changes in health care and retirement benefits will continue to be driven in part by outside forces. With the growth of managed care and the creation of new strategic alliances between health care providers and insurers, many organizations will probably move to a single, highly flexible, point-of-service plan, rather than offer a variety of plans.

Retirement plans are another story. While many organizations have moved away from defined benefits plans, some experts believe that they will make a resurgence. Their argument: Left to our own devices many of us will ultimately retire with insufficient funds to live out the rest of our lives. Thus, organizations will be forced once again to take up the slack. They raise an interesting issue, one that will no doubt continue to generate debate, especially in the United States, given the uncertain future of our Social Security program.

As farfetched as such changes may have sounded a decade ago, ten years from now they may be the norm; another creation of the changing organization. In the next chapter, we will look at how another important aspect of the organization—its leadership—has changed, and how these evolving leaders should be rewarded.

7
Rewarding Leadership in the Changing Organization

He was the CEO of a mid-sized pharmaceutical company and, between mouthfuls of his in-flight dinner, was chewing on his lot in life. "My company is much leaner than it was eighteen months ago," he said. "But the market doesn't seem to know that—it sure hasn't given us any breaks. Nor have our employees. They are certainly more demanding, but they aren't always ready to reciprocate. Their values seem to be different. In fact, everyone's values are changing—even mine. I used to be a rigid, bottom-line-focused manager, heavy into commanding and controlling—sort of a corporate Vince Lombardi. Now I'm asking my people to assume responsibility for decisions I used to make. I'm encouraging them to take risks, work hard, even be creative and have fun. If they do all of that, I tell them, the success—the winning—will follow."

He took another bite of his reconstituted chicken, stared out at the dusk, and shook his head. "I just don't know. Sometimes I wonder if it is worth all the trouble. There are just so many unknowns, so many changes. There is only one thing I know for certain: It isn't easy being a leader these days."

It certainly isn't. It doesn't matter whether you lead a small work group, a company, or a nation, the leadership paradigms have shifted. Not only have the rules of the game changed, but also the players and—so it appears—their ethics and values. No wonder leadership-bashing, long a popular pastime, has been elevated to a major spectator sport. Not a week goes by that the business press doesn't report—frequently with a certain amount of glee—the collapse of yet another supernova of corporate power.

When the high-profile William Agee was ousted from his position as CEO of Morrison Knudsen Corp., it was reported that employees, some of whom had slipped damaging information to the board of directors, celebrated and blew noisemakers.[1] While such antics may be extreme, they nonetheless point to massive changes in how leaders are perceived. Anointment for life—be it from God, the board of directors, or the CEO—is out, replaced by constant reappraisal: what you did today, this quarter, this year, as measured by your supervisors, your peers, even your subordinates—in short, your full range of customers.

"Why does it have to be that way?" lamented the flamboyant Pat Riley, then-coach of the New York Knicks. "Why shouldn't it be the other way? The way it always was?"[2] Riley, who led the Los Angeles Lakers to four National Basketball Association Championships, was speaking specifically about the tendency of high-paid professional athletes to tune out and ultimately force out their coaches. But he could just as easily have been speaking for the ranks of frustrated corporate executives and managers who have come to believe that the inmates are in control of the Big House.

Not that the inmates, by the way, feel any better. The level of frustration of employees over the issue of leadership also is mounting. And it is not just ineffective executives and managers fueling the fire. More and more frequently, employees are being handed the mantle of leadership and responsibility—in a work group or a project team setting perhaps—with little training or support. Like those leaders above them, they are expected to perform marvelously from Day One, without the benefit of the necessary skills and competencies, or a safety net, should they fail.

Indeed, at a time when many organizations are proclaiming the need for empowered employees, the leadership needed to foster that empowerment often is lacking. As Warren Bennis, noted author, educator, and expert on the subject wrote, "Leadership can be felt throughout an organization. It gives pace and energy to the work and empowers the work force. Empowerment is the collective effect of leadership."[3]

THE NEW LEADERSHIP PARADIGM:
DIFFERENT ROLES, DIFFERENT REWARDS

The challenge most organizations face today is selecting, developing, and rewarding leaders during a time when everything—including the leadership paradigms themselves—is quickly changing. In assisting numerous organizations to redesign work and successfully maneuver through cultural transformations, we are often called upon to help identify the leadership competencies needed in the "new" or "redesigned" organization, and to determine how these leaders should be compensated.

Traditionally, of course, that leadership was defined as the executive or senior management team—nothing more. As a result, the selection, development, and compensation of leaders was focused primarily on that small group of individuals with a narrow range of roles and responsibilities, individuals who were found at the top of the organization. As we helped more and more organizations through this process, however, we began having problems with this definition—for several reasons.

First, while the leadership-from-the-top-only paradigm works well in the traditional functional organization with its deep hierarchy and top-down approach to life, it plays poorly in the flexible, flatter organizations that have evolved. These new organizations, with their shifting work cultures, their emphasis on empowerment of employees, and their focus on teams, require leadership at all levels—from the executive boardroom to the assembly-line floor. In such organizations, the role of the project work team leader is an integral part of the enterprise's management, right along with the CEO.

The roles of the two, of course, are quite different, which led to our second concern. As work has fundamentally changed and new work cultures have evolved, a need has been created for new forms of leadership. The traditional handful of top leaders have been supplemented—not supplanted—by a variety of other leaders. Leadership today comes in many shapes and sizes (not to be confused with styles, which is another subject entirely). Among the evolving leadership roles most prevalent in organizations are:

• *Team Leaders*, formal heads of teams created for specific purposes or ongoing processes, such as customer service enhancement, quality improvement, or the facilitation of internal communications. Traditionally, these positions have been filled by managers and supervisors. But the roles of such leaders have shifted, and now emphasize coaching and mentoring rather than the more traditional command and control.

• *Innovators and creators*, recognized experts on important issues such as research or quality. These are the thought leaders, the intellectual and creative minds whose vision extends far into the future. Creators and innovators are found at a variety of levels within the organization. They are sometimes located at the very top of the organization: those forward-thinking owners/executives who have created not just new products and services, but entire organizations. These are the Bill Gates and Steven Jobs of the world. Or, they may be found deep in the organization: individuals who are highly influential not because of the number of people they manage or are responsible for, but because of their knowledge and expertise in a specific area. They might be the key economists in a financial organization, for example, or the software creators in a high-tech firm.

• *Translators*, professional and technical leaders who produce marketable new ideas or concepts for the organization to commercialize. Translators take the ideas of the innovators and creators and, using their technical expertise, turn them into marketable products and services. Depending on the organization, they might be the engineers, for example, or the product designers, who transform the dreams and ideas of the research and development department into reality.

• *Producers/orchestrators*, leaders who have been put in charge of specific projects or task forces that involve the marshaling of people and other assets to achieve very specified goals, such as penetrating a new market or developing a new product or service. Unlike the team leader, producers and orchestrators often play a temporary role—once the new product is developed, or the new market penetrated, they move on to another assignment. These are the individuals who head the new product development teams, for example, or take leadership roles in the creation of new markets or services.

• *Change agents*, those responsible for bringing about major, wholesale changes in the strategic direction of the organization. These individuals often are seen as the "champions of change" who implement broad and bold new visions. They too are found at a variety of levels within the organization. They may take the form of the "hired gun" CEO, who is brought on board to change or save the organization—leaders such as IBM's Louis Gerstner, for example. Or, they might be found far deeper in the organization; someone, for example, who is chosen to lead or sponsor a specific change initiative such as reengineering or TQM.

TRUE LEADERSHIP VS. MANAGEMENT

Another problem we found in attempts to force the traditional leadership paradigm into a changing organization was that what is needed today—at all levels of the organization—is *true* leadership, not simply management. Put in its simplest form, the key function of leaders is to establish a basic vision or mission, while the key function of managers is to implement that vision.[4] Where managers have positions that are built around their ability to command, control, plan, or direct, leaders must be able to create vision, facilitate, coordinate, and build teams. Where the manager's power base is largely derived from technical expertise and an appointed position in the hierarchy of the organization, the true leader's source of power is his or her ability to share that power with others, to manage resources effectively— be they intellectual or financial—to influence the direction of the organization, and to create value.

As Max De Pree, CEO of Herman Miller, wrote in his book *Leadership Is an Art*, "The first responsibility of a leader is to define reality. The last is to say thank you. In between the two, the leader must become a servant and a debtor."[5] That is not to say that managers can't lead or that leaders can't manage. Increasingly, the roles tend to overlap. Still, the two aren't necessarily interchangeable.

True leaders also tend to be risk takers who do things in spite of the odds. They are not, however, organizational daredevils who leap before they look, but rather are steady, studious individuals who understand the issues before they act. This attitude was borne out by a Hay survey of financial traders which found that the defining characteristic of top performers was not their intellect or risk-taking ability, but rather how disciplined they were.

By understanding the competencies and distinguishing characteristics of true leaders, organizations can begin to identify the added value that they can bring to an enterprise. They can then determine how to value that contribution and how to construct an appropriate reward program.

FOUR LEADERSHIP ROUTES:
ASCENDERS, INHERITORS, AGENTS, AND ACHIEVERS

As the roles of leaders have changed, so have the routes to achieving positions of leadership. Until the early part of the twentieth century, most leaders were self-made ascenders to positions of power. They were the owner-leaders or creator-leaders, the entrepreneurs and visionaries who built organizations from the ground up. They were the John D. Rockefellers, who—for better or worse—brought their own vision, money, and rules to the table. This self-made, self-styled form of leadership survives today in a few individuals such as Microsoft's Bill Gates, and is most frequently found in telecommunications, entertainment, and high-technology industries. But unlike their predecessors, such leaders today tend to be viewed more as mavericks than as mainstays of industry.

After the ascenders came the inheritors. These were, and in some cases still are, the descendants—the children or other close relatives—of the ascenders. Inheritor-leaders continue to reign in many organizations, although their numbers and power tend to diminish as the mantle of leadership is passed from one generation to the next. In today's highly competitive marketplace, inheritors seldom survive on their genes alone, and are true leaders only to the extent that they exhibit true leadership competencies. Yet if they have those competencies, they can be powerful forces in the organization. Ford Motor Co., for example, recently named William Clay Ford, Jr., chairman of the board of directors' finance committee. As both a fourth generation Ford *and* a highly respected leader in his own right, he can very legitimately continue exerting the family's influence over the organization. Had he not demonstrated true leadership competencies, however, the legitimacy and credibility of his role no doubt would have been suspect.

As businesses began outliving the individuals and families who had built them, the actual ownership was often transferred to a multitude of institutional investors. While this new form of ownership provided a seemingly endless supply of capital, it also greatly diluted the leadership that had been so critical in creating the organizations. The new leaders in these organizations, especially at the upper levels, were, in essence, agents of the institutional owners. They were—and are—the hired executives who hold forth in most boardrooms today. There certainly isn't anything inherently wrong with such a leadership model. In fact, most of these individuals are highly capable and competent. But there is no doubt they have less of a sense of ownership, bring a different set of skills, competencies, and values to the role, and require different motivation than did their owner/inheritor predecessors.

While these agent leaders continue to play a dominant role, especially at the top of the organization, more and more they are finding it necessary to share their leadership with others throughout the organization. Increasingly, they are finding they need to rely on individuals who, through their achievements, have developed a certain level of expertise or influence that is needed to move the organization forward. Managers, for example—at least those who have been fortunate enough to survive the recent barrage of downsizing and delayering—are finding themselves cast as producers, orchestrators, or coaches on project teams and work groups. And, although they frequently are handed these roles based on their achievements within the organization, they are expected to forsake the traditional supervisor/manager role for one of true leadership. As Lawrence Bossidy, chairman and CEO of AlliedSignal says, "To execute, you need people who can lead. Managers have to understand that they don't *manage* anybody."[6]

Managers are by no means the only individuals who find themselves thrust into these leadership roles. To be successful, most organizations are finding that they also need the innovation and creative direction of thought leaders and the expertise and experience of the technical and professional leaders. And, although these creators and translators may not have the formal authority of the CEO or manager—at least in the traditional sense of leadership—their importance to the organization cannot be overlooked.

THE NEED FOR CULTURE/LEADERSHIP ALIGNMENT

How these new leadership roles and routes are best applied and adapted depends on the individual organization. In many ways the evolution of leadership has paralleled the evolution of work cultures. Each culture requires a different leadership approach that can most effectively align both individual and organizational goals to achieve the desired results. In the functional culture, for example, the individual goals are often completely divorced from the organizational goals. "My job is to make reliable widgets; the company's goal is to make profits." In the process and time-based cultures, there is a higher degree of compatibility between organizational and individual goals: "We—the team, work group, or organization—want to improve customer service or complete this project on budget and on time. At the same time, we're interested in how our effort impacts the company's performance." In the network culture, there may be a greater mutuality of goals. "Whatever our individual roles, our overriding goal is to complete the venture. We're all in this together."

To achieve this alignment, the functional culture may continue to rely successfully on a limited number of leaders who are primarily situated in the upper reaches of the organization, and who are responsible for keeping large groups of people focused on specific targets for production, quality, or customer service. A manufacturing company, for example, may continue to require only a few leaders at the plant and executive level. That should not, however, imply that the functional organization can continue to depend on the same leadership model that has served it well for decades. With the dwindling ranks of managers, the increased emphasis on technology, and greater attention on the customer, even the most conservative of functional organizations may find it necessary to develop and support more leaders at the technical and professional levels.

In process and time-based cultures, the opportunity and need for leadership increases throughout the organization. While both cultures may continue to have a traditional formal leadership hierarchy at the top of the organization, they also depend heavily on professional, technical, and thought leaders to direct and support team efforts and work groups. In a process culture, for example, these mid-level leaders may be moved around to lead various work teams. In time-based cultures, they may be given accountability for various pieces of a project or oversee entire projects.

As many organizations move from functional to process or time-based cultures, they are quickly discovering just how important these new leadership models are. One could even argue that the Republican victory in the 1994 U.S. congressional elections was an indication of a cultural shift and the need for a new kind of leadership. Seeking a more quality- and customer-oriented government, the voters, or so it appears, attempted to replace traditional team leaders and translators—elected officials who were at best managing and maintaining the status quo—with creators and change agents. Only time will tell whether they were really successful.

Perhaps the most dramatic shift in the leadership paradigm takes place in the network culture. Here there is little room for the rigid chain of command and the traditional appointed leader who has lots of time and authority to slowly and carefully develop and nurture loyalty and support. To be effective, the network leader must be able to lead externally—quickly forming and managing business and professional relationships outside his or her normal sphere of influence in order to achieve the desired results. To add to the complexity of the issue, those being led in the network organization are frequently professional, technical, or thought leaders themselves—free agents with their own goals, values, egos, and agendas. How hard is it to lead such individuals? Just ask the real estate developer who must orchestrate the efforts of architects, suppliers, and builders, or the producer who is trying to pull together actors, directors, and screenwriters for a single movie.

Take the case of the best-seller turned blockbuster movie, *The Bridges of Madison County*. The initial director didn't like the screenplay. Leading man Clint Eastwood did. The director wanted a foreign actress to play the leading lady, the studio wanted a young American. The director quit. Eastwood took over, went back to the original script, and hired Meryl Streep.[7] Had a functional approach been taken, *Bridges* would, no doubt, still be just a highly profitable book of questionable literary merit.

SELECTING AND DEVELOPING THE NEW LEADERS

Once an organization has determined the necessary leadership roles and competencies that it needs, it can begin to build the structure for selecting, developing, managing, and ultimately rewarding its leaders. Despite those that claim otherwise, most effective leaders are made, not born. Whatever their role, they require careful nurturing, mentoring, and training, even if they have been wildly successful in previous endeavors. Consider, for example, Michael Dell, who at the age of twenty founded the Dell Computer Corp. Realizing that while he had good instincts, he needed to improve his leadership and management skills if his company was to continue growing successfully, he took university classes, read books by management gurus, and surrounded himself with mentors who were successful, experienced leaders in their own right. "The nature of our business is that everything is changing," he said. "I've learned you have to take advantage of change and not let it take advantage of you."[8]

Organizations facing changes like Dell would do well to formalize this approach, implementing leadership selection, development, and succession planning strategies that are aligned with their culture and values. In an operational sense, leadership development is a key part of the business process and not merely a staff or human resources sideline.

Such strategies can take a variety of forms. Functional organizations tend to have well-established leadership paths (supervisor, manager, department head, vice president, senior vice president) as well as formalized leadership development programs. Such paths and programs tend to be less formal in the emerging work cultures. In a process work culture, for example, individuals who have experience in leading work teams can be given responsibility for mentoring and developing other potential leaders. In time-based cultures, emerging leaders can be given accountability for pieces of special projects while they are being developed to take on overall responsibility for larger programs. In the network organization, those individuals identified as emerging leaders can be given responsibility for producing, directing, or negotiating small projects or elements of the larger overall project.

The developmental time for new leaders also will depend to a great extent on the culture in which they work. In network cultures, which tend to attract individuals who have already attained a relatively advanced level of skills and competencies, the developmental time is relatively short. In process and time-based organizations, the development of leaders tends to take longer. This is because the team or project work groups that such cultures embrace often require more cross-training and the acquisition of a broader range of competencies and knowledge, and the number of leadership positions is somewhat limited. In the functional culture with even fewer opportunities and highly structured pathways, the development of leaders may take even longer.

DEVELOPING LEADERSHIP REWARD STRATEGIES

Ultimately, of course, organizations must develop compensation strategies that reward their leaders for their ability to conceive, empower, and inspire. To be truly effective, these strategies must promote a sense of fairness for leaders at all levels throughout the organization while at the same time acknowledging the unique—and often very different—roles and contributions these individuals make.

Even within the universe of leaders, distinctions must be drawn to reflect the varying impact that each leader can have. Take for example the conductor of an orchestra. On one level he might add value through his ability to bring a diverse group of individual performers together to produce pleasing music. On another level, he might add value through his ability to interpret classic works in new ways. On yet another level, he might pack the house for every performance because of a marketing genius that rivals his musical skills. Or take the team leader who, in addition to the value she adds to her own team, also provides leadership for nine other team leaders. In both cases, the added contributions need to be considered as reward packages are developed.

Just how critical it is to develop a leadership compensation strategy that is aligned with the organization's culture, is fair to a wide range of leaders, and at the same time truly fosters performance can be seen in the case of one of Wall Street's top trading houses, Salomon Brothers Inc. In October 1994, Salomon introduced a new, two-tiered, performance-based pay plan, which segregated the proprietary trading business from its customer-driven businesses. Unfortunately the plan was perceived as highly inequitable, especially for the managing directors in the customer-driven businesses. Not only did the customer service businesses have far more employees sharing the same sized ($2 billion) equity pot that had been allocated to both groups, but incentives in the customer-driven businesses were based on total results, over which the managing directors had limited control. As a result, the managing directors could make only a small fraction of what the proprietary traders could earn—even in a good year.[9] Not surprisingly, several months later, after more than two dozen managing directors in the customer businesses left the firm, the organization announced it would scrap the new plan in favor of one that would be based on "performance and market compensation levels."[10]

THE FOUR Rs OF LEADERSHIP

Organizations can begin developing effective leadership reward strategies by looking at four basic elements of all leadership paradigms: role, responsibility, risk, and results.

The Role.   Each of the role models—team leaders, creators, translators, producers, and change agents—requires a different set of competencies and skills that should be considered in establishing compensation. For the team leader, this may be the ability to facilitate, coordinate, and harmonize the efforts of the group. For the translator it may be the exceptional depth or breadth of knowledge or skills that fosters credibility among those being led. For the producer/orchestrator, it may be the ability to negotiate deals, as well as coordinate the efforts of a wide range of talented individuals.

For creators, the primary competencies might be knowledge-based creativity and the ability to translate that creativity into reality. Similarly, change agents must be successful at turning vision into action by articulating that vision, allaying fears, and creating the necessary buy-in.

The Responsibility.   The amount of responsibility varies greatly from leader to leader. Factors that must be considered include the size of the group—or number of individuals—being led, the size and importance of the project or process, the overall shadow of influence the leader casts over the organization, and, of course, the size of the financial or strategic responsibility.

The Risk.   For true leaders, the mantle of responsibility always comes with a certain level of risk. Traditionally the formula for determining the amount of risk was quite simple: the more responsibility, the more risk. While still an appropriate equation in many cases, it is not, as history shows, always applicable. The past twenty years have seen an onerous shirking of individual responsibility and risk taking especially at the top levels of the organization. This trend has been reflected in the creation of many fail-safe executive compensation programs that tied only a nominal percentage of pay to performance, thus minimizing the amount of risk an executive was expected to take. Based on the exposure and criticism generated by a number of high-profile cases, this no-risk attitude is changing. As we will see in the next chapter, many organizations are beginning to understand the need to tie a greater percentage of executive compensation to performance, thus greatly increasing the risk and establishing a mutual set of interests with the shareholders.

But risk isn't limited to the executive suite. An element of risk is inherent in most of the new leadership roles. Take, for example, agents of change. In today's organization, which seems to be continually shrinking, these individuals often are asked to lead change initiatives that may ultimately result in their own obsolescence in the organization. They may be directing changes that eventually will place them in different roles, or perhaps even eliminate their roles and those of others. Few individuals are willing to take such risks without being provided some sort of reward commensurate with that risk.

It's not just the organizational reengineers who face such risk. Project leaders in time-based organizations often are faced with the fact that the projects they lead are only temporary. Sooner or later—probably sooner, if they do their job well—they will be out of an assignment, or even a job, if new assignments are not developed. That uncertainty and the risks involved must also be recognized. So too must the risks that thought leaders must continually take in creating new concepts, many of which may never make it off the drawing board or the assembly line. While the risk may not appear as great for these individuals, it is nonetheless very real and should, through compensation, be recognized and rewarded in some way.

The Results.   Ultimately, of course, the success of leadership must be measured by the results—the outcomes—it generates. Like the other elements, this varies from leader to leader. The desired results for the CEO and the executive team may be the long-term financial health of the organization. For the work team or technical leader, it may be a measure of productivity or quality, or the creation of a new product on time and under budget. For the change leader, it may be successfully effecting major strategic or structural shifts within the organization.

Whatever these results are, they must be quantified and articulated before the fact, carefully measured during and after the process, and ultimately rewarded. And as can be seen, these rewards and their structures will be quite different from the traditional "one-size-fits-all" approach of the past. In fact, they will be different for each leadership situation.

PAYING FOR PERFORMANCE

Most existing development and rewards systems do not properly recognize these four elements of the leadership paradigm. Outside of the executive level, they focus primarily on role and responsibility, while giving less weight to risk and results as measured by performance. Thus, as Figure 7–1 shows, at the manager and translator level there typically is a heavy emphasis on base pay. Only executives—those traditionally viewed as leaders—are paid to a significant extent based on their risk and results. And even that mix may be wrong, given today's performance issues. The focus, for example, may be far too great on short-term performance, when the real issue is long-term stability.

Figure 7–1

Common Compensation Mixes

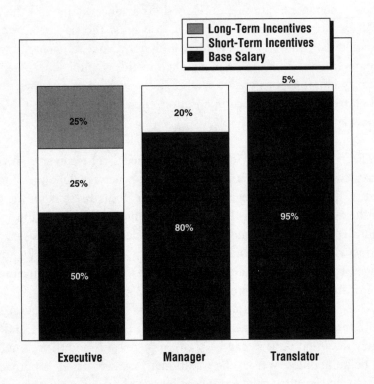

Because leaders have broad accountability—whatever their level within the organization—they tend to have a great impact on the business results. This impact should be reflected through a total remuneration approach that puts more pay at risk through incentives tied to both short- and long-term results, and offers participation in special equity-based or wealth-developing programs.

As Figure 7–2 shows, the percentage of total compensation that should be tied to risk and performance depends in part on the leadership role. Because the performance of creators and innovators, along with change agents, is so critical to the overall success of the organization, a large por-

Figure 7–2

New Leaders: Total Compensation and Percentage of Cash at Risk

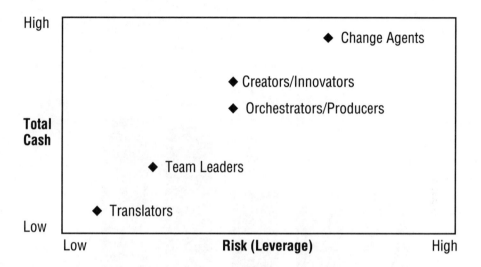

tion of their compensation should be linked to that performance. And, as Figure 7–3 shows, because their leadership spheres frequently encompass a broad range of organizational goals, and they typically must balance both short- and long-term objectives, their compensation should reflect a relatively equal balance of short- and long-term incentives. The specific balance, of course, depends on the level of thought leadership. Those who are creating new products and services, for example, or who are adding innovations to current ones, may require more emphasis on shorter-term measures of quality and customer satisfaction. On the other hand, those creating entire new industries and markets need to be focused on longer-term growth and development issues, and thus should have a greater percentage of pay tied to long-term incentives.

A similar heavy emphasis on performance and a need to balance long- and short-term incentives can be seen in the pay of orchestrators/producers (see Figure 7–3). Here again, the balance between short- and

Figure 7–3

How the New Leaders Are Paid

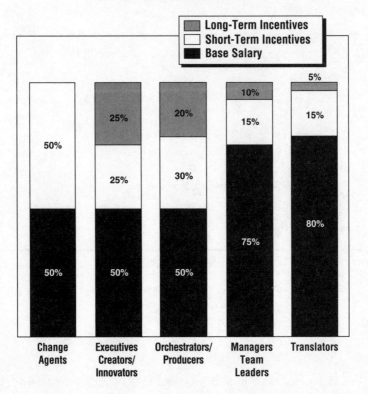

long-term incentives should be determined by the specific roles of the leaders. If they are responsible for the development of a new product, more emphasis probably should be placed on annual incentives. If, on the other hand, they are involved in the development of a broad new business venture, longer-term performance is critical, and thus long-term incentives become more important.

Although performance-based pay for change agents tends to place more emphasis on short-term incentives, here too the need for balance arises. Change agents involved in narrowly defined initiatives are better served by incentives with emphasis on short-term performance, since such leaders are responsible for realizing generally immediate goals. Indeed, come the long term, such leaders often are long gone—having "changed" themselves out of a job and moved on to other challenges. Incentive programs for these change agents typically include very large annual plans based on key milestones for the change, such as the redesign of work in a certain area, perhaps, or the achievement of a specific level of cost reduction. Frequently, however, an additional—often significant—bonus is given at the conclusion of the program for the risk the individual has assumed.

Change leaders at the top of the organization—those hired gun executives we spoke of earlier—need a better balance of both long- and short-term performance measures. After all, they certainly must achieve specific short-term goals. But at the same time, they also must be concerned about the organization's viability over the long haul. To that end, their compensation profile might appear more like that of the executive in Figure 7–3.

Like the managers they often replace, team leaders usually have far less pay tied to performance—typically only about 25 percent. What has changed, however, are the performance measures. Where managers were typically part of an executive incentive program that emphasized organizational results, team leaders are usually part of an incentive program that involves the entire team. While they still may be eligible for a small long-term incentive based on the organization's performance, their short-term incentive will be based primarily on the results of the team.

Like team leaders, translators typically have a smaller percentage of pay tied to performance. To be effective, their incentives should create some degree of productive tension between short- and long-term performance. They may, for example, be eligible for a short-term incentive tied to their specific market, product, or customers, but also be eligible for a small, long-term incentive based on their bigger contribution to the organization.

AN EMPHASIS ON TOTAL REMUNERATION

It should be clear at this point that while the emphasis on performance is important in leadership compensation, the proper blend of short- and long-term incentives depends on the specific role, responsibility, risks, and expected results of the individual leader. For that reason, when designing reward systems for leaders it is essential that organizations recognize the importance of the total remuneration package in linking leadership to business results.

Traditionally, compensation packages were built around a base salary that was determined by market comparisons. Incentives and benefits and perquisites were added on. A more effective approach is to first consider the total remuneration needed to attract, retain, and motivate a leader, and to work back from that figure to achieve a proper balance between incentives and base pay. Say, for example, that the appropriate level of total remuneration is determined to be $100,000. Based on the expected responsibility, risk, and results, as outlined above, that $100,000 is then divided into short- and long-term incentives, benefits, perquisites, and other elements, including base salary.

It is important to note that after the $100,000 has been divided in this fashion, the individual's base pay could actually be less than that of a peer in a nonleadership role. Although it is highly unlikely, if the leader was promoted from a nonleadership role, he or she could conceivably even experience a drop in base salary. Such an approach can obviously have negative ramifications if not properly communicated, or if those affected don't understand the positive long-term outlook for maximizing their leadership potential along with their pay. True leaders, however, should not be offended at the prosect of a reduction in base pay, as long as they can clearly see that they eventually have significant upside potential in direct proportion to the value of their contributions.

THE IMPORTANCE OF INTRINSIC REWARDS

In developing leadership compensation strategies it also is important to remember that money isn't everything. True leaders often are motivated and influenced as much through intrinsic rewards as they are by extrinsic ones. In the past, these intrinsic rewards have come in the form of traditional perquisites and benefits—a company vehicle, perhaps, or a club membership.

But as the cultures and values of both the organizations and those who work in them change, so too do the intrinsic rewards. Today's leaders, especially those in nontraditional roles, tend to be motivated by—and seek out—nontraditional intrinsic rewards. This might be something as simple as special recognition for an outstanding effort. More frequently, it might be something that makes their personal and/or professional life easier— flex time, special time off, travel, or perhaps some special piece of equipment or technology such as a certain computer or their own lab.

As speed, flexibility, and creativity become increasingly important drivers of organizational success, intrinsic rewards that reduce obstacles or increase efficiency may become even more important, since leaders in such environments tend to have little patience with such hurdles. Consider Ted Selker, the creative genius behind IBM's TrackPoint and a number of other innovations. When Selker wanted to modify an IBM ThinkPad for use with an overhead projector, and the company refused to give him one, he simply bought his own and went on to develop another successful computer application.[11] Leaders such as Selker let little stand in the way of their goals, and are often highly motivated by even the smallest gestures that eliminate such barriers.

One highly successful aerospace company capitalized on that motivation through an unusual, three-tiered incentive program that offered both extrinsic and intrinsic rewards to its research and development teams. On one level, team members shared equally in rewards for achieving key milestones tied to measures such as quality, perceived marketability, and speed. A second level pitted team members with different theoretical orientations against one another, with the member who first arrived at the needed solution or idea "winning" the award. The third level of the incentive program was based on past successes: Each year the organization performed a seven-year "research retrospective," rewarding ideas that at the time of their conception had little known value but later were proven marketable.

Even more creative than the plan itself were the rewards, which could be taken in any combination of cash, stock at a discounted price, and funding for their own research. If the last option was chosen, the award was doubled. In other words, a $40,000 cash award equalled $80,000 in lab or computer time. Since anything team members created was considered the intellectual property of the company, such personal research was welcomed.

THE ULTIMATE GOAL: CULTIVATING PEOPLE, REWARDING PERFORMANCE

Whether they are designed to reward the vice president who is directing a large cross-functional work group charged with developing an important new product, or the employee who is leading a five-person team overseeing quality improvement on the assembly line of a small subsidiary of that corporation, effective leadership compensation strategies must be developed to meet today's changing environment. Yet because of the limited use of such programs, the select and often important group of individuals that they involve, and the fear of creating inequities and potential havoc, many organizations are hesitant to develop new programs or change old ones.

They shouldn't be. Today, leadership competencies are more important than ever, and rewarding those competencies should be an integral part of any organization's reward strategy. After all, designing a dynamic compensation program for leaders is really no different than designing a pay strategy for employees. Once the dynamics of leadership are understood, the same basics apply. In the end it comes down to the alignment of pay with the organization's culture, values, and strategic goals. Ultimately it is about motivating people, and improving and managing their performance.

That is not to say, however, that developing such a strategy is an easy task. Always important, leadership compensation today is also often a highly visible, highly charged issue. Nowhere is that more true than in the area of executive compensation, the subject of our next chapter.

8

Reconsidering Executive Pay

Frequently maligned, often misunderstood, executive compensation remains one of the most controversial issues organizations face today. Critics point to huge salaries, sweetheart incentive programs, and luxurious bundles of benefits and perquisites as symptoms of—and reasons for—many of the excesses and failures of major corporations. The huge compensation packages paid many CEOs are, they say, exorbitant and inequitable, based more on avarice than on accountability or achievement. "Is it not grossly unfair that such favored individuals should earn fifty, one hundred, even two hundred times the average pay of working people who toil away at much less interesting jobs?" asked former Harvard president Derek Bok, in his book *The Cost of Talent*.[1]

Those who defend such high-dollar compensation packages, however, say they are driven not by greed but rather by the competitive demands of the marketplace. Simply put, you get what you pay for. And, if you want the most talented, highest performing individuals to lead your organization, then you must pay, and pay dearly. Those on the receiving end of executive compensation tend to agree. In a Hay survey of more than two hundred CEOs from some of the largest companies in the United States, 86 percent said that they believed less than a quarter of the CEOs of the country's top one thousand companies were overpaid.

Before rushing to any sweeping conclusions about the appropriateness of executive compensation today, it is important to look beyond the most exorbitant examples that continually are showcased by the media and the critics. No doubt such cases exist. But by their extreme nature, they tend to skew the perception that most executives are overpaid. A much more reliable indicator of executive compensation trends can be found in more extensive studies, such as our own annual survey of more than five thousand executives, which reveals a wide variety of practices.

For example, according to our survey, a 13 percent increase in incentives coupled with a 4.8 percent increase in base salary raised the total cash compensation of the "typical" CEO 7.6 percent. Add a 9 percent increase in long-term incentives, and that same "typical" CEO received a 10.5 percent increase in annual total direct compensation.[2] These individuals received a much greater increase than that given to employees in the rest of their organizations, which, depending on their level, ranged from 3 percent to 6.7 percent.[3]

But the data also reveal that many CEOs were less fortunate. For starters, as Figure 8–1 shows, the reward structure and actual compensation level depend a lot on the size of the organization, with the CEOs of large organizations making considerably more than those of smaller companies. There are other notable variations as well. A full one third of the organizations surveyed did not increase their CEOs' base salaries, 42 percent of the CEOs saw their bonuses decline, and 25 percent experienced a drop in their total cash compensation. In fact, after factoring in these trends, the median change in total cash awards was only 4.9 percent.

Given the intensity of the arguments and the ammunition available to both sides, it is clear that the executive compensation debate will continue for some time. Certainly there are many highly effective executives deserving of every dollar they earn, given the value they create for the organization. But there are also those who are ineffective and overpaid. And because some of the charges of excess pay ring true—at least in part—most organizations today would be well served to reevaluate their executive compensation programs.

A NEW EMPHASIS ON VALUE AND PERFORMANCE

Where should an organization begin its examination of executive compensation? Certainly market data and comparisons remain an important part

Figure 8–1

Levels of CEO Reward

(All Incumbents)

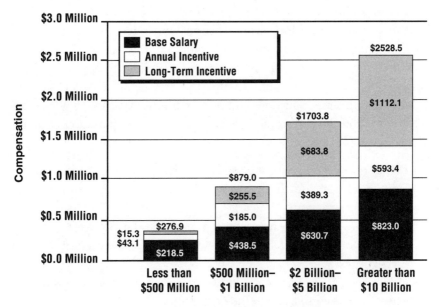

Note: Figures above each bar indicate total direct compensation.

Source: 1994 Hay Executive Compensation Report—General Industry

of the executive compensation equation. After all, the overriding goals of most executive pay strategies are in many ways the same as those of the pay programs for the rest of the organization: attracting, retaining, and motivating talented, high-performing, value-creating people. And, if organizations are to remain competitive—be it at the executive or hourly level—they still need to determine where their position is in relation to the rest of the market.

Yet, while it is certainly appropriate to look at the size, scope, and responsibility of a specific executive position in relation to the market, such comparisons can only go so far in determining an effective reward strategy. As with other areas of compensation today, the primary roles played by internal equity and external competitiveness in driving executive pay are rapidly giving way to issues of performance and value. Rather than merely reexamine the amounts of pay and the vehicles for delivering it (which in many cases are the same vehicles that are used for paying other leaders), organizations first need to determine whether their executive compensation philosophy is reasonable, defendable, and aligned with their organizational culture and values. They also must determine whether the performance of their executives truly adds value to the organization—whether the shareholders are getting a good return on their "CEO investment."

Answers to these questions can best be found by addressing four key elements that should be part of any executive compensation strategy. Theses elements are:

- *Degree of risk*. What are the "stakes of the game" for the executives? How much risk are they expected to assume through performance-based compensation?
- *Performance measures*. Are incentive measures and performance goals realistic? Do they stretch the executive's performance and lead to excellence?
- *Degree of ownership*. How much real or perceived ownership is the executive expected to build in the organization?
- *Total remuneration*. Does the mix of compensation, including base pay, variable pay, and perquisites, send the right messages and create the right culture?

Once all of these issues have been answered, the organization can begin the process of refining or rebuilding its executive compensation program.

A GROWING EMPHASIS ON RISK

The concept of paying executives based on their performance is not a new one. If you were to ask most corporate boards, they would tell you that they have been tying executive pay to performance for years. The executives would no doubt agree. In fact, in our CEO survey, 60 percent of the respondents said that more than three fourths of the CEOs at the one thousand largest U.S. companies were paid based on their performance.

They are correct—up to a point. Many organizations traditionally *have* emphasized performance, usually through some sort of bonus or short-term incentive program. One failure of such strategies, unfortunately, is that while they paid a premium for success, there was very little downside risk. Granted, a CEO might not have taken home a huge bonus at the end of a mediocre year. Still, he had a hefty base salary that was untouched, along with a very comfortable benefits package, not to mention his perquisites.

Only in the past few years have organizations begun to understand that performance-based rewards pack a much stronger motivational message when there is a substantial element of risk involved. To that end, a growing number of organizations are creating executive compensation programs that are embedded with true risk. As investor Warren Buffett notes in the annual report of his holding company, Berkshire Hathaway Inc.: "It has become fashionable at public companies to describe almost every compensation plan as aligning the interest of management with those of shareholders. In our book, alignment means being a partner in both directions, not just on the upside. Many 'alignment' plans flunk this basic test, being artful forms of 'heads I win, tails you lose.' "[4]

In an effort to achieve such true alignment, many organizations have "raised the stakes" for their executives by increasing the percentage of total direct compensation that is based on performance. When Kmart Corporation hired CEO Floyd Hall in an effort to bolster its sagging performance, it linked the new executive's compensation tightly to the organization's performance. In addition to his $1 million base salary and options to buy 3.45 million shares of stock, Hall receives 500,000 shares of restricted stock and a bonus of $1 million a year if Kmart achieves its performance goals.[5]

Other organizations are taking similar approaches. Just how much pay is put at risk varies, of course, from organization to organization, depending on a number of issues, including industry and size. According to our research, for example, the percentage of total compensation that is tied to such incentives tends to increase dramatically for the higher paid executives. (See Figure 8–2.)

How well do such performance-based compensation strategies work? The answer really depends on both the type of incentives used, and the performance measures that are tied to them. Our research, for example, shows a direct correlation between the pay of CEOs and their performance—in terms of annual profits.[6] As Figure 8–3 shows, overall CEO compensation rose when profits increased, and declined when they dropped. While such linkage may be important, it doesn't address two

Figure 8–2

Mix of Total Direct Compensation

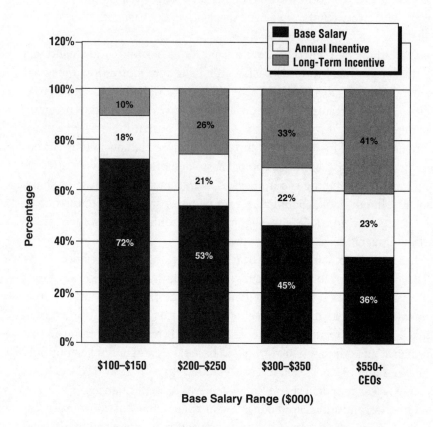

Source: 1994 Hay Executive Compensation Report—General Industry

critical issues: First, whether the measures—in this case profits—are a true judge of performance; and second, what the impact is of the CEO's compensation on long-term performance.

DETERMINING THE RIGHT MEASURES

Many organizations are finding that the traditional methods of measuring performance are no longer aligned with their cultures or business strategies. Simple accounting measures such as return on investment, for example,

Figure 8–3

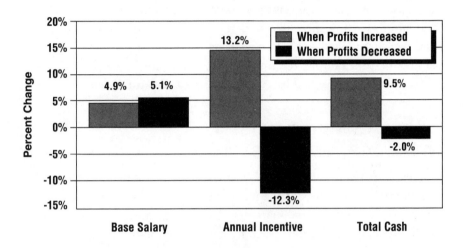

Median Percent Change in CEO Compensation
(Same Incumbents)

Source: 1994 Hay Executive Compensation Report—General Industry

tend to overemphasize one aspect—albeit an important aspect—of the organization's equation for success. But such measures do not fully capture the much more complex dynamics of today's organization.

Functional organizations, for example, need to measure reliability as it is perceived by its markets, not as it is perceived by its own financial department. Process organizations must measure performance in terms of quality and customer satisfaction. Time-based organizations, which tend to emphasize speed to market, must measure performance in terms of its ability to capture new markets. And networks, of course, must measure the success of their ventures or enterprises.

To broaden their performance perspective, many organizations are turning to more comprehensive economic measures that strike at the heart of their strategic intent—measures such as economic value added (EVA), and market share and dominance. These measures not only provide a more accurate indication of performance, but when tied with the appropriate incentives, go far in balancing the interests of the organization, its shareholders, and its executives.

Such measures, of course, can be linked to a variety of incentives. Take, for example, a typical stock option plan. In the past, such a plan might have been linked to return on equity. In today's organization, depending on the culture and business strategy, it might be based on market share. Incorporating these new, more dynamic, more relevant measures does not mean, however, that organizations should suddenly begin ignoring the traditional accounting measures that they have long depended on. Such measures should instead be used as incentive plan "triggers." An incentive plan could, for example, require that a certain return on equity must be achieved before any award based on other measures can be granted.

CREATING OWNERSHIP AND INVESTOR/ORGANIZATION BALANCE

Whatever the measures, recent history has shown that merely linking pay to performance or increasing the mix of performance-based, at-risk variable compensation provides no guarantee that an organization's performance will improve, especially over the long haul. As a number of organizations discovered during the 1980s, executive compensation plans that emphasize maximizing short-term returns, as many did in that decade, wind up satisfying the institutional investor at the expense of the company.

Although the business failures and takeovers that often resulted from this shortsighted strategy may have appeared to be the result of some sort of conspiracy among executives and shareholders, the real culprits, more often than not, were compensation strategies that failed to support the agency theory that is at work in the upper echelons of most organizations.

As we explained in the previous chapter, most executives are in reality agents rather than owners. As such, they tend to have different objectives than the owners—usually to maintain the status quo. To shift those objectives so that they are more aligned with those of the owners, these agents should assume more risk, be afforded a longer decision-making horizon, and be compensated to a great extent as if they were owners. (This view of executives, by the way, strikes at the heart of the argument that executive compensation should be limited to a certain multiple of the compensation paid the top employees. It should be clear that, while there is a need for reasonableness, the ability of an executive to direct the business and impact its performance over a sustained period cannot be relegated to such a simple formula.)

Until recently, such ownership alignment was created primarily through relatively simple, nonrestricted stock options. Although such programs had the potential to create true ownership and risk, there was usually very little of either. Instead, since executives were not required to hold onto the stock for any length of time, they tended to act like any other investor who was seeking short-term growth, rather than true owners, who are more interested in long-term performance. As a result, they would unload their stock as quickly as they got it, or hold it just long enough to realize a reasonable profit from the organization's short-term performance—performance that they played an important role in achieving. Needless to say, such motivation and the resulting behavior did little to create long-term organizational viability and value that could weather the inevitable changes in the market.

What most organizations hadn't yet realized was that performance is not an annual issue and that compensation programs that generate huge incentive payouts based solely on annual performance miss the mark. The critical issue is actually one of long-term, *sustained* performance. Seeing the error of their ways, those organizations that have been fortunate enough to survive have begun shifting the emphasis of their executive compensation programs to long-term incentive programs that generate true risk. That's not to say, however, that annual performance should be ignored. It is still critical. But the rewards for that short-term performance should, at least in part, be deferred—perhaps for up to five years—after which the viability and sustainability of the executive's performance can more accurately be assessed.

The critical issue that organizations must wrestle with is creating a certain level of productive tension between maximizing annual performance and the creation of long-term value. When a choice must be made, however, the plan should reinforce the longer-term value. What form such incentives should take is up for debate. As Figure 8–4 shows, organizations today are using a variety of long-term incentives. Whether or not they are right for your organization should depend not on their popularity in the marketplace, but on whether or not they can support your organization's culture and values, and whether they can help you achieve your long-term business strategy.

A number of organizations have begun developing executive compensation programs that combine some of these more dynamic incentives and measurements. One of the most highly publicized is that of Michael Eisner, CEO of the Walt Disney Company. Under his 1989 employment agreement, Eisner receives two percent of the company's profits beyond a predetermined return on capital. How Eisner achieves that goal is left up to him.[7]

Figure 8–4

Long-Term Incentive Plans

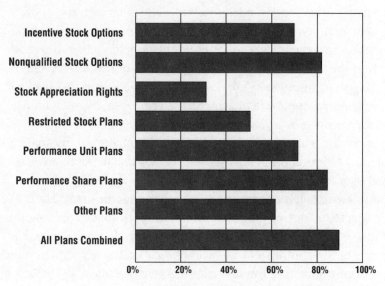

Percent of Eligible Executives Receiving Awards

Source: 1994 Hay Executive Compensation Report—General Industry

If Disney's performance is any indication—in 1995, *Fortune Magazine* ranked it as one of the ten most admired companies in the country—this trend of emphasizing performance-based rewards by putting more executive pay at risk and increasing the use of long-term incentives and more comprehensive measures will, we believe, continue in the coming years. And, while it won't silence the critics, it should increase the level of accountability and performance—legitimate issues that fueled the debate over executive excess in the first place.

Indeed, board members themselves may soon find their pay linked more closely to the organization's performance and the interests of its shareholders. A commission formed by the National Association of Corporate Directors recently unveiled a plan that urged companies to consider paying directors primarily in stock, to establish substantial stock ownership guidelines, and to abolish all benefits programs for board members because they "often reward longevity rather than performance."[8]

BENEFITS AND PERQUISITES:
MORE COMPLEX, BUT STILL USEFUL

Of course no debate over the merits of executive compensation is complete without some discussion of benefits and perquisites. That these important elements of executive compensation are often maligned should come as no surprise. Because they have not been viewed as an integral element of many compensation programs, but rather as lower-profile, less-scrutinized extras, they have been abused by some executives. Read any story about executive excess and you are sure to find a reference to some potentially damning "perk," be it the private jet, the island retreat, or the limo.

Certainly the annals of business are filled with stories of executives who have been undone by greed, characters who abused organizational power to gain personal pleasure, and in the process gave perks a bad name. But if used properly, benefits and perquisites can be effective, economically sound tools for attracting, rewarding, and retaining those high-performing individuals that are so demanded by organizations today.

Like the rest of the organizational paradigm, perquisites have changed significantly over the past few years, primarily in response to the changing tax code. The Deficit Reduction Act of 1984 (DEFRA) required that most perquisites be included when calculating the tax on employee income. Yet only two years later, the Tax Reform Act of 1986 reduced the maximum tax rate from 50 percent to 33 percent, significantly lowering the employee's tax cost of various perquisites.

More recently, the Omnibus Budget Reconciliation Act of 1993 reduced from $235,840 to $150,000 the annual compensation that could be considered in determining an executive's qualified retirement plan. In essence, the act limited the level of compensation that could be counted in determining an executive's retirement benefits. The 1993 act also eliminated the deduction for dues for clubs used primarily for business purposes, and cut entertainment deductions by 50 percent.

As a result of such legislation, many organizations are modifying their executive benefits and perquisite packages. In light of the 1993 act, for example, many employers have begun implementing nonqualified supplemental executive retirement programs or SERPs. These plans, which unlike the more traditional qualified plans are not government approved or protected, and in most cases are taxed only on receipt of the benefits, offer executives—especially those not far from retirement—a supplemental avenue for accumulating capital without incurring tax-related penalties.[9]

Such legislation also has taken its toll on perquisites, which, as they have become taxable, have lost much of their lustre. Still, they remain an attractive, important element of executive compensation, in part because of the status they connote. As Figure 8–5 shows, among the more popular executive benefits and perquisites today are cars and car allowances, mobile telephones, and financial and tax counseling. This last one, although popular with executives, cannot be justified by many organizations because of its high cost and potential liabilities.

Country and luncheon club memberships also continue to be popular, although these perquisites are being scrutinized by many companies to ensure that they are being utilized for the proper purposes and remain aligned with the organization's culture and values. Shifting cultures and values have also sped the decline of individual life insurance policies, such as key person plans, which reinforce the outdated belief that certain individuals are irreplaceable.

Also disappearing are the golden parachutes that were so popular in the 1980s, which many organizations have replaced with employment contracts and severance pay programs. Such hefty and frequently questionable escape vehicles simply don't fit today's business climate in which executives live and die by their performance, and in which mergers, acquisitions, organizational restructuring, and short tenures are the norm. Indeed, in today's business climate, such plush escape vehicles raise red flags among most shareholders. The disclosure, for example, that the former president and chief executive of W. R. Grace & Company, J. P. Bolduc, had left with a $20 million severance package that included the buyback of $12.2 million worth of stock he owned, led several shareholders to file lawsuits against Grace's board.[10] Ironically, Bolduc reportedly left Grace after clashing with the company's chairman, J. Peter Grace, in part over perquisites the chairman had received. According to The Wall Street Journal, even after his retirement as CEO, Grace continued to receive $165,000 annually for full- and part-time nursing care, $200,000 for security guards, $74,000 to maintain a New York apartment, and a full-time cook.[11]

Many organizations are avoiding such potentially damaging incidents by getting out of the perquisite business. In their place, they are providing ex-

Figure 8–5

Benefits and Perquisites Prevalence

	Percentage		
Insurance programs	**1994**	**1992**	**1990**
Executive group life insurance	24	23	20
Split dollar insurance	11	11	9
Key person life insurance	11	13	13
Executive long-term disability	21	23	18
Waiver of insurance waiting periods	10	10	13
Medical expense reimbursement	13	15	15
Physical examinations	46	49	51
Excess personal liability insurance	8	9	10
Executive retiree medical	5	6	—
Nonqualified programs			
Deferred compensation	36	34	34
Supplemental retirement plans	38	38	38
Employment guarantees			
Employment contracts	37	36	31
"Golden parachutes"	18	21	24
Executive severance pay practice	39	38	31
Travel-related perquisities			
Company aircraft	18	18	16
Paid spouse travel expense	20	19	20
Company cars/car allowance	71	69	69
Chauffeur	11	12	12
Mobile car telephones	39	33	25
Executive parking	47	48	45
Other perquisites and benefits			
Executive vacation schedule	35	32	38
Club memberships			
Athletic club	18	20	19
Country club	33	33	38
Luncheon club	26	27	34
Executive dining room	11	12	15
Personal financial counseling/ tax preparation	32	33	35
Personal legal services	6	5	6
Executive flexible benefits plan	4	3	—
Apartments/houses/suites	5	—	—

Note: All percentages based on the number of respondents to each perquisites practice.

Source: 1994 Hay/Huggins Benefits Database

ecutives with a commensurate value in compensation, and are allowing them to create their own perquisite programs.

It should be apparent by now that, like the rest of the compensation puzzle, executive benefits and perquisites to a large extent depend on the organization's culture. In the functional organizations, perquisites tend to be utilized only at the top of the organization, but are not excessively large or overly emphasized. Their use drops in process cultures, which emphasize teamwork and a certain sense of equality, even at the top of the organization. In time-based and network organizations, however, they become an extremely important part of the compensation package. In both cultures, the high-performing "stars," who come together for a specific project or venture, demand perquisites. They are, after all, often putting it all on the line—their talent and expertise, their time, their careers—and they expect something more for that extra effort they make and the risks they take.

As cultures continue to change, so will the emphasis on executive benefits and perquisites. As rigid hierarchies continue to disappear and organizations become even flatter, perquisites in particular will tend to be utilized in much more targeted ways and for specific purposes. Yet for those individuals who give extraordinarily of their time and talent, and who at the same time are given an extraordinary amount of risk and responsibility, the rewards will be extraordinary.

Such carefully tailored approaches already are in place in more forward-thinking organizations. For example, partners at Goldman, Sachs & Company, the prestigious investment banking partnership, are expected to work long hours, sacrifice their personal lives, assume a high degree of risk—in short, give their all to the organization—and then retire early, often by the age of fifty. For that, they collect salaries of about $200,000 a year, not a lot for such a high-performing Wall Street firm. At the same time, however, they are allocated a share of the firm's profits, which must be reinvested in Goldman until they retire. The result: Despite their relative short partnership tenure, they can count on nest eggs of at least $10 million when they retire.[12] The compensation strategy not only rewards their extraordinary efforts, but reinforces the pressure on sustained performance.

Such a program may at first sound overly generous, or even excessive. But on closer examination, it may be a very appropriate reward, given the nature of the organization. The Goldman strategy in fact squarely addresses those questions that must ultimately be asked: Is the compensation program truly aligned with the organization's culture and goals? Does it, in the final analysis, add value to the organization?

ACHIEVING THE RIGHT TOTAL REMUNERATION MIX

An effective executive compensation strategy, of course, requires more than an attractive benefits and perquisites package, or a well thought out variable pay initiative. To best support the goals of the shareholders and the organization, executive compensation, like any other level of compensation, should encompass a total reward package—base salary, incentives, benefits, and perquisites.

Finding the right mix of those elements is a critical part of developing a sound strategy. While performance and ownership should, to a large extent, drive most executive compensation strategies today, their role and the vehicles used to carry them vary depending on an organization's values, goals, and culture.

As we have already noted, executive compensation is not immune from the forces of shifting cultures. Although the culture/compensation alignment issue may not be as dramatic as it is at the lower levels of the organization, there is a definite need to shift the emphasis of an executive compensation program as the culture changes.

At the executive level, however, the alignment strategy is somewhat unique: Rather than play a supporting role as it does at other levels of the organization, compensation here should help *lead* the cultural change. Executives should not be rewarded for merely conforming to the values and goals of their current cultures, but should be paid for their roles in leading the charge through the change process and toward the organization's new vision. They should, in essence, be establishing the right behavior and values for the other levels of the organization to follow.

To ensure that the organization is maintaining the proper alignment and is really getting what it pays for, it must first have established exactly what it *is* paying for through a clear executive compensation philosophy and policy. That philosophy should be tailored to and driven by the organization's culture, mission, and strategic objectives, while of course complying with the current tax code. (Unfortunately, many organizations continue to get these steps backwards, designing executive compensation around the tax laws rather than around the goals and interests of the business.)

The philosophy should address why, what, and how the organization wants to reward. And it should be included in a written compensation policy that also establishes the pay processes, such as when and how merit increases, incentive payouts, and bonus payments are distributed.

In establishing the philosophy, policy, and processes, the organization should use credible survey data so that it knows where it stands in relation to the market in which it must compete for top executive talent. But at the same time, it should take a hard look at where the organization is going— its business goals, its strategies for getting there, and the type and cost of talent it needs for both the short- and long-term journey. It also must honestly assess its willingness and ability to pay for the level of talent it wants to attract and the performance it wants that talent to achieve.

In addition to its primary role in establishing an effective reward strategy, a carefully designed, well-documented compensation policy can be highly effective in informing the executive team as to what is expected of it, in terms of both performance and rewards. But beyond that, it is an excellent tool to use in educating boards, shareholders, employees, and— when the need arises—the public. It also can provide an excellent first line of defense should critics attack the executive compensation program as being excessive.

The compensation strategy and policy should be written, administered, and annually reviewed by an independent compensation committee rather than the full board of directors. To be effective, this committee should be small—four to seven members—and include the board chairman as well as chairman of the audit or finance committee. Where outside consultants are used, they should clearly work for the compensation committee.

AN ISSUE OF RESPONSIBILITY, ACCOUNTABILITY, AND RETURN ON INVESTMENT

Consultants, of course, are not immune from attack in the debate over executive compensation. Consultants are, some critics claim, co-conspirators in the scheme to make executives ever richer—highly paid "yes persons" who tell boards and executives only what they want to hear. Graef Crystal, the reformed executive compensation consultant who has made a second career of attacking the excesses of executive pay, goes so far as to say that while he doesn't believe the majority of compensation consultants are prostitutes, "the system more or less forces them to please their clients if they are to eat."[13]

No doubt there are those consultants who have, along with certain boards and executives, given executive compensation a bad name. But they are the exceptions. And, while Crystal makes some excellent points in his criticism of executive compensation, he misses the mark when it comes to blaming outside experts. Consultants should offer ethically and economically sound advice. But ultimately, the responsibility and accountability must rest with the board.

The board must take responsibility for selecting and retaining the right people—the right "agents" for its executive team. It must take responsibility for establishing a compensation philosophy that is aligned with its mission, values, and culture. It must be accountable for following that philosophy.

In the final analysis, the executive compensation debate will not be resolved through more legislation, additional surveys, or yet more criticizing and philosophizing. The real answers will be found in sound, responsible business decisions about executive pay—decisions that result in a fair and reasonable return on investment for the organization, and high, sustained value creation for its shareholders and agent-executives.

9
Pay and the Changing Role of Human Resources

Richard Trickett, vice president of organization design and worldwide remuneration for Holiday Inn Worldwide was talking to us about the massive changes his organization had gone through in the past five years as it transformed itself into a high-performance service organization. He talked about changes in Holiday Inn's culture, the need to develop new leadership competencies, and the new compensation program that was implemented to support those changes.

Trickett spoke fervently about the challenges that his organization had faced before ultimately achieving success. But when the subject turned to human resources, there was even more passion in his voice. HR, he said, had basically become a second-class citizen. "We were caught in the middle—facilitators of senior management on one hand, the advocates of the employees on the other. We were just servicing the company and the compensation plan, making sure the vehicle followed the road map.

"But when the organization changed, that old paradigm went out the window very quickly. Suddenly we had to take a share of responsibility for the organization's performance—its profits, its growth. We had to understand not just compensation, but broader business issues."

205

Although he may not have recognized it as he spoke, Trickett had just eloquently described one of the most important—and most frequently overlooked—aspects of developing an effective compensation strategy: the integration of compensation with other human resource processes and the changing but critical role of human resources and compensation professionals.

HUMAN RESOURCES: HINDRANCE OR HELP

It should come as no surprise that as new compensation programs are created, other critical HR processes are frequently overlooked completely or they are left until everything else is in place. They are, after all, usually viewed as ancillary, bureaucratic functions of a highly bureaucratic department. Typically, one group of HR people handles compensation, another benefits, and yet a third training and development. So, why should any of these specialized experts be concerned about the issues outside of their bailiwick?

To add to the problem, traditional human resource departments, as Trickett observed, are not considered major players by the rest of the organization. Sadly, in many cases they have become the proverbial Rodney Dangerfields of the organization, getting little or none of the respect they think they deserve. In just how low esteem they are held can be seen in a recent study we did with a number of managers from both within and outside the human resource departments. Both groups described the HR function as having little influence within their organizations. Non-HR managers went even further, saying that human resources was not only a nonplayer in the change process, but also was frequently an impediment to effective organizational change.

The perception that human resources is the last bastion of the "organizational old school," filled with traditionalists who care more about rules and regulations than they do about people, performance, or business results, unfortunately is reinforced by some human resources professionals themselves. In a recent Hay survey of more than 1,500 human relations professionals, only 30 percent said that reengineering work processes was a top priority. Even fewer—9 percent—said that asking employees about the company and their work was an important objective. And only 8 percent thought adapting to workforce diversity was a burning issue. Those are interesting perceptions, considering the growing importance of reengineering to improve business results, and the increased importance of people and the valuable diversity they bring to the organization.

A NEED TO SHIFT THE HR ROLE

Our research confirmed what we had long suspected: The traditional human resources department is frequently a major barrier to the development of a new compensation program. And, if an organization is really serious about creating a new, more dynamic culture that makes a positive impact on business, it needs to begin shifting the focus and role of the HR function long before the new pay program is implemented.

In today's organization, the myriad of narrowly defined human resource boxes, housing narrowly defined functions, must give way to a continuous series of processes that address how people enter the organization, how they evolve within that organization, how their performance can be maximized, and how finally they exit. Under this new paradigm, the human resource function must be viewed not from the HR professional's perspective, but from the employees' and customers' perspectives: What do the employees need to help them become more productive, valuable organizational assets? What do the customers—frequently line managers—need to help them more effectively lead and utilize these important human assets?

Ultimately, of course, the departmentalized, highly functional human resources structure must give way to a smaller, leaner organization. Human resource processes must be shifted from highly centralized administrative units and become fully integrated into the broader business operations. Line managers should handle many of the activities that formerly were handled by the HR department. In some cases, certain HR activities may even be more effectively and economically outsourced.

One organization that effectively decentralized its HR processes around the issue of compensation was the University of Texas Medical Branch at Galveston, which, although it had nine thousand employees in four schools, two institutes, seven hospitals, and 109 outpatient facilities, had no formal pay program. Under a new decentralized compensation strategy, administrators have the capability—within institutional guidelines—to develop salary programs that support their specific goals and objectives. Rather than controlling compensation, the HR professionals act as consultants, helping the various departments find solutions to their compensation needs.

Like compensation, the human resource processes must also be consistent with the culture they support. For instance, in the process organization, the line managers become the internal customers of the human resource department, and take over the day-to-day execution of many HR processes, such as performance assessment and pay. To best serve these managers, the compensation professionals must part with their centralized offices and spend most of their time in the field, on their customers' turf, meeting their changing needs. They may even be assigned to specific divisions or groups.

In the time-based organization, line management will claim even greater ownership of the compensation program, fully controlling such processes as the selection, development, and compensation of their employees. In such an atmosphere, compensation/HR professionals become true internal consultants. Working behind the scenes, they provide the tools and expertise that management needs to make sound HR decisions. If necessary, they can help facilitate the decision-making process.

The human resources consulting role becomes even more extreme in the network organization. Here, because of the diversity of players, values, and employment agreements, the HR professional must be creative, highly flexible, and be able to rapidly deliver a variety of solutions in an atmosphere that is both varied and chaotic. Such individuals must have the ability to quickly develop "special deals" that can effectively pull a network together on very short notice.

At first, this dramatic shift in roles may sound unappealing to HR professionals. They are, or so it may appear, losing both position and power as many of their current duties are given to line managers, outsourced, or embedded in the system. Actually, just the opposite should be true. Rather than continue their roles of administrative housekeepers and organizational bit players, the HR professionals, if fully utilized, become key strategists in the business process. If, on the other hand, they refuse to budge, and cling tenaciously to the traditional structures and strategies, they will be seen as part of the problem, and will indeed be left out of the process.

At Holiday Inn, HR has become an integral part of the organization. It took some effort. As Trickett says, human resources had to "get out of a defensive mode and an HR frame of mind and into a business frame of mind." HR professionals had to demonstrate where they could add value, and provide expertise that resulted in better work.

Today human resources at Holiday Inn strives to be viewed as an equal business partner, providing just as much meaningful input as finance, marketing, and the other key business processes. Says Trickett: "We are invited to the table when decisions are being made, and if we are not, we should demand that we be there."

LINKING COMPENSATION WITH OTHER HR PROCESSES

HR professionals, of course, aren't going to be invited to the table unless they have something to offer. For the compensation professional, that means understanding not only the specifics of today's more dynamic pay strategies, but how those strategies must be linked to other human resource processes.

We have already discussed in detail the need to consider compensation within the broader context of the organization—its business strategies, its work cultures, its future vision. Equally important is the need to consider compensation within the context of other human resource processes. As Figure 9–1 shows, this includes the full range of performance management issues, including:

• *How work is designed*. As we have already noted, work today is shifting from very specific, narrowly defined jobs, to broader roles that encompass a wider range of responsibilities. It also is moving from a total focus on individual performance to at least some emphasis on the efforts of groups and teams.

• *How people are selected*. These expanded roles and responsibilities often require new skills and competencies. Finding the people with these competencies and capabilities is critical to the organization's ongoing success.

• *How employees are developed*. Training and development programs, always important, are even more critical during this time of change. New skills and competencies, new behaviors, even new values, are seldom acquired through osmosis. They must be taught, developed, and nurtured.

• *How their performance is measured*. The traditional individual appraisal, typically one-dimensional and less than effective, must be replaced by more comprehensive, dynamic measurement tools that will provide a fair, accurate readout of employee performance.

Figure 9–1

Five Processes That Shape Human Resources System

How these human resources processes, along with compensation, *all* must be integrated can be seen more clearly by examining the steps an organization typically takes as it goes through any major change. Consider, for example, the traditional functional business that is moving toward a more process-oriented culture. Not only must the organization redesign work—in this case probably around cross-functional teams—but it also must rethink which people will be most effective in that team situation. Then it must determine what criteria should be used to select the best people for new roles, and what training and development will be necessary to bring them up to speed—a course in negotiation and conflict resolution, perhaps. Finally, it must establish a new method to more accurately assess performance in those new roles—perhaps incorporating feedback from both internal and external customers as well as other members of the team.

TIMING THE OTHER HR PROCESSES

Like the compensation process to which they are linked, the timing of the selection, development, and assessment processes within the greater change process is critical. Typically, these processes should begin once work has been redesigned, processes reengineered, new roles created, and old ones eliminated (the change management issues we discussed in Chapter 3), but before the compensation program is designed.

The reason for this sequencing is simple: Like compensation, these processes can support and reinforce change, but cannot drive it. All too often organizations facing a crisis try to initiate change by creating new selection criteria, revamping their training program, or implementing a new assessment process. They reason that a different kind of employee, some new training on teams, or a performance assessment tool will transform their organization. Instead, they find they are facing the same issues. The new messages they are sending through the new processes they have implemented are simply adding confusion to an already chaotic situation.

SELECTION

Once work and roles have been redesigned, the first of these processes that should be examined is selection. Ideally, the newly created roles should be filled by individuals who best exhibit the competencies that are needed in the new culture. Where the old organization may have favored individuals performing narrowly defined, highly repetitive tasks, for example, the transformed organization might require individuals who can move from one task to another with ease, can make sound decisions on their own, and can work well with other members of a team.

In most organizations, there is a tendency to try to retrain and redevelop current employees to fit the new model. Certainly there are many employees who can, through training and development, adapt to a new culture. And most organizations want to help them make the transition. But it is sometimes more efficient and economically effective to select new people for the new roles rather than try to retrain and develop current employees. Obviously determining the right balance between retraining employees and selecting new ones who already have the necessary skills and competencies is a critical issue that organizations must face. Their decision must be determined by the culture, the amount of resources—both financial and human—the degree of change, and the speed with which it must be implemented.

Trickett's organization, Holiday Inn, took such an approach when it transformed its North American headquarters in Atlanta into a more aggressive, service-oriented organization. Holiday Inn first identified eight competencies it believed were critical to its future success. These competencies, which ranged from creative problem solving to customer service orientation, were then used in the initial screening of applicants for headquarters roles. Ultimately, of approximately 1,000 jobs available in Atlanta, fewer than 300 were filled by people with the capabilities and willingness to make the move from the old Memphis headquarters. In addition to the 100 or so jobs people already held in the Atlanta worldwide headquarters group, some 630 were filled from outside the organization. According to Trickett, the process has been highly successful. After three years, turnover is well below local market averages—a sign that the selection methods were effective. "We feel we ended up with a very different employment population than we had started with," Trickett says. "When you hire from these competencies, you hire very motivated people."

LEADERSHIP SELECTION AND SUCCESSION PLANNING

As high-performing as they may be, even the most well-selected, best-developed employees still need effective leadership. Attempting to change employee behavior while maintaining old leadership values will quickly be seen as duplicity, and will most certainly cripple the entire change initiative. Obvious though this may appear, many organizations resist putting change initiatives into the hands of an aggressive, forward-looking leader, and instead pass the task off to one of the organization's "old" leaders—typically someone they view as expendable, a vice president, perhaps, who is a couple of years from retirement and has nothing better to do. After all, they reason, as important as this change may be, the organization still has to operate a successful business.

It is a logical assumption, perhaps, but flawed. The "old" leaders are probably averse to both risk and change, and more than likely will be dragging along the very organizational baggage that needs to be jettisoned. And, because they probably continue to act and behave as they always have, their value as role models is at best nonexistent, at worst detrimental. Although few organizations have the courage to do it, if they truly want to shift their culture, they need leaders with not only a vision of the future, but also the new values, competencies, and expectations that they want to instill throughout the organization. If the organization is going to be successful in achieving its desired state, it must select and develop leaders who, at all levels of the organization, model the new values, core competencies, and desired behaviors. For that reason, early in the change process, along with the creation of a new selection strategy for employees, the organization must begin to establish new criteria for selecting leaders along with a succession strategy for developing them and placing them in key roles.

In the face of mounting competition, Kaiser Permanente, the giant and highly successful health maintenance organization pioneer, determined it needed to begin shifting its culture and enhancing performance. It also determined that achieving such change would require unprecedented leadership throughout the organization. To create such a high level of leadership it modified the process by which it selected and developed its regional presidents. At the heart of the new process is a leadership effectiveness model that identifies the major roles and responsibilities of these critical leaders, the expected performance outcomes, and the competencies necessary to achieve them. Among the required attributes are the ability to lead the organization through the major changes rampant in the health care industry, and the ability to develop future leaders.

TRAINING AND DEVELOPMENT

In many organizations, training programs have taken on a life of their own. Any time a new organizational initiative is implemented, or so it seems, a new training program is also started. The result, all too often, is the generation of a little knowledge and a lot of conflict and chaos, as employees struggle to keep up with the latest trend or program without understanding how it fits with all the other changes and training they've undergone while trying to do their job.

To avoid such confusion, it is important that, rather than simply add another raft of courses, the organization carefully assess its current training program to determine what works, what should be eliminated, and what should be added to support the new culture. To make that assessment, the organization needs a baseline understanding of employees' current skills and knowledge in relation to the new competencies, behaviors, and expected outcomes.

Training doesn't have to be approached as a massive, company-wide process. Rather, it can start small, in a key division, perhaps, or in parts of the operation that are noticeably different from the rest of the organization, and which will have to make greater transitions to the new culture. We have found that in many cases the best approach is a 1990s version of on-the-job training. Typically, certain key roles and jobs within the organization are natural training centers—points at which employees can gain experience and learn behaviors critical to their—and the organization's—future success. These jobs and roles are far too valuable to be maintained as permanent career positions, filled by people who cannot advance. Instead they should be identified and used as temporary developmental positions—three- to four-year assignments during which time the employee or manager learns the necessary competencies and behaviors needed for broader roles. These "enterprise roles" are critical, and must be carefully identified and wisely used. Ultimately, they become the crucibles in which the new competencies and behaviors are forged.

Consider, for example, the general management positions in organizations that have flattened their structures, eliminating a number of supporting management positions. Formerly career-level jobs, these positions, where managers first learn how to integrate a number of complex business processes, become "learning" roles for future vice presidents and organizational leaders.

Such positions should be identified at all levels of the organization, and integrated with the formal training program. Indeed, if an organization spends millions of dollars on training, yet fails to determine what is really being learned through certain jobs such as these, it is missing the mark.

That is not to say, however, that formal training and course work are not important. They can be. But only if they are tied to the new behaviors and competencies that the organization wants to develop, and are timed to support them. Kaiser Permanente, for example, didn't simply create a new set of expectations for its regional leaders and then walk away, leaving those leaders on their own to survive or fail. Instead, it is continually building on its state-of-the-art leadership initiatives that include both developmental centers and "virtual training" through interactive software.

Like the other human resource processes, training must be carefully timed to support, not drive, other changes. Otherwise it will be at best ineffective, at worst damaging. We once were asked to provide communications training for a large, very formal, highly functional organization that wanted to develop a strong process culture with lots of interaction between individuals and teams. The first day of training the employees appeared puzzled. Why, they asked, were we teaching them to write memos and make presentations? After all, they said, their organization frowned on such behavior. In reality the company had made little real progress in changing its culture. The employees continued to operate under the old rules—including seldom putting anything in writing—and the training merely confused them and increased their cynicism.

No matter how effective the new selection and developmental processes, there will always be the difficult process of eliminating, or finding, special roles for those members of the workforce—employees, managers, even top leaders—who simply cannot change their behaviors and develop the competencies needed to move to a new level of superior performance. That does not mean, however, that the organization should summarily "execute" the 15 percent of the workforce that will fall into this category. Such a broad reaction runs the risk of creating too much conformity and reducing diversity below a healthy level. At the same time, however, there must be a realization that not everyone will be able to accept change. Plans must be made for identifying and addressing that segment of the workforce that simply cannot "get with" the new program. In most situations there will be a segment that must be moved out. While this must be done with dignity and sensitivity, nonetheless it must be done, and relatively early in the process. The longer it is avoided, the more disruptive it will be when it finally happens.

PERFORMANCE MANAGEMENT

It is at this point that many organizations attempt to implement their new compensation programs. After all, they have new selection criteria and a new training program. Now, if they really expect the employees to accept the organization's new, highly touted values, take on unfamiliar roles, and behave differently, they need to motivate them with one of those new, dynamic compensation programs.

Well, yes and no. Ultimately they do need to create a reward strategy that is aligned with the new culture they are creating, but not until after they establish a new process for assessing and managing performance. A new culture requires careful monitoring of the organization's return on compensation to ensure that performance is commensurate with pay. Performance management in today's organization, like the other human resources processes, should be based on outcome-focused competencies rather than skills, and should be aligned with and support the organization's culture.

In a functional culture, for example, with its emphasis on individual performance, measuring excellence in individual contributions remains critical. In the process culture, with its emphasis on teamwork and customer service, the measures should center on how well—both as individuals and as team members—employees have served their customers, and how their customers view the level and quality of service they are receiving. In a time-based culture, with its focus on work groups, speed, and cost effectiveness, the emphasis should be on how the individual's performance impacted the group's, as well as how the group performance impacted the business results of the organization or business unit. In the network, the key to judging performance is the impact the members of the network have on the specific venture in which they were involved.

Performance management today involves far more than the traditional assessment process, in which once each year, as per the personnel department's request, supervisors fill out an assessment form and then in a hastily called meeting review it with the employee. Such an approach—which subjectively measures individual skills, objectives, goals, or even personality traits, stresses form over process, and always comes after the fact—is neither a fair nor adequate measure of performance.

To be effective, a process should be developed in which expectations are linked to business objectives, performance is planned, people are motivated and coached, and individual and team results, along with competencies, are rewarded. Such a process should be owned and managed by line managers, not the personnel department, and should include a full range of evaluators. In today's environment, restricting the assessment process to one person—usually the supervisor—is not only shortsighted, but it also limits its value.

Praxair Incorporated, an industrial gas manufacturer, undertook a more dynamic approach to performance management in an effort to reinforce a new culture that emphasized continuous improvement, empowered employees, and encouraged teamwork. In place of its existing appraisal format that was one-way, passive, and perceived by some employees as at times inequitable across departments, Praxair developed a competency-based process that involved three critical steps—performance planning, a joint process done by employee and manager together; performance coaching, an ongoing formal and informal interaction between the employee and manager; and performance review, which emphasized developmental needs and provided a final rating. (See Figure 9–2.) The result was an ongoing process that not only reinforced the organization's new values and improved employee dialogue, but also more fairly and accurately measured performance.[1]

THE 360-DEGREE ASSESSMENT

As a final step in this thorough, balanced approach to performance management, a growing number of organizations are creating what are commonly known as 360-degree assessment processes, in which input is gained from a variety of key people. These frequently include not only supervisors, but peers, subordinates, the employees themselves, and internal and external customers—who might include people in other departments, suppliers, and contractors. In short, anyone who has a stake in or is impacted by that person's performance may be involved in the process.

While such processes have the potential to provide highly accurate measures of development and performance, 360-degree assessment requires more than simply garnering opinions from a few additional people. Like the rest of the performance management process, any assessment tool should measure the development of critical core competencies rather than focus on the skill and knowledge that a person has to acquire. Competencies provide the best platform for the 360-degree assessment because they are research-based, are proven to impact performance, and are behaviorally anchored. To be effective, however, these competencies must be clearly stated and understood by those involved in the evaluation.

The assessment tool also should be designed for simplicity and ease of use. Too often such programs become cumbersome administrative nightmares. They have too many dimensions, and eventually die of their own weight. Because of the inherently complex nature of such assessments, organizations should also consider scrapping the traditional paper-and-pencil approach in favor of a more user-friendly one that incorporates technology that is readily available. Getting input through E-mail, for example, can be far easier, more secure, and less time consuming than burying the evaluators in a blizzard of forms.

Like many organizational changes, the move to a 360-degree assessment process can be a shock for both employees and managers—especially when peers and subordinates are involved in the evaluation process. Peers chosen to be evaluators cannot merely be pals with whom an employee spends breaks. They must be individuals with whom the employee has

Figure 9–2

Performance Management Process

• **Critical goals** • **Professional and managerial competencies**
• **Development plan** • **Weighing of goals and competencies**

• Critical goals • Professional and
managerial competencies
• Development plan • Overall rating
• Final comments • Signatures

• Informal coaching
• Periodic results reviews
• Critical goals • Professional and
managerial competencies
• Development plan

regular business interactions and upon whom the employee has a significant impact.

To help ensure the acceptance of a 360-degree appraisal, the process needs to be clearly communicated to employees. They need to understand more than merely how the new assessment differs from the old. They need to understand the underlying reasons for its use. They need to understand that it is not a sneaky way to get fellow employees to "tattle" on their peers, but rather one aspect of a much bigger change in how all members of the organization work together, support each other's work, and impact the organization.

To alleviate the pain and anxiety that the 360-degree appraisal often creates, some organizations have even begun allowing the employees to select their own evaluators. Still, it is often difficult to gain widespread trust in the process. Many people, after all, are not used to giving or receiving honest input, and may need some training to develop those skills prior to initiating the program. Honeywell Inc.'s air-transport systems unit, for example, spent three years training its employees to deliver constructive feedback. And workers at Eastman Chemical's Tennessee unit must go through one to two years of courses that include topics such as building self-esteem in coworkers, listening, asking for help, and encouraging one another.[2]

The 360-degree appraisal also can play a major role in helping the organization change its culture. Shifting to this more democratic approach sends out a very strong message to employees: They are now integral players on a much bigger team. And their effort—their performance—is critical to the success of that team. No longer can they view themselves purely as individuals, accountable only to themselves and to their supervisors. Everyone, including their peers, has a vested interest in how well they do, and ultimately a voice in judging how well they are performing.

Ultimately, the 360-degree evaluation provides the people-to-people leverage that is not found in traditional performance management processes. Organizations that have implemented 360-degree assessments find that people—employees and managers alike—become not only more productive, but also a little nicer. They are more caring, cooperative, and, ultimately, more trusting. After all, they now live in the same "universe of consequence," where mutual accountability is critical to the success of the organization and everyone in it.

TYING HR TO MISSION: ONE ORGANIZATION'S STORY

Creating such a universe may sound like a formidable challenge for all but the most progressive New Age organizations. The fact is, by incorporating a seamless series of people processes into its culture and strategy, such a universe can be created by even the most traditional organization. Consider the case of one large Catholic health care system. One might argue that a health care system run by a religious order would be the last place to implement massive changes in its people processes. This forward-looking system, however, knew better. If it were to survive both the religious and secular changes that were assaulting its $1.5 billion health care system, it had to take swift and dramatic action.

Like many organizations embroiled in change, it was caught in the crossfire of clashing cultures. On the one hand, it knew it had to embrace some tough, modern business values if it were to succeed in an industry that, with the explosion of managed care, is continually growing more competitive. On the other hand, its leaders knew such success would ring hollow if the organization failed to maintain many of the basic values that had been imbued by the order when it founded the health care organization—values that supported a mission of fidelity, empowerment, stewardship, and excellence.

The balancing act was made even more difficult by the fact that the stakeholders themselves were changing. The order itself, like many today, is dwindling. Only 750 nuns remain. As the elderly members pass on—at the rate of twenty-five or so each year—sadly, no one is there to take their place. Like it or not, ultimately the continued survival of the order's hospitals will have to be placed in the hands of the laity.

The health system determined that if it were to be successful in moving from religious to lay management—if it were to maintain its mission and cultural fabric while embracing new business values—it would have to do so through the transformation of its people systems. Those systems, it was decided, would have to be aligned with the organization's core values, in order to pass those values on to the laity who will eventually take over the organization's reins.

The confluence of mission and margin was clear. The real issue was getting the right performance the right way. As one member of the religious order put it: "We have to get our laity thinking like our nuns. If we don't, we ultimately will lose the essence of who we are."

The organization began by identifying the core competencies of its top one hundred leaders and performers from throughout its eight-hospital system. These were people who best embodied the organization's mission and had a significant impact on the business. It was determined, for example, that stewardship required high degrees of ethical discernment and social and resource accountability. Empowerment, on the other hand, required the ability to lead change and to develop others consistent with this performance value standard.

These core competencies are now being incorporated into the organization's entry, evolution, and exit process. For example, a 360-degree appraisal process is being developed, in which supervisors, peers, and subordinates will provide feedback so that employees can, over time, develop those core competencies that they lack. To help further support the culture shift, these same values and competencies are also being incorporated into the organization's evolving roles. The chief financial officer, for example, can no longer simply be the top number cruncher who traditionally was responsible for an important but narrowly defined set of tasks. In today's change-grow-and-compete environment, the CFO must be responsible for the much broader role of developing new business. The individual in that role will need to understand not only finances, but also the changing, turbulent health care market. He or she will have to perform the role of dealmaker, in addition to his or her more traditional responsibilities.

Ultimately, a new pay process will be developed that will include both base and variable elements, and will be quite different from the old program. Traditional emphasis on external and internal comparisons, for example, will be downplayed, along with merit increases. Instead, people will be paid at what the organization determines is a just rate based on their performance, contribution, and demonstration of core competencies. In addition, an annual incentive plan will be implemented that will be based on the achievement of certain business results and tied closely to a profit-sharing plan.

At the same time that the health system is making these changes it also is decentralizing many of its human resource processes. In the future, its HR professionals will, in effect, operate as consultants, helping the client entities, such as the individual hospitals, with planning and strategy.

LESS EMPHASIS ON ADMINISTRATION

Whenever we discuss with human resources professionals initiatives such as those undertaken by the Catholic health care system, and the need to integrate compensation with other HR processes, not to mention *their* changing role in the equation, the same question is always raised: But what about pay itself? Who is going to administer the compensation program?

The simple answer: everyone—the compensation professional, the line managers, even the employees. Indeed, the administration of many of the pay programs we have discussed should be integrated throughout the organization. We're not talking, however, about administration in the traditional sense. As Figure 9–3 shows, in the organization of old, more than two thirds of a compensation professional's time was spent on routine administrative issues—fielding questions, updating position descriptions, analyzing the market; distributing, retrieving, reviewing, and filing performance appraisals; and collecting, analyzing, and reporting compensation data. Little time was spent on service and delivery issues such as the architecture of the compensation program and vehicles for communicating it. Even less time was spent in strategic planning. Like so many other issues revolving around pay, that equation too must change drastically if an organization is to develop a successful new compensation program. As Figure 9–4 shows, the traditional administrative housekeeping should amount to only about 20 percent of the effort. Instead, the most emphasis should be on service, delivery, and strategic planning.

AN INCREASED EMPHASIS ON AUTOMATION

Much of this shift in balance can be accomplished through automation. Efficient organizations will put data on jobs, competencies, roles, persons, and the market into one system, and will then seamlessly move from one element to another. The advantages of such a system are clear, for example, in the process of developing a position description. Traditionally a line manager would draft the description and send it to a job analyst for expert review. The analyst would then pass it on to a committee to evaluate and price. Finally, after weeks or months, depending on when the committee met and whether additional market data was required, the final draft would be sent back to the manager.

In an automated setting, the manager can simply log onto a PC and, using special software, query similar role or position descriptions or job summaries. If no documentation is available, the manager can complete an on-line questionnaire, from which a matching salary range, band, or level is produced. This can also include an incentive opportunity, as well as the performance indicators. If there are questions about the range, a search of additional data on comparable positions can be made. In a few minutes, the description is complete.

Compensation software isn't limited to the more traditional administrative chores of comparing work and writing job descriptions. We have developed software that allows organizations to create their own innovative measurement tools customized to their specific cultures. Given the increased focus on competencies and performance, this same software also allows organizations to build their own competency models, compare people and jobs to determine the best selection, and then track superior performance.

Such automation can, with the proper security, extend beyond technical and administrative operations. With the right software, for example,

Figure 9–3

Current Emphasis of Compensation

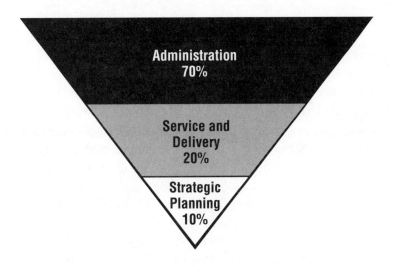

Figure 9–4

Ideal Emphasis of Compensation

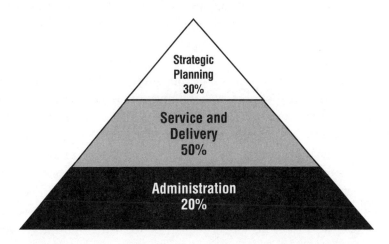

employees logging onto the network can do everything from acquiring routine information on their benefits to checking the performance of their 401(k) plans—even shifting investments if they choose.

MEASUREMENT AND REVIEW STILL CRITICAL

Deemphasizing and automating the administrative aspects of compensation doesn't mean eliminating the ongoing measurement and review of pay programs. Indeed, one of the key roles of the compensation professional in the changing organization should be to provide expertise and guidance in helping the organization determine if in fact it is getting a good return on its investment. Are the high performers actually getting decidedly more pay than the low or even average employees? Or has the organization resumed the far too prevalent "peanut butter" approach in which compensation is spread relatively evenly, no matter what the performance?

Despite the new emphasis on competencies and roles over skills and specific jobs, there is still a need to measure work and make market comparisons. An organization still must make sure it establishes the right touch points within its markets and continually monitors those points. For a functional organization, that means continuing to use relatively standard job measurement, internal equity, and market comparisons to determine how jobs are paid in the markets and where the organization's practices and policies fit. As the organization begins to shift toward one of the new cultures, however, much of that title comparison market data loses its relevance. In its place, new measures must be found to accurately assess the roles and competencies that are unique to specific organizations.

In such organizations some of the more traditional market data can still be utilized to determine base pay, but it must be applied in a different fashion, based on the performance of both individuals and teams. An organization, for example, that has traditionally paid at the 75th percentile for a specific job may choose to pay at the lower 45th percentile for filling a basic role or providing a specific service, increasing pay beyond that point only when the growth in competencies and performance warrants it.

In determining the variable pay aspect of compensation, however, new measures will need to be added to chart performance and the growth of competencies. To establish such measures, accurate survey data is more critical than ever. That doesn't mean that all the survey data to this point must be scrapped. Indeed, many organizations can effectively incorporate established, highly reliable data—such as that found in Hay's Guide-Profile Chart Methodology and database—into new matrices that more accurately capture the values of the new work cultures, be it in terms of work, roles, or team contributions.

Organizations also should continually monitor their programs to make sure that they comply with all regulations concerning equal opportunity, affirmative action, and the like. Just because an organization has chosen to replace its traditional compensation program with the dramatic new performance-based strategy doesn't mean it can ignore compliance with all applicable laws and statutes.

We recommend organizations develop a regular review process, reexamining the pay programs in a quarter to a third of their operations each year. Some organizations may even want to take the review process a step further, and actually set a "sunset" date for their programs, after which they will be terminated unless they are proven to be viable, value-adding processes. That doesn't mean that the entire program should automatically be scrapped on a predetermined date. Rather, it forces the organization to examine its program regularly, and to change and upgrade it as necessary. As radical as this "sunset" approach may at first sound, it fits perfectly with the concept of pay as a dynamic element of the organization, an element that must evolve as the organization evolves. Indeed, with regular review and modification, today's well-designed pay program can continue to be a viable, sustainable program far into the future.

ELIMINATING THE HUMAN RESOURCES PROBLEM

It should be clear by now that compensation and human resources professionals still play an important role in the compensation process. Yet in many organizations their stock has slipped dramatically. They have, in effect, become the major whipping boys for those organizations that are struggling unsuccessfully through change. Unfortunately, much of that criticism is deserved. Too often the human resources department has come to epitomize the bureaucratic foot dragging that has slowed and, at times, blocked perfectly fine change initiatives, including the development of dynamic compensation strategies. HR in far too many organizations remains a narrowly focused, outdated, malfunctioning department, made up of equally narrowly focused administrators.

And yet, how were they to know it was time to change? Who gave them their marching orders in the first place? Chances are, it was the organization's senior leadership—leadership which may have neglected to tell the HR folks that the rules had changed. Top leadership, however, shouldn't shoulder all the blame. Let's not forget line managers, who have been only too eager all these years to let HR play the role of administrator and enforcer.

That said, rather than merely blast the human resources professionals for their lack of vision, they must be given a new vision. Line managers, who most likely will take over much of the day-to-day responsibilities now handled by the HR professionals, must be given a much better understanding of the processes—not the least of which is compensation.

At the same time, the human resources professionals must, with the support of top leadership, evolve from bureaucratic policemen into true professionals who provide expert advice—a key responsibility that has for too long been buried under administrative debris. The fear of and resistance to change that human resource professionals are exhibiting must be acknowledged and dealt with. Such feelings and behavior are only natural. They are, after all, no different than any other group of employees which is facing a major change. They are not immune from the insecurity that wells up inside all of us, creating a certain degree of resistance. The "new" must be made "familiar" through a compelling vision and a new partnering of HR with the rest of the organization. While their concerns need to be addressed, they must be made to understand, however, that the transformation of their roles and responsibilities is inevitable, and that a "functional mindset" is no longer appropriate and will not be accepted.

Ultimately, of course, it is the human resource processes that must be transformed. Like the organization it is supposed to support, human resources must evolve into a dynamic series of intertwined processes that are aligned with the organization's culture and vision. The centralized, bureaucratic, functional approach must be replaced by a seamless process that supports people from the day they enter the organization until the day they leave.

10
Communicating Pay

The call came from the general manager of a large metropolitan governmental agency. He needed help quickly. His organization had spent thousands of dollars and hundreds of hours designing a state-of-the-art incentive program. The intent of the program was good. It was designed not merely to cut costs, but to improve productivity, advance customer service, generate improvements in work processes, and create employee involvement. Hopes for success ran high, but after only a few months, the program was going nowhere fast. Production was flat. Customer complaints had not dropped. And the employees were behaving as they always had. Only a few had even bothered to turn in suggestions for improvements.

"We've stuck our neck out here," the GM said. "We've promoted this as a progressive initiative. The local media have reported it. If we don't get some results soon, the public is going to have a field day tearing us apart. We *have* to get this program going—again."

We asked what the agency had done *initially* to get the program going.

"Oh, you know, the usual implementation drill," the manager replied. "We had a big kickoff, developed a theme with a catchy name, put up posters, created a video, sent a letter to all the employees."

What the general manager described is all too frequently standard operating procedure for communicating a new pay strategy. In typical fashion, after a new pay program is designed and approved, thoughts finally turn to how it should be communicated to the workforce. A whiz-bang package is quickly developed and the program is rolled out—usually long after unfounded rumors have scared the heck out of employees. There is a big announcement, even a round of employee meetings, perhaps. That's it. Then, silence.

What's left to say? Management is satisfied. After all, *they* created and championed the program. The human resources and public relations departments are proud. *Their* video on the new program won a national award. But the employees are perplexed. They know their pay has changed, but they aren't sure why. Coming on the heels of a recent downsizing, they can only assume it is another management ploy to increase productivity and cut costs. So much for the new compensation program—a program that was designed to motivate; a program that was designed to send positive new messages about the organization and its values.

UNDERSTANDING THE ROLE OF COMMUNICATIONS

Although we've saved it for one of the final chapters, we in no way want to suggest that the communication of a pay strategy should be a minor, after-the-fact, administrative exercise. It is an integral step in creating and implementing an effective compensation program. How a new pay strategy will be communicated should be one of the initial considerations in designing and developing it. The communication itself should start early—long before the new strategy is implemented—and continue through the life of the program.

Communication of a new pay plan has to be carefully planned and well executed in order to set the tone for what will follow. It must, in rapid fashion, eliminate fear, educate, and ultimately create employee buy-in. Once the new pay program is up and running, its status should be reported on a regular basis. At that point, the communication of pay must be fully integrated into the organization's broader communications and performance strategies. After all, if employees' pay is tied to their performance and that of the organization, then they need to know more than the bare necessities (How much do I make?) of pay. They have the right and need to know—on a regular basis—how well they and the organization are doing. Are they achieving their goals? If not, what should they be doing differently?

Unfortunately, most organizations have taken the approach that the metro agency had taken: a big rollout, replete with high-tech visuals, slogans, and slick brochures. Certainly there is nothing wrong with a high-profile kickoff—if it fits the organization's culture. But all the hype and histrionics in the world won't carry a new compensation program—however well designed—very far.

To effectively support today's more dynamic compensation programs, communication must be a thread that runs throughout the process from beginning to end, tying it together, and covering the full range of issues. It must be fully integrated into the organization's strategies and systems, and viewed as one of the key processes, on equal footing, for example, with its reward system.

It also must be dynamic in scope and function. The communication of a new compensation program cannot, as was frequently the case in the past, take place in a vacuum. Pay must be discussed in terms of the other changes and initiatives the organization has undertaken. It is, after all, a true reinforcer of those changes and initiatives, and must be linked to them. If a new incentive program is built on quality and customer service measures, then it is critical that the employees be kept fully informed—and not just in terms of pay—about the organization's quality improvement and customer service efforts. That doesn't mean just *telling* the employees what the organization thinks they need to know when they need to know it. In today's organizations, employees need constant access to information. They want to be able to ask questions, get answers, make comments.

Finally, compensation communications must be open, honest, and straightforward. Employees should be told in plain, understandable terms—sans technical jargon and corporate hype—how their pay is determined and what they need to do, if necessary, to make the most of the program. As we already know, fear of anything—including pay—is largely based on the unknown.

The problem, unfortunately, is that traditionally pay has been a mystery of sorts, a tightly held organizational secret. Outside of general pay policies, little was known. Organizations either guarded their pay strategies as if they were trade secrets known only by their compensation experts, or else they spoke in a strange technical language, and ranked jobs through a complex system that only they understood.

The importance of effective compensation communications is widely acknowledged, and yet in many organizations it remains a paternalistic, functional task. Messages cascade down from the top of the organization, usually after the fact: This is your pay. This is how it was determined. Now run along. There is little discussion, dialogue, or feedback. Indeed, when it comes to talking about pay, employees still tend to be treated like Victorian children—seen but not heard, speaking only after being spoken to.

Take, for example, a new benefits plan. In the traditional organization, such a plan would, on the request of senior management, be developed by the HR department. After it was designed it would be blessed by top leadership, and then handed off to the internal communications or PR department to develop the necessary communications pieces.

Such an approach, while less than satisfactory, may have been accepted by employees a decade or two ago, when most of the other news they received was positive—continued organizational growth, increased profits, and large pay increases—and they were used to having very little say in the pay process. But in today's flatter, more dynamic organizations, in which much of the news employees are receiving is downright depressing—cutbacks, shrinking profits, minimal merit increases—such a reactionary, authoritarian approach is counterproductive.

Always a highly charged issue, compensation is even more explosive during periods of dramatic change, when employees are hypersensitive to everything, and nothing goes unnoticed. In such an atmosphere, treating compensation as a "black box" process—where no one, except those folks in the compensation department, knows the secret formula—can have a negative effect. Empowered, team-oriented employees who are paid based on how well they and the organization perform want to be told not just *what* they are paid, but also *why* they are paid as they are, and *how* they can better their pay. Once the sole bailiwick of top management and perhaps the HR or PR departments, communications today are everyone's responsibility. As a growing number of organizations are discovering, to inform employees about compensation—or any other issue, for that matter—communication must be redesigned along with the rest of the organization's processes. It must reinforce and reflect the organization's cultures. It must be consistent with the organization's other business processes in terms of design, scope, and implementation. Otherwise, it sends out mixed signals, creates confusion, and destroys credibility.

LOW MARKS FOR CURRENT COMMUNICATIONS

This changing role of communications is difficult for many organizations to come to terms with, given perceptions and beliefs that have evolved over the years. As one stunned senior executive said upon hearing details of a complex strategy for communicating a new compensation program and linking pay to a major reengineering initiative, "I always viewed communications as a simple task or routine function. I never realized that it was a major area of responsibility."

But a major responsibility it is, especially if one examines the rather dismal marks that employees give to communications. According to our research, while most employees—from middle managers to hourly workers—still think that much of the information they receive is believable and credible, that trust and credibility is steadily declining. This should come as no surprise. After all, the downsizing, delayering, and other massive changes that most organizations are undergoing have taken a toll on even the most loyal and trusting employees.

More and more frequently, employees say that while they still believe much of what they are told, they don't believe they are getting the full picture. As one employee said, "You're not lying, maybe, but you're only telling me what you want me to know."

Even worse, as Figures 10–1 and 10–2 show, a majority of employees believe their employers are neither listening to them nor taking action when employees have problems or concerns. Again, such a response might not have been cause for alarm a decade ago, when employees generally felt safe, secure, and satisfied. But today that security and satisfaction are fading as employees are told they must assume more responsibility for the organization's success as well as their own, and that there are no guarantees for long-term employment. Given these changing values, it is only natural that employees have many questions, concerns, and suggestions. They want to be heard. And as many organizations are discovering, when they *do* listen, they find employees are providing them with some innovative, valuable ideas and solutions.

Not only are employees concerned about *what* information they're getting, but they're also concerned about *how* they're getting it. As Figure 10–3 shows, the old grapevine continues to be a major source of information. This is disturbing for two reasons. First, if you believe the

Figure 10–1

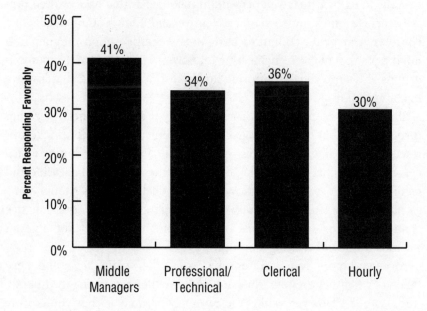

Does your employer listen to you?

Source: Hay Research for Management Employee Attitude Database

communication theorem that "the size of the grapevine is inversely proportional to the effectiveness of formal communications," then it points to an obvious weakness in the process. Second, as this figure also shows, employees prefer getting information from other sources.

This preference, however, should not be interpreted as a mandate to create yet another publication. Most employees we've surveyed—from senior managers to entry-level laborers—say they are overwhelmed with the blizzard of memos, bulletins, and other written missives that they must plod through every day. As one supervisor pleaded: "No more memos. I already have to come in on the weekend just to catch up on my current reading."

What employees really want is to be dealt with personally. Almost 75 percent prefer to get information directly from their supervisors, and nearly

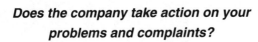

Figure 10–2

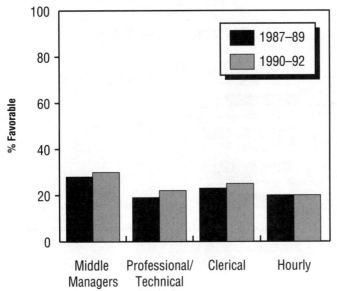

Does the company take action on your problems and complaints?

Source: Hay Research for Management Employee Attitude Database

half want to be informed through meetings with their managers. Why? Such forums offer a chance for dialogue and the possibility that their ideas and concerns will be heard.

That doesn't mean, of course, that all communications should be delivered face-to-face. Communicating effectively with today's diverse workforce requires a similarly diverse arsenal of tools and sources. Different people also process information differently. Some prefer verbal communications, while others want to see it in writing. Still others are more comfortable with hi-tech vehicles. The highly computer-literate engineering division of one organization, for example, said that compensation and benefits communications delivered through E-mail would better suit its informational processing needs. Another organization found that an MTV-style video it produced to communicate a new pay program was highly effective with the

Figure 10–3

How Employees Feel About Communications: Sources

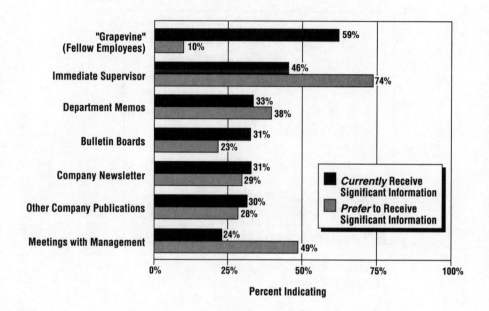

Source: Hay Research for Management Employee Attitude Database

under-thirty-five crowd, but confounded the older workers, who were put off by the jerky movements of the hand-held camera.

Most employees want information from a variety of sources. If it is a major announcement about the company's performance—good or bad—they want to hear it directly from the CEO or another senior leader. In many organizations, unfortunately, such leaders are all too frequently invisible. (See Figure 10–4.) If it is about their individual performance, they probably want to hear it from their supervisor. If it is less urgent, perhaps more complex and informational, such as a new benefits program, they will also want it in writing, so that they can study and review it, and perhaps share it with their spouse.

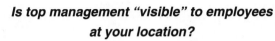

Figure 10-4

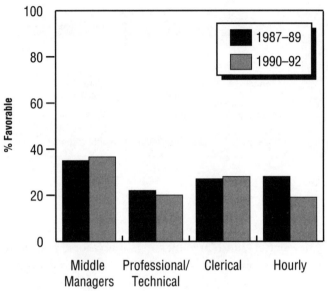

**Is top management "visible" to employees
at your location?**

Source: Hay Research for Management Employee Attitude Database

CULTURAL ALIGNMENT: A CRITICAL FIRST STEP

So how can an organization determine the best strategy and "message mix" to use in communicating a new compensation program? As with many other organizational issues, it starts with alignment. Like compensation, communications should be considered in the context of an organization's work cultures. (See Figure 10–5.) Moreover, compensation communications must be placed in the broad context of both individual and organizational performance. They must emphasize not only pay, but results and how those results are achieved.

As we've already noted, communications in traditional, functional organizations tend to be formal, and delivered through static vehicles such

Figure 10–5

Aligning Communications with Work Culture

Work Cultures	Functional	Process	Time-based	Network
Communications				
Style	Formal	Formal & informal	Formal & informal	Informal
Frequency	Scheduled	Constant	As needed	As needed
Path	One-way	Multidirectional	Multidirectional	Multidirectional

as memos, newsletters, and large meetings. Functional communications also tend to be one-directional—cascading down the organization—and regularly scheduled. Messages are delivered at the discretion of senior management. It decides *what* the employees need to be told and *when* they should be told. And it doesn't spend a lot of time explaining why certain actions are taken, nor does it worry much about soliciting feedback. Frequently, communications about pay follow this pattern. Beyond being informed every year about how big a raise employees are getting, there is very little communication. The only time people are told in detail why they are paid as they are is when they ask—a behavior that is often discouraged.

To be effective today, however, even the functional organization needs to change how it communicates issues of performance and compensation. People need to be told more of the whys—the organization's compensation philosophy, for example, and how their specific pay is determined. They also should be told on a regular basis about their individual performance, and if that performance is tied to compensation, how it is impacting their pay. And, there should be more openness in addressing compensation issues, including providing a vehicle for seeking and answering employee questions in a nonthreatening manner.

As we move toward the process- and time-based cultures, communications patterns begin shifting. Communications become less formal, and much more dynamic in scope. In the process organization, with its emphasis on cross-functional teams, the communications must be constant and interactive—which is consistent with the emphasis on continuous improvement and quality. Both in groups and as individuals, employees need instant access to a wide variety of information. Team members must be in constant communication with each other in order for the process to be effective. Because their pay is probably linked to the performance of the team, and perhaps even to the performance of the organization, they need to be provided with timely information about their team's performance and how it is impacting the organization's overall performance. At the same time, they need to be able to communicate to other teams and to individuals within the organization about issues such as improving customer satisfaction and enhancing quality.

The same sort of dynamic communications also are required in the time-based culture, with its emphasis on project work groups. Although here the communications may be less frequent, employees must have access to information when they need and want it, not just when the leaders deem it necessary. They also need to be able to communicate directly with a wide range of other employee and management groups, without having to negotiate through rigid protocols. Time, after all, is of the essence. A project group may be working on a new product, and need immediate access to certain R&D data or marketing numbers. Group members can't simply wait around until someone decides to give it to them. By the same token, R&D and marketing may need access to product development teams, so that they can get information that is essential for making broader strategic decisions at the organization or business unit level. While little of this communication may be directly related to compensation, it nonetheless has a major impact on the performance of the project teams, and, ultimately, their pay.

In the network organization there are few signs of a rigid communications structure. Members of the network communicate very informally with each other, sending and receiving messages when they need or want information that will help them make sound business decisions and ultimately achieve the goals of the venture. Communications on pay issues are similarly informal and infrequent, and also are often tied to the bigger issue of performance. Network members, for example, probably will have little need for specific details on a regular basis about their pay. Instead, they will want information about the venture that will insure that they maximize their pay potential. Is the venture on schedule? Is the budget being met? What more can be done to ensure its ultimate success?

THE COMMUNICATIONS PROCESS

The alignment of compensation with specific work cultures requires a more proactive, carefully thought-out approach to communications than most organizations have traditionally taken. To communicate changes in the compensation program, organizations frequently need to modify their broader communications strategies based on the cultural direction in which they are heading. If, for example, the organization is moving toward a process culture, and is implementing a pay program based on team performance, then it needs to develop a strategy both for communicating how the new program works and for keeping team members informed of the progress they are making toward achieving their goals. The traditional approach, in which communications were very infrequent—usually a single, annual individual employee evaluation—is no longer acceptable.

In developing a specific strategy for communicating a new compensation program, we advise clients to follow a well-defined four-step approach, which treats communications as an ongoing process rather than a series of separate pieces. We also recommend that the communications strategy be developed by a small (four- to seven-person) cross-functional team of key stakeholders, which includes, but is not necessarily run by, representatives of the PR/communications and human resources departments.

Step 1: Assessing Current Communications.   Before an organization can develop an effective communications strategy, it must determine what works, what doesn't, and what needs to be eliminated or changed. To that end, a periodic communications assessment is critical. Through a combination of focus groups, surveys, and a review of past communications, an organization should examine the credibility and effectiveness of the communications vehicles it uses, as well as those within the organization who are frequently called upon to be the "messengers." These range from the CEO and other senior leaders to middle managers, to those employees who are the informal "opinion leaders" and grapevine "editors."

The results of these assessments are often stunning to those closest to the process. The communications department of one organization we worked with, for example, was extremely proud of its professionally designed, full-color, *USA Today*-style employee newsletter. Even we had to admit that it was a great-looking product. The employees, however, were not impressed. It was, in the words of one employee, "corporate propaganda." What they read—and believed—was the frequent, single-page, photocopied, highly informal bulletins that the CEO distributed.

The communications department of another organization had produced a highly professional video in which the CEO offered details about a new compensation program. It was immediately challenged by some employees who wondered—out loud of course—why the CEO couldn't meet with them in person, and how the organization could afford a fancy video when it had recently gone through a major cost-reduction effort.

Yet another organization was very proud of the groundwork it had laid for a major change initiative that included a new compensation program. It had sent out numerous memos and letters, and even held departmental meetings. What it didn't realize was that despite the hard work, the rumor mill continued to outdistance the organization's efforts. People were not just scared, they were leaving the organization in large numbers. Ultimately, senior managers had to take to the halls, talking one-on-one with employees to stop the hemorrhaging.

One of the best, yet perhaps unconventional, ways of assessing the credibility of "official" organizational communications is to determine the size and scope of the grapevine, as well as the number and credibility of unofficial publications, which are so popular in the age of desktop publishing. (One organization we worked with had at least fifteen of these "rogue" publications.)

A thorough communication assessment also will unearth discrepancies in the credibility of key messengers. The CEO may have a long tradition of delivering credible messages; but if his or her most recent message was bad news—a major downsizing, perhaps—that credibility may be tarnished, at least for the time being. If so, the organization may need to find a different messenger/leader to champion the new compensation program. The same holds true for middle managers, who frequently are called upon to play a large role in communicating a new compensation program. Consider the managers' role and credibility prior to the new communications effort. Is their stock high with employees? Will they lend credence to the message?

An assessment also is an effective tool for identifying other communications barriers. These can range from general perceptions about the organization—its values, ethics, and culture—to more specific views about compensation. If, for example, there is a long history of announcing new initiatives with drumrolls and fanfare and then forgetting them six months down the road, a huge kickoff of the new compensation program probably will be met with skepticism. Similar levels of skepticism will probably be generated if an organization that has traditionally kept the employees in the dark suddenly overwhelms them with information. Such was the case of one manufacturing firm, which, after years of financial secrecy, suddenly opened its books to employees as part of a new incentive program. Disbelieving employees had to be convinced that there weren't actually two sets of books; one real and still secret, the other open but phony.

Or consider the large health care organization that was attempting to move from a traditional base-plus-merit program to a performance-based plan. A survey of employees found that most believed their current merit raises were actually cost-of-living allowances. They also considered five-percent increases insufficient, and believed experience alone should govern pay. Obviously an intense education program had to take place before the performance program could be implemented.

Step 2: Understanding the Communications Objectives.　Before developing a strategy for communicating a new compensation program, a consistent set of objectives needs to be established and understood. Traditionally the objective was merely to inform. Employees were told how the program worked and how they were affected—nothing more.

Certainly there is still a need to inform. But in communicating today's more dynamic compensation program, especially one that is tied to performance, that is only the beginning. It is also necessary to educate: To create the necessary awareness, acceptance, and ultimate buy-in, employees must be shown how the new compensation program works, but they also have to understand why it has been changed and how it will benefit both them and the organization.

Once the program is in place, the organization must chart progress to show employees how the program is working and how they and the organization are performing. At the same time, successes must be celebrated and failures acknowledged. Unless this ongoing communication takes place, the organization will have difficulty changing behavior, which ultimately is a key goal of most new compensation programs.

Take a new gainsharing program, for example. First the program must be introduced. After all, for many employees it is a strange, even frightening concept. They will no doubt want to know how it works and how much money they will receive if the goals are achieved. To achieve those goals, however, they will need to know how the program fits in with the organization's broader strategies and other initiatives, what they need to do, and how they need to change. But it doesn't stop there. Once the program has been implemented, the employees need to be shown—frequently—how their efforts and involvement are impacting the success of the program. They must know not only what other employees are doing to achieve and surpass the goals (the successes) but also what may be impeding their achievement (the failures).

Step 3: Developing a Strategy and Plan.   This is the point, unfortunately, at which efforts to communicate new pay strategies often come unglued, the victims of insufficient planning or inadequate follow-through. During this phase the organization must develop a communications strategy based on its objectives and assessment, as well as a very specific action plan that includes who is going to be told, what they are going to be told, who is going to tell them, and the sequence of communications.

The devil, as usual, is in the details. Key audiences need to be identified, along with the key messages and appropriate messengers and vehicles. What and how an organization tells senior management about the compensation program may be somewhat different than what it tells its managers. And what those managers—who most likely will become the main communicators of the program—are told may be somewhat different from what they in turn tell employees. The executive team, for example, will probably want information about the overall strategy and how it will impact the organization's performance. Middle managers will need to be told not only how the pay program affects them personally, but how they must present it to the employees. Even among the various employee groups there may be a need for different messages. Hourly workers, for example, may require a less complex approach than the professional staff.

If the program is highly visible or controversial, or if the organization is public, a separate message may be necessary for customers, shareholders, even the public. This may be a simple statement that can be used should questions be raised, or it may be a proactive announcement of the new program, stating how it will benefit not only employees, but also the customers and shareholders.

Finally, to assure that nothing is left to chance, the plan should be put in writing. Organizations should develop a script, talking points, and a list of common questions and answers. This is especially important if a large group of middle managers will be key communicators of the new program. While they all may be highly credible messengers, each may interpret the program differently based on his or her own fears, opinions, and understanding. By carefully scripting the communications, this quite natural and often unintentional distortion of the facts can be minimized and a high level of consistency achieved. (An example of talking points one organization used in communicating its gainsharing plan can be found at the end of this chapter.)

The plan also should be developed from a marketing perspective. After all, products aren't sold by simply describing how they work, but also by explaining their benefits. Consider the last time you purchased a car. Chances are, you didn't base your purchase on an explanation of the internal combustion engine, the drive train, and the suspension, but rather on how well the car performed. The same goes for compensation. Employees certainly need to know how the new program works, but their acceptance of it depends more on how they will benefit from it—and this statement of benefit needs to be highly personalized.

As a last step in the plan, a time line for both rollout and ongoing communications should be established and followed. Timing is critical. All too frequently, communications lag behind the development of new compensation programs, resulting in the generation of fear and rumors that can slow, if not scuttle, the acceptance of such programs. Although it happens far less frequently, communicating too much ahead of the implementation of a compensation program can also wreak havoc, creating false hopes and expectations.

Step 4: Evaluate and Modify.   The communications strategy, like the pay program it is supporting, is a work in progress. It needs to be evaluated regularly and modified as necessary. Through focus groups, surveys, or interviews with representatives of various audiences, the effectiveness of the communications should be evaluated. Did the audiences understand, accept, and commit to changes in the compensation program? What worked? What didn't? Has the level of credibility risen or fallen? Are there any new barriers? The feedback can be used to adjust both the communications efforts and the compensation program.

DECENTRALIZING THE COMMUNICATIONS PROCESS

Once a compensation program has been implemented, most organizations traditionally hand the responsibility for ongoing communications—what few there are—to their human resources and compensation experts. In today's decentralized organization, however, much of the responsibility for communication, as with other responsibilities, should be pushed "deeper" into the organization. Not that the human resources and communications professionals should be ignored. In fact, their expertise and advice are often crucial. But for the most part, the actual communications should be handled by a variety of others within the organization. Indeed, the key stakeholders should be brought into the process.

In the most effective programs we've seen, the CEO and the rest of the senior leadership team have taken responsibility for championing the program initially. Certainly they left explaining the details to those lower in the organization. But they spent a great deal of time making the rounds of employee meetings, talking about the importance of the program, and tying it to the bigger organizational picture.

The details of the program in such cases are often left to the line managers. This is only natural, considering that they not only are frequently responsible for dealing with compensation issues on an ongoing basis, but also are usually the employees' most credible, accessible sources of information. They cannot, of course, be expected to communicate effectively without understanding the compensation program. That is why it is so important that a thorough, well-scripted communications package be developed and rehearsed prior to taking it on the road.

As good as those managers may be, communications should not end with them. When it comes to compensation, the employees themselves can be very effective messengers. In fact, they should be involved from the beginning and consulted throughout the developmental process. There are a number of ways to solicit employee involvement. At the very least, their ideas and concerns should be heard. To that end, once the program is designed, but before it is fully communicated, the organization may want to test it through a series of employee focus groups. Such forums can generate excellent feedback, and can also provide a vehicle for preselling the program to employees who are highly influential, highly vocal, or both. Getting such individuals on board early will obviously make the broader sales process much easier.

When Reuters decided to modify its benefits program, for example, it involved employees throughout the process. Initially about a dozen human resources representatives were trained to conduct focus groups. Additionally, an employee group was involved throughout the process, including the final approval of the communications changes. As a result, the new benefits plan not only was accepted with little resistance, but it also paved the way for other supporting compensation and human resources changes.

The involvement of employees in the actual design of a compensation program may sound extreme. Yet more and more organizations have found that their participation can be very effective. It's not just the large organizations with professional staffs who are taking such an approach. The water and sewer department of one municipality involved all of its employees in the design of a new skill- and competency-based compensation program. First, a series of informational meetings were held to discuss the issues and get feedback. Next, a design team was created that included crew chiefs, who participated in the design process, and became key communicators, carrying the message of the plan's progress directly to their crews. One year after the first employee meetings were held, the program was implemented with little difficulty. Its acceptance, in large measure, can be linked to employee involvement.

As these examples show, a carefully designed communications strategy that involves employees can effectively advance a new compensation program in a variety of organizational settings. Employee involvement alone, however, cannot save an otherwise ill-communicated pay program.

To be successful, compensation communications must be dynamic, ongoing, fully integrated into the organization's strategy, aligned with the organization's work culture and values, and closely linked to its broader goals and initiatives. Most important, communication must be considered a key organizational process, no less important than the compensation program it helps advance.

Talking Points for a New Incentive Program

The following talking points were used by one organization to help communicate a new gainsharing program. Written as a series of questions, they were used by managers and supervisors to provide consistent answers to some key concerns.

I keep hearing about a new program called gainsharing. What is it?

Gainsharing is a new pay program we are starting. Now, in addition to your current base pay and benefits, you will be eligible for an additional financial reward annually, based on your performance and that of the organization.

Who will be eligible? Aren't bonuses usually given only to executives?

Every employee will be eligible. While it is true that incentives have traditionally been used to reward executives, we believe it is critical to the success of our company to involve every one of you.

Why this sudden interest in the involvement of employees?

As you know, we have gone through a lot of changes in the past year. Some of these have been created by our own rapid growth, while others have been caused by the changes in the industry. We have worked hard to meet these challenges through our strategic quality management efforts and a number of related initiatives. The gainsharing program is part of these efforts. It will help us:

- Better focus attention on key corporate, regional, and departmental goals
- Strengthen the link between performance and pay
- Attract and retain quality people
- Motivate both individual and team performance

All of that sounds good. But how does it work?

Your supervisor will explain the plan in detail. Simply put, we will share a portion of our revenues above a 5 percent net operating margin with the employees, provided we also meet certain quality improvement and customer service standards.

How much more will I make? And when will I get it?

Again, the size of the gainsharing award will depend on how well the organization does. It could be a few dollars, a few hundred, perhaps even more. The awards will be paid at the end of each year. But remember, if we don't reach our customer service and quality goals, nothing will be paid out, no matter how well we do financially.

So what's the catch? Will my base pay shrink? Will I have to work harder?

There is no catch. Your base pay will not shrink. Merit and cost-of-living raises will continue as they have in the past. As for the need to work harder—that depends on your performance. If it is below company standards, then yes, you probably will. Remember, even though your individual contribution may not be measured, your performance will have an impact on the overall performance that determines the incentive payout. That said, it is important that you:

- Work not necessarily harder, but smarter. That means always providing the most efficient, cost-effective, high-quality service to your customers, including your peers in others departments.
- Work together as a team, sharing responsibility and efforts.
- Always be aware of the importance of your contribution, not only as an individual, but also as part of the company.

What if I have questions?

The plan will be explained in detail by your supervisor. If you have any questions, doubts, or concerns you can talk to your supervisor, someone in human resources, or dial our incentive hotline and someone will get back to you with an answer within two working days.

11

Nine Principles of Dynamic Pay

S even-step self-help programs. Top-ten talk show lists. Twelve-step recovery plans. All the complexities of life, it seems, have been reduced to abbreviated, enumerated lists. What follows is our own checklist for creating a successful compensation program.

Don't misunderstand; we certainly don't propose that a subject as important and complex as pay can be covered in a list of simple statements. Based on our experiences with clients, however, we know that far too frequently those complexities overshadow some of the more basic principles of an effective compensation strategy. The fact is, some otherwise well-designed programs fail because one or more of these principles are either not understood or overlooked.

If you take little else from this book, remember these principles. They form the foundation of any successful compensation strategy. Regardless of the specifics of the programs they support, they are universally applicable. They also are unchanging. Although we would like to believe otherwise, much of what we have written will be outdated fifteen, ten, or even five years from now. These principles, we believe, will stand a much longer test of time.

1. *Align your compensation with your organization's cultures, values, and strategic business goals.* When the dust finally settles, the failure of most

compensation programs today can be traced to a lack of alignment. Older, established programs fail because they no longer support the evolving work cultures. New programs fail because they are designed without a recognition of those cultures. That is why it is so critical to not only understand how cultures have changed, but also to determine where your organization is in the cultural universe and to assess where it needs to be headed.

2. *Link compensation to the other changes.* Yes, pay is important. But don't put it on a pedestal or keep it in isolation. Compensation should support and reinforce other change initiatives and be fully integrated with them. Pay today is about far more than security or status. It is a tool that, when tied to performance, can be used effectively to motivate and empower employees, increase productivity, and improve quality. A compensation program that is suddenly introduced amid dozens of other changes such as reengineering or quality improvement, but which is not presented in the context of those changes, stands a good chance of not just failing, but backfiring—creating mayhem where there should be momentum.

3. *Time your compensation program to best support your other change initiatives.* As in sports, business, and most of life's other pleasures, so in compensation: timing is everything. Simply knowing where your organization is and where it is headed doesn't mean you're ready to implement a new pay strategy. All too frequently, new compensation plans are introduced too early in the change process. Many organizations believe—wrongly—that compensation is the ideal catalyst to propel the organization through change. Certainly pay is a powerful motivator. It is an excellent vehicle for reinforcing new values and behaviors. But it cannot *drive* or *lead* the change process.

4. *Integrate pay with other people processes.* As important as compensation is today, it alone cannot provide the support that the people in your organization need. Rather, it must be developed in the context of a more complex human resources system that includes how work is designed, how people are selected and developed for that work, and how their performance is managed.

5. *Democratize the pay process.* To centralize pay decisions or to decentralize them, the debate continues. Do neither. Instead, democratize the process. Do not condemn compensation to the "black hole" of human resources. Make every executive, manager, and supervisor accountable for

their part of the compensation program. Certainly there are aspects of compensation, including policy and core administrative issues, that should be centralized. But many of the ongoing day-to-day activities surrounding compensation—including most communications and specific performance/pay issues of both individuals and teams—should be handled at the line, the department, or the team level. If you are really going to give people more power, if you are serious about asking them to share in the success of the organization, then you'd better be ready to give them more authority for the rewards that supposedly will result from their new-found responsibility.

6. *Demystify compensation.* You can't, of course, expect people to be accountable for something they don't understand. If pay is truly going to motivate people and help support change, then—like many other organizational processes—it needs to be hauled out of the safe, unwrapped, and displayed for all to see. That doesn't mean that the pay of individual employees should suddenly become public information. Certainly sensitive, confidential issues remain. But the bigger whys and hows of compensation should be known throughout the organization. Communicate continually. Inform, educate, share success, and acknowledge setbacks. Although this is a lot of work, we guarantee it is worth the effort.

7. *Measure results.* There is no use tying pay to performance if you can't or don't measure that performance, or if you are unwilling to pay significantly more for superior performance. The measures you use depend on your organization and its goals. They may be based on financial performance, productivity, quality improvement, economic value added, shareholder value, or customer service. Many organizations find a combination most appropriate. Whatever the measures, they must be understood by the employees in the program. The bottom line: If performance can't be accurately measured, if employees don't understand how it is evaluated, or if they can't see the link between their efforts and the desired results, the program won't work or will be less than fully effective.

8. *Refine. Refine again. Refine some more.* Call it CCI—continuous compensation improvement. Once your new compensation program is implemented and running smoothly, don't turn your back and walk away. Instead, review it on a regular basis, refine those elements that need improvement, and change those that aren't working. You may, for example,

find that an incentive program that once worked well is now reinforcing inappropriate behavior and advancing the wrong goals. Or, you may find that your employee benefits program—the one that everyone used to think was wonderful—no longer meets their needs. Remember, pay is not a static process. To maintain its effectiveness, it must continually change as the organization evolves.

9. *Be selective. Don't take to heart everything you hear or read about pay.* When it comes to compensation, there are no miracle cures. There is, however, a seemingly endless supply of new theories and strategies about how people should be paid. Some are valid, value-adding options if—an important if—they fit your organization. So be selective. Don't grasp at the latest trend, or follow the lead of a competitor. Explore all the available options and then decide on the solutions that are right for your organization, your culture, and the changes you are going through.

Epilogue: Paying for People

I t's only fitting that we end this book back where we started. The major league baseball strike that we wrote of in introducing the subject of pay has ended. Gone, as they say, but certainly not forgotten. It left behind a lot of upset employers, unmotivated employees, and unsatisfied customers. The players, who didn't get the pay, perks, or other benefits they wanted, are sullen. The fans, who feel cheated, are staying away from ballparks in record numbers. The employers—well, let's just say it hasn't been a banner year in terms of the business of baseball.

No one is happy. There are no winners.

After reading this book, of course, that should come as no surprise. How we reward people for the work they do is a very important matter. As you have seen, compensation, if aligned with an organization's values, mission, culture, and business strategies, can play a major role in helping that organization successfully run the gauntlet of change, and come out stronger, more successful, and more competitive. Pay can, if used properly, be a critical key to improving performance, be it in terms of bigger profits, increased value, better products, higher quality work, or happier customers.

Most important, pay is a powerful force in motivating people. It's far more than the overly simplistic carrot-and-stick concept that critics use in attacking today's dynamic performance-based pay programs. People, as we have noted, are the heart and soul of the organization, not to mention the mind. A sophisticated, well-designed, carefully aligned total compensation strategy can help transform even your "average" employees into more involved, more responsible, high-performing individuals. And, it can help turn that disjointed, even dysfunctional group of people into a cohesive team.

But that's not all. In writing from the perspective of the employer—the organization—we have perhaps underemphasized the other, more personal, side of pay. Certainly pay can improve the performance of people. But it also can boost their self-worth, their level of personal satisfaction, their sense of well-being.

We remember the first time we visited LEGO Systems, Inc.'s Connecticut plant. After talking at length with the managers, we were invited to tour the operation. Our guide was a young woman who worked as a team leader on the production floor. No one else went along. Unlike other operations we've visited, there was no phalanx of nervous PR types, jittery VPs, and uptight managers to sanitize what we saw or heard. The woman talked openly about the company. While she was frank about the struggles of moving toward a team environment and the problems that she and others had to overcome, she was very optimistic about the direction the company was headed. She was also excited about the direction she was headed. She had enrolled in college and was taking business classes in the evening. LEGO, she proudly noted, was already adopting many of the leading-edge strategies that her professors were discussing. But that wasn't the only benefit from working at a forward-looking company: The team skills—communicating, negotiating, group dynamics—she had developed at work, she said, laughing, had even improved her relationship with her husband at home.

Our tour guide may have been an hourly worker on a packing operation, but unlike most of the highly paid major leaguers we've watched this season, here was someone who clearly enjoyed her job. She was excited about the organization and where it was going, and proud of her role and contribution.

Which brings us to a second reason for ending where we started—for coming full circle. Such continuity, after all, symbolizes compensation today—an ever-evolving, living, continuous process, with no beginning and no end. If the first lesson you take from our book is the importance of people, the second should be the concept of compensation as a process that must constantly change as your organization changes. If you walk away from this book thinking that broadbanding, or gainsharing, or pay for competencies, or pay for teams is *the* answer to all your compensation worries, then you've missed the point. Take the book back to the store. Demand a refund. We obviously have failed.

Remember, the secret of compensation today lies not in the specific strategy you choose. To use compensation successfully to enhance performance and effect change, you must align your pay strategies with your constantly evolving culture, values, and business strategies.

And, even more important, you must put people first.

Notes

Preface

1. Peter Block, *Stewardship* (San Francisco: Berrett-Koehler Publishers, 1993), p. 173.

Chapter 1: The Compensation Lag

1. Fred R. Bleakley, "The Best Laid Plans," *The Wall Street Journal*, July 6, 1993, p. 1.

2. "Deming's Demons: The Management Guru Thinks U.S. Corporations Are Crushing Their Worker Incentive," *The Wall Street Journal*, June 4, 1990, p. 39.

3. Willie Sutton with Edward Linn, *Where the Money Was* (New York: The Viking Press, 1976), pp. 119, 120.

4. The 1995 Hay Human Resources Professionals Survey.

5. Charles Handy, *The Age of Unreason* (Boston: Harvard Business School Press, 1989), p. 31.

6. Charles Handy, *The Age of Paradox* (Boston: Harvard Business School Press, 1994), p. 3.

7. Barbara Lloyd, "Secret of Success Is in the Design" *The New York Times*, May 11, 1995, p. B8.

8. Dori Jones Yang, "When the Going Gets Tough, Boeing Gets Touchy-Feely," *Business Week*, January 17, 1994, p. 65.

9. Gary Hamel and C. K. Prahalad, *Competing for the Future* (Boston: Harvard Business School Press, 1994), p. 131.

10. "Researchers Say U.S. Social Well-Being Is Awful," *The New York Times*, October 18, 1993, p. B7.

11. *Changing Employee Opinions About Quality, Competitiveness, and Management Performance*, The 1994 Hay Employee Attitudes Study.

12. *Workforce 2000* (Indianapolis: The Hudson Institute, Inc., 1987), pp. xix, xx.

13. Shawn Tully, "The Real Key to Creating Wealth," *Fortune*, September 20, 1993, p. 38.

14. Jose Pagoaga and James B. Williams, "Dynamic Pay for Health Care's Changing World of Work," *Hospitals & Health Networks*, September 5, 1993, p. 24.

Chapter 2: Work Cultures

1. Walter Kiechel III, "How We Will Work in the Year 2000," *Fortune*, May 17, 1993, p. 39.

2. For a more detailed examination of Chrysler's time-based strategy, see *Time Based Competition*, a video-based program produced by Harvard Business School Management Programs.

3. Barbara Presley Noble, "On Bosses, Barriers and Beliefs," *The New York Times*, March 6, 1994, p. 25F.

4. Wendy Bounds, "Kodak Under Fisher: Upheaval in Slow Motion," *The Wall Street Journal*, December 22, 1994, p. B1.

Chapter 3: The Role of Pay in Organizational Change

1. A. J. Vogl, "The Age of Reengineering," *Across the Board*, June 1993, p. 33.

2. Thomas A. Stewart, "Reengineering, the Hot New Managing Tool," *Fortune*, August 23, 1993, p. 41.

3. 1994 Hay Compensation Conference Participant Survey.

4. Hal Lancaster, "Managing Your Career: 'Re-engineering' Authors Reconsider Re-Engineering," *The Wall Street Journal*, January 17, 1995, p. B1.

5. 1992 General Electric Co. Annual Report, p. 5.

6. Peter F. Drucker, "A Turnaround Primer," *The Wall Street Journal*, February 2, 1993, p. 14A.

7. 1995 Hay Hospital Compensation Survey.

8. Gilbert Fuchsberg, "'Visioning' Missions Becomes Its Own Mission," *The Wall Street Journal*, January 7, 1994, p. B1.

Chapter 4: Dynamic Compensation Strategies and Tactics

1. "The Perilous New World of Fair Pay," Jaclyn Fierman, *Fortune*, June 13, 1994, p. 57.

2. 1994 Hay Compensation Conference Participant Survey.

3. Fierman, "The Perilous New World of Fair Play," p. 57.

4. Executive Summary, *Workforce 2000*, Hudson Institute, 1987, p. xxi.

5. Charles Handy, *The Age of Unreason*, Harvard Business School Press, 1990, pp. 51–52.

6. Tom Peters "Going 'Horizontal' in Your Career," *Industry Week*, January 4, 1993, p. 47. (From Peters' book, *Liberation Management*, New York: Alfred A Knopf, 1992.)

7. Alfie Kohn, *Punished by Rewards* (Boston and New York: Houghton Mifflin 1993), p. 16.

8. Barnaby J. Feder, "Recasting a Model Incentive Strategy," *The New York Times*, September 5, 1994, p. 17.

9. Terry Maxon and Martin Zimmerman, "Southwest Pilots Ratify Contract with Stock Options," *The Dallas Morning News*, January 13, 1995, p. 1D.

10. Bob Ortega, "Life Without Sam," *The Wall Street Journal*, January 4, 1995, p. 1.

11. Bruce N. Pfau and Steven E. Gross, *Innovative Reward and Recognition Strategies in TQM*, The Conference Board Report No. 1051, 1993, p. 22.

12. Ibid, p. 26.

13. Doron P. Levin, "Compaq Storms PC Heights from Its Factory Floor," *The New York Times*, November 13, 1994, p. 5F.

14. Hay Compensation Database, Team-Based Pay, 1994.

15. John R. Katzenbach and Douglas K. Smith, *The Wisdom of Teams* (Boston: Harvard Business School Press, 1993), p. 26.

16. 1994 Hay Compensation Conference Participant Survey.

Chapter 5: Aligning Cultures and Compensation

1. Steven E. Gross and Bruce N. Pfau, "Innovative Reward and Recognition Strategies in TQM," Conference Board Report No. 1051, 1993, pp. 19, 20.

2. Richard Corliss, "Hey, Let's Put On a Show!" *Time*, March 27, 1995, p. 57.

Chapter 6: Benefits in the Changing Organization

1. 1994 Hay/Huggins Benefits Report.

2. Shawn Tully, "America's Healthiest Companies," *Fortune*, June 12, 1995, pp. 99, 100.

3. Ellen E. Schultz, "'Time-Off Bank' Lets Employees Choose," *The Wall Street Journal*, September 27, 1994, p. C1.

Chapter 7: Rewarding Leadership in the Changing Organization

1. Joan E. Rigdon, "William Agee Will Leave Morrison Knudsen," *The Wall Street Journal*, February 2, 1995, p. B1.

2. Bob Drury, "The Street Fighter Within," *Men's Journal*, February 1995, p. 48.

3. Warren Bennis, *Why Leaders Can't Lead* (San Francisco: Jossey-Bass Publishers, 1989), p. 22.

4. Edwin A. Locke and Associates, *The Essence of Leadership* (New York: Lexington Books, 1991), p. 4.

5. Max De Pree, *Leadership Is an Art* (New York: Bantam Doubleday Dell Publishing Group, 1989), p. 11.

6. Noel M. Tichy and Ram Charan, "The CEO as a Coach: An Interview with AlliedSignal's Lawrence A. Bossidy," *Harvard Business Review*, March–April 1995, p. 77.

7. LynNell Hancock, "A Place in the Heart," *Newsweek*, June 19, 1995, p. 72.

8. Scott McCartney, "Michael Dell—and His Company—Grow Up," *The Wall Street Journal*, January 31, 1995, p. B1.

9. Leah Nathans Spiro, "Turmoil at Salomon," *Business Week*, May 1, 1995, p. 150.

10. Anita Raghavan, "Salomon Throws Out Proposed Pay Plan," *The Wall Street Journal*, June 12, 1995, p. C1.

11. Laurie Hays, "Abstractionist Practically Reinvents the Keyboard," *The Wall Street Journal*, March 6, 1995, p. B1.

Chapter 8: Reconsidering Executive Pay

1. Derek Bok, *The Cost of Talent* (New York: The Free Press, 1993), p. 227.

2. 1994 Hay Executive Compensation Report.

3. 1994 Hay Compensation Database.

4. 1994 Berkshire Hathaway Inc. Annual Report, p 11.

5. "Pay for Kmart Chief Tied to Performance," *The New York Times*, June 15, 1995, p. C8.

6. 1994 Hay Executive Compensation Report.

7. G. Bennett Stewart III, *The Quest for Value*, Harper Business (New York: HarperCollins Publishers, 1991), p. 5.

8. Joann S. Lublin, "Give the Board Fewer Perks, a Panel Urges," *The Wall Street Journal*, June 19, 1995, p. B1.

9. Joseph K. Sapora and Thomas P. Flannery, "Developing Supplemental Executive Retirement Programs," *Health Care Executive Briefing*, (Philadelphia: The Hay Group), 1994.

10. Kenneth N. Gilpin, "Grace's Board Votes Changes Demanded by Big Investors," *The New York Times*, April 7, 1995, p. C1.

11. James P. Miller, Thomas M. Burton, and Randall Smith, "W. R. Grace Is Roiled by Flap Over Spending and What to Disclose," *The Wall Street Journal*, March 10, 1995, pp. A1, A6.

12. Laurence Zuckerman, "The Good Life after Goldman," *The New York Times*, October 16, 1994, p. 1F.

13. Graef S. Crystal, *In Search of Excess, The Overcompensation of American Executives* (New York: W. W. Norton, 1992), pp. 13, 14.

Chapter 9: Pay and the Changing Role of Human Resources

1. Bruce N. Pfau and Steven E. Gross, "Innovative Reward and Recognition Strategies in TQM," The Conference Board, 1993, p. 18.

2. Sue Shellenbarger, "Reviews from Peers Instruct—and Sting," *The Wall Street Journal*, October 4, 1994, p. B1.

Index